Anglophone Verse Novels as Gutter Texts

Anglophone Verse Novels as Gutter Texts

Postcolonial Literature and the Politics of Gaps

Dirk Wiemann

BLOOMSBURY ACADEMIC
NEW YORK · LONDON · OXFORD · NEW DELHI · SYDNEY

BLOOMSBURY ACADEMIC
Bloomsbury Publishing Inc
1385 Broadway, New York, NY 10018, USA
50 Bedford Square, London, WC1B 3DP, UK
29 Earlsfort Terrace, Dublin 2, Ireland

BLOOMSBURY, BLOOMSBURY ACADEMIC and the Diana logo
are trademarks of Bloomsbury Publishing Plc

First published in the United States of America 2023
Paperback edition published 2025

Copyright © Dirk Wiemann, 2023

For legal purposes the Acknowledgements on p. x constitutes as an extension
of this copyright page.

Cover design: Eleanor Rose
Cover image: © Ursula Meyer

All rights reserved. No part of this publication may be reproduced or transmitted
in any form or by any means, electronic or mechanical, including photocopying,
recording, or any information storage or retrieval system, without prior
permission in writing from the publishers.

Bloomsbury Publishing Inc does not have any control over, or responsibility for,
any third-party websites referred to or in this book. All internet addresses given
in this book were correct at the time of going to press. The author and publisher
regret any inconvenience caused if addresses have changed or sites have ceased
to exist, but can accept no responsibility for any such changes.

A catalog record for this book is available from the Library of Congress.

Library of Congress Cataloging-in-Publication Data

Names: Wiemann, Dirk, author.
Title: Anglophone verse novels as gutter texts : postcolonial literature
and the politics of gaps / Dirk Wiemann.
Description: New York : Bloomsbury Academic, 2023. | Includes
bibliographical references and index. | Summary: "A systematic analysis
of contemporary verse novels and how textual gaps serve as symbolic
interventions into current debates on the planetary and the
post-national"– Provided by publisher.
Identifiers: LCCN 2022053354 (print) | LCCN 2022053355 (ebook) | ISBN
9781501399503 (hardback) | ISBN 9781501399541 (paperback) | ISBN
9781501399510 (ebook) | ISBN 9781501399527 (pdf) | ISBN 9781501399534
(ebook other)
Subjects: LCSH: Novels in verse–History and criticism. | Novels in
verse–Technique. | LCGFT: Literary criticism.
Classification: LCC PN1445 .W54 2023 (print) | LCC PN1445 (ebook) | DDC
809.1/3–dc23/eng/20230428
LC record available at https://lccn.loc.gov/2022053354
LC ebook record available at https://lccn.loc.gov/2022053355

ISBN: HB: 978-1-5013-9950-3
PB: 978-1-5013-9954-1
ePDF: 978-1-5013-9952-7
eBook: 978-1-5013-9951-0

Typeset by Newgen KnowledgeWorks Pvt. Ltd., Chennai, India

To find out more about our authors and books visit www.bloomsbury.com
and sign up for our newsletters.

For Tania

CONTENTS

List of figures ix
Acknowledgements x
List of abbreviations xi

1 Introduction: In the gutter ... 1
   1.1 Gutter texts and the politics of form 3
   1.2 Verse novels as gutter texts 17
   1.3 Gappiness and incompleteness 35
   1.4 Connexionism and minor cosmopolitanisms 41
   1.5 Gappy planet and incomplete nation: Michael Cawood Green's *Sinking* 51

2 Volcanic verses: The planet as verb 61
   2.1 Sibylline cures: Derek Walcott's *Omeros* 63
      Naming and wounding 63
      Volcanic wounds – volcanic cures 67
   2.2 'Links between geology and character': Anne Carson's *Autobiography of Red* 74
      Exorcizing epic masters 75
      Psychogeology 80
      Light writing – life writing 84
   2.3 The space that connects: Albert Wendt's *The Adventures of Vela* 89
      The appealing/appalling precolony 93
      We have never been not modern 98
      The Va 102
      The gospel according to Vela/Alapati/Wendt 108
      An ongoing planet 111

2.4 The planet as praxis: W. S. Merwin's *The Folding Cliffs* 113
    History, genealogy, socioecology 115
    Volcanic syllables, volcanic silences 127

3 In/verse Britain: The poetics of the post-nation 133
  3.1 A million epiphanies now: Kae Tempest's *Let Them Eat Chaos* 134
    The state of the nation in verse 135
    Clima(c)tic truth events 139
    Apophenia revisited 142
  3.2 'But I dreamt of creating mosaics': Bernardine Evaristo's *The Emperor's Babe* 145
    Chick lit as imperial romance 146
    The right to be stupid 149
    Fame fatale 154
  3.3 Detoxing England: Patience Agbabi's *Telling Tales* 158
    The nation between incompleteness and wholeness 158
    Toxic ingredients 162
    Not by rap alone 166
  3.4 Untelling tales: Anagrammatic Blackness in M. NourbeSe Philip's *Zong!* 171
    The archive of enslavism 173
    The *Zong* case 176
    A new narrative address 179

4 Epilogue: ... looking at the stars 193

Bibliography 201
Index 223

FIGURES

1.1 NASA *Blue Marble* (1972) 9
1.2 NASA *Blue Marble* (2012) 10
3.1 M. NourbeSe Philip, *Zong!* 181
3.2 M. NourbeSe Philip, *Zong!* 186
3.3 M. NourbeSe Philip, *Zong!* 188
3.4 M. NourbeSe Philip, *Zong!* 191

ACKNOWLEDGEMENTS

I thank all the friends and colleagues who have been so generous and patient all through the time that it took to bring this project into the shape it now has. I am especially grateful to Ira Raja for her constant support in so many ways, and to Anke Bartels, Lars Eckstein, Harald Pittel and Satish Poduval who read earlier drafts of some of these chapters and offered helpful comments, important critique and, where applicable, approval.

In conversation and correspondence, I benefitted immensely from the ideas and comments of Benjamin Lewis Robinson, Anja Schwarz and Nicole Waller, and from the continuous discussion with everybody at the Research Training Group 'Minor Cosmopolitanisms', especially Judith Coffey, Sérgio Costa, Ina Kerner, Shaswati Mazumdar, Francis Nyamnjoh, Rajni Palriwala, Regina Römhild and Madhumeeta Sinha.

Gigi Adair, Kylie Crane and Vira Sachenko were immensely supportive in the process of translating this project into a book. Daisy Nikoloska was a most meticulous proof-reader but at the same time managed to make manuscript revision so much fun.

I am especially grateful to NourbeSe Philip for her generous comments and for kindly granting permission to include reproductions from *Zong!* in this book.

The editors and assistants at Bloomsbury, most of all Amay Martin, Hali Han, Saranya Manohar and Nandini, were extremely helpful, responsive and flexible throughout: thank you so much for all the support.

Most of the first draft of this book was written during a replacement semester granted by the German Research Association (DFG) to whom I am very grateful for their generous funding.

My deepest gratitude goes, as always, to Tania Meyer for making bridges out of gaps. Du Wunder!

ABBREVIATIONS

C	Kae Tempest, *Let Them Eat Chaos*
EB	Bernardine Evaristo, *The Emperor's Babe*
FC	W. S. Merwin, *The Folding Cliffs*
O	Derek Walcott, *Omeros*
R	Anne Carson, *Autobiography of Red*
S	Michael Cawood Green, *Sinking*
T	Patience Agbabi, *Telling Tales*
V	Albert Wendt, *The Adventures of Vela*
Z	M. NourbeSe Philip, *Zong!*

1

Introduction: In the gutter ...

"We are all in the gutter, but some of us are looking at the stars", quips the frequently quoted Lord Darlington in Oscar Wilde's 1893 comedy, *Lady Windermere's Fan* (Wilde 2008: 44). Wilde's gutter-and-stars witticism pivots on the incongruence between a situatedness in the debased here-and-now and an intention towards the sublime. It projects a subjectivity that shuttles back and forth from cynicism to enchantment, from the disillusioned acceptance of a drab existence in the prosaic fallen world to a weak commitment, all the same, to some residue of romance (cf. Pittel 2019). The explicit endorsement of a hard-boiled reality principle rubs shoulders with an increasingly ironic fidelity to the shrinking remnants of utopia. Some thirty years after the first publication of Wilde's play, the German sociologist Karl Mannheim registered a similar structure of feeling in the polarized cultural and political climate of the late Weimar Republic. He diagnosed the widespread friction between a 'situationally congruent' resignation to the given situation on the one hand, and a 'situationally transcendent' longing for that which established reality withholds: "All those ideas which do not fit into the current order are 'situationally transcendent' [the German original has '*seinstranszendent*', i.e. 'transcendent of existence/being'] or unreal. Ideas which correspond to the concretely existing and *de facto* order are designated as 'adequate' and situationally congruous" (Mannheim 1979: 175). It is within this tension between *Seinstranszendenz* and *Seinskongruenz* that, according to Mannheim, modern subjectivities take their shape. To 'take shape' obviously is a matter of form, and for Mannheim, the formation of subjects is indeed to a large extent tied in with "the general historical-social *form* of existence" (ibid.: 116; emphasis in the original), that is, the assemblage of material infrastructure, social relations, meaning-making narratives and epistemic premises of any given situation. In this rigorously historicizing perspective, the situatedness of subjects delimits their intellectual, affective and even physiological horizon as "not everything is possible in every situation. [...] Certain experiences, actions, modes of thought, etc., are possible only in certain places and in certain epochs" (ibid.: 121). This, however, does not lead Mannheim to full-blown determinism; to the contrary, his sociological ideology critique is primarily concerned with the phenomenon that subjects tend not to comply with the fait accompli of their situations; that they obstinately uphold horizons that are situationally transcendent; that they won't let go of looking at the stars from the gutter. Like many of his contemporaries – Ernst Bloch or Erich Fromm come to mind – Mannheim thus diagnoses a specific utopian version of modernity's hallmark disposition, the unhappy consciousness. But where Bloch or Fromm tend to postulate the utopian impulse as anthropologically constant energizer of world-historical betterment, Mannheim is more particular and less generous in his insistence on the difference that *form* makes: when it takes the wrong shape, when it goes awry, situational transcendence turns into starry-eyed romanticism at best, and into fascist ressentiment at worst.

Form makes a difference: this holds true even for Lord Darlington's quip, which is both an integral part of the script of a comedy of manners and a self-standing 'saying' in the generic sense proposed by André Jolles. Jolles discusses the saying as a simple form that manifests in multiple concretizations as proverb, maxim or aphorism, all of which serve as formal correlates of "an asymptotic world" (Jolles 2017: 123) that is not experienced as seamlessly continuous. Rather, an 'asymptotic world' is apprehended "as a multiplicity of discrete perceptions and discrete experiences" whose constituent moments remain distinct "in their scattered idiosyncracy [and] cannot flow together" into one coherent whole (ibid.). Therefore, the world of the saying is "not a *cosmos*; it is things in dispersion" (ibid.; emphasis in the original): a collage of weakly articulated segments. As a saying – more accurately, an aphorism – Darlington's quip comes in/as an emphatically moveable form, which is perhaps most apt for the task to give expression to a structure of feeling that oscillates between gutter and stars. For however deeply embedded and 'situationally congruent' with its larger dramatic context it may appear, Darlington's witticism does never belong only there. Quite literally it retains some degree of 'situational transcendence' as a mobile, self-sufficient, self-enclosed unit that calls out to be transplanted and to be allowed to resurface elsewhere – as calendar motto or epigraph to books and magazine articles, on fridge magnets, bumper stickers and T-shirts, in Fatboy Slim lyrics or introductions to Nietzsche: new settings and contexts where it will not appear primarily as an extract from an absent larger text but rather as the core and perhaps the germ of a story yet to be unpacked. It is not so much a fragment as a segment. Already in its original context of Wilde's comedy, it displays its extraordinary reproducibility, punctuating the flow of the dialogue of which it nevertheless remains a part. Darlington's interlocutor, Dumby, immediately repeats the memorable phrase and thereby foregrounds its iterability. As a result, the aphorism stands as a bounded unit that refuses to fully dissolve into a contextual continuity. It thereby subtly introduces into the Wildean script of elegant repartee a moment of pause where uninterrupted conversation briefly stumbles and points to the parts of which it is made: segments. Whenever continuity is caught wrong-footed in even the slightest way, the illusion of seamlessness and organicity gives way to an insight into the fabrication of the text as an assemblage of heterogeneous units. An impediment to prose's "careful determination to move steadily onwards, one step at a time" (Moretti 2013: 56–7), the aphorism has a halting effect and points to the patterning of language. Instead of a continuous sequence, the text then becomes a constellation of segments that are held apart and yet connected by the separating gaps between them. Like the stars looked at from the gutter, these assemblages invite the viewer to make up their own connections.

It remains to be added that stargazing is never a simply individualistic affair. True, the patterns that appear as heavenly script across the dark folio of the night sky are nothing but the effect of perspectivist tricks of the eye that looks up from the gutter. But that 'eye' is never individual for the constellations above are the same for other stargazers in other gutters: an apparently universal script, based entirely on the imaginary relations that the viewer constructs rather than construes between actually disparate, unconnected distant suns. From the base camp of Planet Earth, the night sky thus appears as a vast panorama of "composed relationalities", which is Anna Kornbluh's shorthand definition for *form* (Kornbluh 2019: 4). But even this is, quite literally, only half the story: there is not one single planetary perspective that everybody shares but rather situated outlooks contingent on location in time and space. For the starry sky changes with the seasons so that summer and winter have their own specific patterns; moreover, the sky is strictly hemispheric so that gazers from the Global South will make (out) completely different constellations, hence an entirely different script, than their Northern counterparts. It is this situational and perspectival difference that complicates the planetary and renders it experientially incomplete without, however, disclaiming its categorical wholeness. The readings throughout this book are energized by this differential quality, this heterogeneity and experiential incompleteness of the planet whose privileged medium of figuration, I will argue throughout, is the gutter text.

1.1 Gutter texts and the politics of form

This is neither a book about Oscar Wilde nor about stargazing but about verse novels as gutter texts – a term I use for any text that wears its own segmental make-up on its sleeve by foregrounding blanks and gaps, both in its typographic materiality and the composition of its various codes. Of course, there is nothing new about this textual strategy, which has important antecedents in medieval chronicles and story cycles, in high modernist montage novels and films, in the collages so typical of avant-garde poetry and visual arts, or in the pointillist and cubist narrativities of experimentalist writers from James Joyce to B. S. Johnson and Danielewski. What is new, however, is the prominence that this formal politics has obtained, and more surprisingly the mainstreaming it has undergone: no longer a confrontative avant-gardist intervention, an "antithesis to mood-laden art" with its projections of a "gapless continuity" (Adorno 1997: 154), the gappiness of contemporary verse novels, and gutter texts in general, is neither iconoclastic nor unreaderly. Rather to the contrary, many of the most popular and apparently most readily consumable textual formats today are conspicuously segmental: TV serials, graphic narrative, story cycles, multi-strand/interlaced novels and verse novels, the form that this book is focused on.

Unlike in Lord Darlington's dictum, the 'gutter' of the gutter text is first and foremost a technical term derived from graphic narrative theory, more precisely from Scott McCloud's influential introduction *Understanding Comics* (1993). For the analysis of conventional graphic narrative, McCloud introduces the gutter as a term to designate the blank space between two demarcated visual blocks. Apparently, nothing but a gap, the gutter is the site where "panel-to-panel transition" (McCloud 1993: 70) takes place. It is therefore not only a gap but also a bridge: a bridge that emerges through the inductive acts elicited in and performed by a recipient who will decode the "intelligible arrangement of the images" (Eisner 2008: 51) on the page. During the course of this reader operation, that which is a merely spatial arrangement – a com*position* – of a set of visual units on a page gets translated, as it were, into a temporal sequence: "In the limbo of the gutter, human imagination takes two separate images and transforms them into a single idea" (McCloud 1993: 66). True, it has always been one of the basic tenets of reception theories from Ingarden, Iser and Eco to the present that the reader cooperates in the actualization of the literary work by negotiating the lacunae and spots of indeterminacy that permeate any text. And yet theorists of graphic narrative have good reason to insist that it is "an undeniable fact (and one of the few that can be claimed positively about the form) that the gutter – the gaps between panels – requires work on the part of the reader of a different nature than other narrative forms" (Gardner 2006: 800). This claim hinges on the gutter's persistence *beyond* that moment of synthesis and sequentialization that McCloud (1993: 63) calls "closure".

The gutter is a blank, to be sure, but not simply a spot of indeterminacy of the sort that any narrative or descriptive verbal text inevitably features. As Roman Ingarden (1973: 50) delineates, "It is impossible to establish clearly and exhaustively the infinite multiplicity of determinacies of the individual objects portrayed in the work with a finite number of words or sentences". These unavoidable "blanks of the represented object" (Bundgaard 2013: 180) are not necessarily made visible on the printed page as typographic gaps or ellipses. Rather, to the contrary, Ingarden habitually uses examples of continuous run-on prose of realism for his model of narrative indeterminacy: an indeterminacy that does not typographically 'show' and that tends to evaporate once the reader has imaginatively concretized and 'filled out' the representational gaps, or, more often, simply read on. As a contrast, the gutter remains visible as an empty space on the page where it functions as a blank that both separates and connects. McCloud does not offer any explanation of the unceremonious term 'gutter' other than that "comic afficionados have named it" so (McCloud 1993: 63). In technical terms, a gutter is a trough or channel to carry away rain or surface water; in figurative speech, the term gives a name to a debased position at the lowest margins of society that the Victorians, as the *OED* testifies, took 'as the typical haunt of persons, esp. children, of low birth or breeding'. Yet, obviously, the gutter was not only the haunt of allegedly natural-born 'gutter brats' but equally the dreaded endpoint of any descent on the social ladder, the gathering place of fallen women, failed entrepreneurs, indebted gamblers and other addicts: that place we all are in, according to Darlington, while looking at the stars.

However, a third meaning of the term appears crucial for McCloud's usage as well as mine. In printing, the gutter names the back margin that is added on a sheet to allow space for binding: a blank that enables the transition from sheet to page. The gutter of an open book is the inside edge where the pages are bound together. As the blank space down the centre, the gutter itself is that part of the sheet which, when folded, partly falls in the back of the book and disappears: "That thing which is not itself a page but makes the page, rather than a mere sheet, possible as such" (Dworkin 2020: 39). In the finished product, the gutter visually runs like a demarcating trench between the recto and the verso, but it is at the same time the space where (at least in traditional book production) the pages are bound together. In a compelling formulation that condenses the gutter's work as both separating and connecting, John Southward's 1875 *Dictionary of Typography and Its Accessory Arts* defines the gutter as "the furniture *separating* two *adjoining* pages in a chase, as between folios 1 and 8" (Southward 2010: 45; emphasis added), that in the printing form need to be held separate in such a way as to ensure a proportionate margin for all pages of the finished product. McCloud's gutter (as the blank between panels) owes most of its efficacy to this technical detail from the art of printing where the gutter serves as a space that demarcates as well as sutures two adjoining pages. It functions like the inside margin of the pages of a book as a site of separation and transition, and even if it partly disappears from view like those parts of the gutter that fold into the back of the printed book, it yet retains most of its visibility.

If McCloud's gutter is already at least partly metaphoric, then I will transfer this term to even more areas of reference and assume that the gutter is not restricted to graphic narrative but a feature of any text that foregrounds its blanks at least to some extent visually, that is by way of a deliberately discontinuous and gappy distribution of print on page. In this respect, the verse novels on which this study focuses display a wide range of different modes of evoking gappiness, and their readings will have to attend to the "materiality of print" (Larkin and Pon 2001: 6) as much as to the numerous other dimensions of these texts. Brian McHale, to whose model of narrative poetry I am largely indebted, has explicitly, albeit only sporadically, taken recourse to McCloud's deployment of the gutter for his own discussion of gappiness as a genre-transcending phenomenon. In his discussion of gappiness, McHale asserts that

> where the text breaks off and a gap (even if only an infinitesimal one) opens up, the reader's meaning-making apparatus must gear up to bridge the gap and heal the breech. A gap is a provocation to meaning-making; we intervene to make meaning where ready-made meaning fails. [...] we are already familiar with this principle from the poetics of graphic novels (McCloud), where it is the gutter between the panels that mobilizes meaning-making, and from the poetics of cinema, where the same thing happens at the cut. For that matter, we know it from narratology, which acknowledges narrative gaps and gap-filling to be one of the engines driving narrative progression. (McHale 2009: 16)

The gap, of which the gutter is one prominent manifestation, here serves primarily as an impediment and simultaneously a trigger for 'meaning-making'. In this capacity the gutter can be a significant blank on the page as much as any other device that demarcates one segment from the next, including among others the line break in a poem; highlighted chapterization in a novel; or the far more elusive 'narrative gaps' that McHale mentions. As a gap that persists even after it has been filled out, the gutter manifestly coexists with and tends to hamper the continuous flow of reading by retaining the boundaries between the individual segments (panels, verses, stanzas, chapteroids, and so on) even after their *articulation* with the sequentiality of narrative.

I use the term 'articulation' here in the sense most commonly associated with phonetics, linguistic morphology and syntax, where it names the integration of segments (phonemes, graphemes, lexemes) into a combination that ideally appears as an organic whole whose segmentive make-up vanishes from view – as in a 1950s mainstream Hollywood movie where continuity editing virtually renders invisible the cuts between individual takes, or as in "the ideology of prose, which requires the illusion that the format is a continuous and uninterrupted precession of text rather than an assemblage of discrete and discontinuous lines" (Dworkin 2020: 44). This integration of elements into the unity of a larger whole has made articulation a fruitful model for political theories from Gramsci, Althusser and Balibar to Laclau and Mouffe, who define articulation as "any practice establishing a relation among elements such that their identity is modified as a result of the articulatory practice" (Laclau and Mouffe 2001: 105) through which elements become "moments" (ibid.) of an articulated assembly. This kind of transformation surely occurs in the reading of graphic narrative where 'elementary' panels convert to 'momentous' story elements; but insofar as the panels yet remain distinct units, this process does not entail the full integration or even dissolution of the hitherto distinct units into some uninterrupted chain as in, say, continuity-edited film or run-on prose narration with its stylistics of virtual naturalness effected by the 'unselfconscious transparency' underscored by "the typography that enshrined it" (Lanham 1993: 74). In contrast, it is this remaining-visible of segments *as segments* that characterizes the texture of gutter texts: texts that (1) point to the parts they have been made of instead of obfuscating their own constructedness under the veneer of organic continuity; texts that therefore (2) exert a particularly weak "reader control" (Eisner 2008: 50) by highlighting the recipient's indispensability to enact and give shape to narrativity in the first place through gap negotiations; texts, then, whose very form (3) allows for the visible though not necessarily harmonious coexistence of two radical poetic principles – sequentiality and segmentivity – whose balance or imbalance persists beyond the ending of the text and thus defies full completion: the gutter text remains at odds with itself even after its closure. Most generally put, then, the poetics of the gutter text implies a particular politics, one that tends towards (1) transparency/democracy, (2) mobilization/enabling and (3) inconclusiveness/agonism.

This admittedly bold and no doubt somewhat simplifying assertion is grounded in the tradition of social formalism that, as Dorothy Hale observes, relies on the (most often) tacit assumption that there is an intimate nexus between literary form and social relations, and that texts by virtue of their structuration are not only expressions but actually embodiments and to some extent co-producers of the composed social relations in which they participate. Hale's is a metatheoretical account of modern conceptualizations of the novel from Henry James to Mikhail M. Bakhtin and Henry Louis Gates, Jr. In this corpus, she makes out a theoretical paradigm grounded in "the belief that the novel instantiates social identity through its form" (Hale 2009: 904). The important pointer is the word 'belief' that runs as a clandestine leitmotif all through Hale's account of social formalism. She defines that approach as "the belief that formal markers [of the novel] can not only express the intrinsically social character of one's identity but embody it too" (Hale 1998: 15). While Hale does not outright reject such social formalist assumptions, she cautiously brackets them as unverifiable and speculative while at the same time acknowledging their persistent efficacy *as belief*: "Despite the truths we have learned from post-structuralist theory, we still *believe* in the ethical imperatives that made social formalism so enduring in the first place" (ibid.: 19, emphasis added). Where Hale thus tends to question social formalist premises on the ground that they are 'merely' speculative, I side with those who endorse them not in spite but because of their anti-positivist unverifiability which I assume to be the basic precondition for any figuration of situational transcendence.

Social formalism, in this understanding, does not merely register but points beyond what is. Hence it will always have to be a speculative formalism that, as Tom Eyers lucidly explains, assumes that form is a productive or constitutive force that invents as much as it reiterates. What Eyers (2017: 189) calls the inconclusive "formativeness of form" involves the literary text, the world and the reader alike, all of them constellated with each other by virtue of the one feature that they have in common: their non-totalizability, "their shared decompletions" (ibid.: 3), and their concomitant processuality. In this understanding, the foregrounded gappiness of the gutter text relates to readers who are themselves posited as ineluctably incomplete and hence constantly becoming, as well as to an ever evolving world that is grasped as a process rather than a given. By pointing to their in-built segmentivity, literary gutter texts thus signpost not only their own incompleteness and fabricatedness; they also generate decidedly incomplete literary worlds. In itself, this is nothing special given that, as Eric Hayot (2012: 61) points out, necessarily "all literary worlds are incomplete". The actual specifics of the gutter text come into view only when we take into account what kind of outside world these texts configure. Hayot posits "completeness as a feature of the actual world" (ibid.); compared to this completed world the inescapably incomplete worlds that literature constructs will always be lacking. Spots of indeterminacy, as Ingarden and his followers pointed out, are unavoidable because of the infinite number of features and determinants of the object that the finite text can represent only partially. On this understanding, the given plenitude of the world confronts the necessary limitedness of its representation and is, somewhat paradoxically, reconfirmed by that limited rendition. Gutter texts, by contrast, are oriented not on a presumably complete but on a processual, unfinished and incomplete world that is always in the making.

The poetics and politics of gutter texts can be best illustrated very briefly *ex negativo* by once again looking towards outer space to determine what a gutter text is *not*. Visual theorist Nicholas Mirzoeff opens his 'introduction to images', *How to See the World* (2016), with a comparison of two *Blue Marble* photographs, that is, pictures of Planet Earth taken from space. The first of these, taken in 1972 (Figure 1.1) from the Apollo 17 on its way to the moon, is a conventional analogue photograph and accordingly of one piece, taken from one place in space at one precise point in time. In it, the

FIGURE 1.1 NASA *Blue Marble* (1972)
Source: NASA/Apollo 17 crew, NASA Johnson Space Centre, 7 December 1972. Not subject to copyright.

ice caps of the Antarctic and the outlines of the African continent, including Madagascar and the Arabian Peninsula, are visible against the deep blue backdrop of the Indian and Atlantic Oceans under the swirl of spiralling masses of white clouds. Taken from a height of some 7,000 miles, the 1972 *Blue Marble* is the first photographic rendition of our home planet as a whole. As such it has had an immense impact on the cultural imaginary worldwide and ranges among the most frequently reproduced single items in the history of photography. Yet even as a one-piece analogue image, the 1972 *Blue Marble* requires to be decoded as a clandestine gutter text. For qua photograph, it is a composite of segments whose composition is rendered invisible by the obfuscation of the gaps between them. As Villém Flusser (2002: 129) notes, "In photographs, the calculation of dot elements (such as molecules in silver compounds) and the computation of these elements into images are [...] apparent. They are not actually surfaces [...] but rather mosaics". To the extent that the gaps disappear from view, what is actually a gutter text – a 'mosaic' – parades as a continuity text.

If this fundamental disjuncture between pixelated deep structure and organically continuous surface is already built into the analogue photograph (and hence, the 1972 *Blue Marble*), then this disparity widens significantly with Mirzoeff's second example: the digital recreation (2012; Figure 1.2) of the iconic 1970s image. This new *Blue Marble* image differs from the original not only in that it centres on the North American instead of the African continent, but more fundamentally in its constitution: it is a composite of an undisclosed number of individual digital pictures taken by the NASA satellite, Suomi NPP, in the course of six orbits over a period of eight hours in

FIGURE 1.2 NASA *Blue Marble* (2012)
Source: NASA 'Blue Marble' (2012). NASA/NOAA/GSFC/Suomi/NPP/VIIRS/ Norman Kuring. Not subject to copyright.

January 2012. The ensuing image, writes Mirzoeff (2016: 8), "is accurate in each detail but it is false in that it gives the illusion of having been taken from a specific place at one moment in time". In effect, "what seems to be a solid whole is actually a composite of assembled pieces" (ibid.: 9): a gutter text, then, that dare not speak its name but effectively conceals its segmentivity. The 2012 *Blue Marble* presents itself, counterfactually, as another version of the 1972 analogue 'original', and like that original it comes in the guise of a continuity text. Due to this intransparency the image denies the viewer any insight into its being-made-ness and hence demands to be accepted as given rather than fabricated, overwhelming instead of enabling its recipient. By feigning complete articulation (in other words, by entirely suppressing its constitutive segmentivity), the composite image finally forecloses all internal formal tension in order to enunciate unequivocally as given truth the visual constative of the planet's haecceity.

It is against such an enforcement of naturalized continuity, wholeness and organicity that the poetics of gutter texts mobilize the segmentive, the incomplete and the internally tense. Adopting Jolles's distinction of the world configured by simple forms, gutter texts don't present or evoke a 'cosmos' but figure 'things in dispersion': not a continuous surface but a mosaic. They do so not least by virtue of what appear to be merely formal features that at closer inspection turn out to be decodable as particular ideological positionings or moves.

A second example (now a positive one) may help illustrate this point. At the time of writing this introduction, one of the most fiercely debated controversies in my home country, Germany, has been fought over the alleged 'guttering' of the German language in an attempt to overcome its androcentrism and gender-binarism. Much linguistic creativity has gone into the invention of various forms of re-articulating German nouns to denaturalize and interrupt the traditional gender assumptions that they communicate and reproduce through the language's grammatical gender system. In German, every professional designation comes with a gender-determining suffix, in most cases with the feminine ending *-in* as an addendum to the 'more natural' masculine *-er*. The German for 'teacher', for example, is *Lehrer*, literally referring to a male person but deep into the 2000s and even today used as a generic and gender-neutral term, whereas the morphological derivate, *Lehrerin*, for a female person, remained gender-specific. Headmasters and headmistresses would hail their assembled staff as '*liebe Lehrer*' ('dear teachers') even if they were addressing an all-female collegiate. Feminist language politics for a long time pressured for the equal inclusion of feminine forms in public speech so that it would be inacceptable not to address explicitly both male and female teachers. More recently, though, the debate has shifted from gender equity to gender pluralization: instead of the binarism of two stable identities formally expressed in clearly masculine and feminine endings, the demand is now for a more fluid and flexible morphology that gives room to the evocation of a wide spectrum (rather than an either/or dichotomy) of possible genders. Enter the gutter. Instead of *Lehrer* and *Lehrerin* ('male teacher' and 'female teacher'), new suggestions try to undo the binarism by designing one-word variants that mark gender as gap negotiation: *Lehrer_in*, *LehrerXin*, *Lehrer:in*, *Lehrer*in*. What is at issue here is the struggle against what Alexander Weheliye has in a different context called "preferred articulations", and the attempt to introduce alternate ones. As Weheliye (2014: 48) explains, "Preferred articulations insert historically sedimented power imbalances and ideological interests, which are crucial to understanding mobile structures of dominance such as race or gender, into the *modus operandi* of assemblages". Therefore, any counterstrategy will have to start with the undoing of those preferred and entrenched articulations. In the attempts to open up the German language to the infinite number of potential genders, the identificatory politics of masculinism as well as gender binarism has to be disarticulated, most literally: the word becomes a gutter text in which a foregrounded gap serves as a bridge, as a space of potentialities and at the same time as a void that renders visible the necessary incompleteness of the word that signals and acknowledges how it never can contain the open multiplicity of possible genders.

In spoken German (by now even in government-sponsored broadcast media), this gap becomes audible as a minimal stop that interrupts the seamless articulation of the word so that the 'feminine' suffix *-in* appears slightly distinct from the rest of the word. What gets thus undone is the naturalness, the apparent cohesion of the word that now points to its own status as a composite. In written, print and digital inscription, the gutter appears as underscore, upper-case X, colon, or – most commonly by far – as asterisk. In this particular usage, the asterisk has been dubbed by Germans as the 'little gender star' (*Gendersternchen*): a star that, for its users, bridges the gutter without closing it in some identity-fixating move, but that for its numerous detractors embodies a violent distortion, a ripping apart of the language's continuity and integrity. In that camp, 'gender' has become a verb that gives a (bad) name to all activities undertaken to make German a more inclusive and indeed situationally transcendent language. 'To gender' is 'to gutter', a provocation for the advocates of a normalized status quo given once and for good, but a space of possibilities for all who uphold the idea of a world that can be changed. Precisely because it denaturalizes the naturalized, the gutter text (starting from the minimal unit of the gutter word) is the natural ally of change: it points out the segmental make-up of the word's (and the world's) ostensible organic unity and thereby, its principal mutability by showcasing how any "'unity' is really the articulation of different, distinct elements which can be rearticulated in different ways because they have no necessary 'belongingness'" (Hall in Grossberg 1986: 53). This is as banal as it is radical.

Not all instances of gutter textuality wear their politics as openly on their sleeves as the practice of the German *Gendersternchen*; to the contrary, in many cases, the gutter text will appear first of all as a purely formal affair. Even so, however, the gutter text points most emphatically to the essential decompletion inherent to form. If form were complete, its effect would be to "amplify and replenish our sense of how things are" (Felski 2009: 34): an exercise in situational congruence, in making peace with the status quo. The opposite, however, is the case: the formal *is* political precisely because of its decompletion and its concomitant formativeness that a reflexive reading will have to reckon with. A current example of such a mode of reading is Alexander Beecroft's theses on the return of *entrelacement* (no doubt a gutter text feature) as a conspicuous formal device of contemporary 'world novels'. Beecroft addresses this surface phenomenon as the defining feature of what he calls the "plot of globalization" where interlacement serves as a device "to project onto the level of form the paranoiac interconnectedness of life in a globalized era" (Beecroft 2015: 283). Beecroft's reading, resonant with the diagnoses of postmodern claustrophobia put forth by Fredric Jameson in his interpretation of conspiracy paranoia as a surrogate for an ever-receding grip on totality (Jameson 1988: 356; 1995: 13), is a highly rewarding contribution to the discussion of world literature as it opens up what appears to be a 'merely' formal textual phenomenon to a *social* formalist reading. As such it may of course be questioned, for example, for omitting the possibility to read interlaced novels *also* as articulations of a "utopian horizon of global interconnectedness" (Osborne 2013: 34). Read as a gutter-text feature, *entrelacement* – a device that "alternately entwines and interrupts" (Mazzoni 2017: 144) and thus foregrounds gaps as much as their negotiation – may be indicative not only of a claustrophobic but also a radically open world insofar as the loose configuration of semi-autonomous narrative strands can plausibly be seen to resonate with minor cosmopolitan practices of decentred and pluralized, yet collaborative, projects of world-making. To the extent that the narrativization of this 'utopian horizon' pushes against the formal constraints of the novel, it forces the novel to morph (back) towards the allegedly obsolete medieval multi-strand poetics and politics of *entrelacement*, hence towards a gutter textuality. Both these readings of *entrelacement* – the one that interprets it as an indicator of paranoia and the one that sees in it the utopian outlook of loosely knit collaborative alliances – are principally in the same camp: that of social formalism that assumes some kind of correlation between the text and the social world, more precisely, the form of the text and the form of the social world.

Modes of social formalist reading have a long and veritable tradition in Mirzoeff's discipline, Visual Studies, dating back at least as far as Erwin Panofsky's iconological study of central-point perspective as symbolic form. That term is derived from Ernst Cassirer's epistemological ventures into the constructive and poietic capacities of cognition as well as the arts, both of which, for Cassirer, "do not merely reflect the empirically given, but rather produce it", as each domain of cultural production brings forth its specific symbolic form that "constitutes its own aspect of 'reality'" (Cassirer 1980: 78). In this vein, Panofsky presents a heuristic model in which the early modern rise of central-point perspective in European painting is embedded in and co-constitutive of a larger cultural shift towards general abstraction and standardization. Not only does Renaissance painting figure and present an essentially geometric, in fact purely mathematical, "infinite, continuous and homogeneous space"; it also reduces

> all its elements, the 'points' which are joined in it, to mere determinations of position, possessing no independent content of their own outside of this relation, this position which they occupy in relation to each other. Their reality is exhausted in their reciprocal relation: it is a purely functional and not a substantial reality. (Panofsky 1991: 29–30)

In this genuinely modern construction of rational space, objects and bodies are conceived of as relational points determined by their position rather than their substance. While their relationality on the one hand renders them commensurable and interchangeable with each other, it ensures on the other hand the endless continuity of the space they are located in. Nothing could be more different from this construction of space than the planar projection so typical of European medieval art, where individual self-enclosed "forms stand in relief against a gold or neutral ground and are arrayed without respect to any previous compositional logic" (ibid.: 48). Here, the painting is more an assembly of items arranged on a 'gold or neutral' surface rather than the simulation of unified space. Yet even if the medieval painting may appear gappy and incomplete to the modern spectator, it would be misleading to read it as a gutter text. To the contrary, for its contemporary viewer, the medieval painting does *not have to* produce (a semblance of) coherence and completeness because coherence and completeness are always already assumed as given in the unquestionable ordo of a god-willed world. Hayden White has argued an analogous point with regards to the European medieval practice of historiography in the pre-narrative forms of annals and chronicle that, very different from the modern "history proper" (White 1987: 8), do not (have to) organize recorded events into meaningful plots precisely because whatever happens in the world is already emplotted with "a cosmological story given in Scripture" (ibid.). A similar phenomenon can be made out in medieval cartography that was not driven by "the idea of drawing a map to show some topographical relationship" (Harvey 1987: 464). Instead of evoking coherent space, the pre-geographic map collates often elaborately embellished topographic representations of individual sites that, for the modern reader, remain as disconnected on the chart as the events of the annals or the self-standing figures on the planar surface of the medieval painting. Or, arguably, the arbitrarily episodic adventures of the heroes of the great epics of the European Middle Ages. In all these cases, a gappy textuality of incompletely articulated segments is conspicuous. This gappiness, however, points not to a lack of coherence but precisely to its givenness – hence in medieval painting, historiography, mapping and literature the absence of that specifically modern demand for contingency containment. Against this foil, modern linear perspective in painting, modern emplotment in historiography or the modern geographic projection of continuous space in cartography become readable as techniques that must compensate for the waning of coherence in the course of the weakening of the medieval theocratic and geocentric "image-world" (Cassirer 1980: 78). The unspecified but persistent ground that envelops the figures in a medieval painting appears to give way to a void. From now on there will be gaping lacunae between these figures and it appears to be the task of the modern text to close these gaps.

As soon as meaning and coherence are no longer guaranteed in and by the world, they must be generated by the visual, historiographic, cartographic or literary text from its own resources, as it were. Hence the 'infinite, continuous and homogeneous space' that Panofsky makes out as the prime effect of central-point perspective and that finds its extension in the post-Mercator projections of geometric cartography; hence the evocation of meaningful historical patterns by way of narrative design in the absence of a cosmological master plan; and hence, finally, the gradual refinement of the manifold literary means of generating amplitude and narrative density, reality and persistence effects. Modernity thus produces its own coherence, one that Panofsky describes as a "purely functional and not a substantial reality" (1991: 30). This reality is by no means limited to the geometric space of central-point perspective that reduces objects to generally interchangeable abstract 'points'. It resonates with similarly standardizing and homogenizing formal innovations in, say, the experience of time, the organization of economic exchange or the modes of imagining social existence as such. Walter Benjamin (1968: 260–2) has famously sketched the chronological regime of modernity as 'homogeneous empty time': a temporality that relies on the *formal* principles of continuous linearity, irreversibility and the commensurability of all points in time; likewise, the advent of a monetarized market economy transforms more and more objects and services into commodities that are indefinitely commensurate due to their "homogeneous exchange value" (Harvey 2010: 24). What Marx (1976: 126) defines as the generalized "price form" (*Preisform*) engenders a pervasive abstraction and de-ontologization due to "capital's mitigating equalization of all things uncommon to each other through the flexible form of money exchange" (Fehskens 2012: 411). This emphatically includes "the ideological illusion that all humans on the global surfaces of the world market are interchangeable" (Hardt and Negri 2000: 395). If the syntax of modern continuity and coherence arguably requires a paradigm of purely abstract commensurate terms that can be smoothly substituted for one another, the gutter text departs form this poetics by insisting on the specific at the cost of continuity. Unlike the segmental medieval text, it cannot rely on a pre-existent given coherence of the world, but unlike the postrenaissance continuity text it will not sacrifice heterogeneity and specificity to the project of seamless continuity. The gaps of the gutter text are the *formal* pointers to its refusal to subject the particular to the abstraction demanded by the "will to coherence" (Wagner 2020: 110).

Form, then, has a social life of its own – a dimension that in literary theory has ironically been neglected especially by most variants of formalism proper (such as the New Criticism) due to their penchant to postulate a dichotomous relation of mutual exclusivity between form and its alleged other, whether grasped in terms of content, matter or substance. Instead of subscribing to such polarities, I hold that neither content, matter nor substance can occur without form, and vice versa. If form, as Sandra Macpherson (2015: 388) puts it, "means a perceptible, perhaps a recurring pattern that makes something the thing it is", then the question arises as to "what could be free from form" (ibid.). All that is the case (in other words, 'the world') will always also occur in some kind of shape or pattern, however precarious, evanescent, fragile or volatile. This kind of political formalism does not postulate a fully articulated totality into whose paradigmatic order everything is inserted; it rather presumes that social life, though essentially structured and patterned, is never fully fixed and, more than that, that there is always a multiplicity of coexistent (symbolic) forms, major or minor. This, to be sure, applies to Renaissance perspectival painting as much as to all other 'image-worlds'. Hans Belting (2010: 527) points out that central-point perspective in Italian painting was deeply indebted to "the historical encounter with Arab science that helped to create the visual culture of the Renaissance"; more fundamentally this cross-cultural genealogy urges to pluralize and decentre the notion of the symbolic form as such: "Studying perspective as a cultural or symbolic form is meaningful only if the goal is to give equal acceptance to other forms and rules for guiding the eyes" (Belting 2011: 255). Whereas the continuity text attempts to suppress this pluralism, gutter texts are premised on its acknowledgment. The formal precondition for this acknowledgment is the incompleteness of the segments' articulation: an aesthetics that correlates with the ineluctable inconclusiveness of sociopolitical integration.

This is exactly what Laclau and Mouffe mean when they claim, in a gesture that hijacks and twists around the Thatcherite adage, that "society does not exist" (2001: 107): no political project or discourse can hegemonize the whole field of discursivity, so that society principally "involves the institutionalization of its own openness and, in that sense, the injunction to identify with its own impossibility" (Laclau 2000: 199). Society's forms are therefore necessarily provisional and ungrounded but for all that, not simply entropic. Even the quirk and the glitch are, in spite of their apparent incommensurability, very much part of the patterned regularity against which alone they can stand out as *ir*regular in the first place. The late Althusser, whose aleatory materialism is frequently misread as a mere anti-formalism, postulates precisely this when he concedes that the world is "just a pure effect of contingency" as its genesis depends "on the aleatory encounter of atoms" (Althusser 2006: 170); yet he adds in a kind of secular deism that, once this encounter has occurred and engendered the crystallization (read: articulation) of a world from what theretofore was just disconnected atoms, contingency is suspended and superseded by "the accomplished fact [*fait accompli*]" of a formed world ordered by "the fact of the forms which 'gives form' to the effect of the encounter" (ibid.: 169–70).

Form, then, is inscribed into the very fabric of the world as soon as it begins to constitute; it is hence not restricted to works of art but indeed a pervasive dimension of the inhabitable and perceptible world. Moreover, "forms, defined as patternings, shapes, and arrangements [...] can organize both social and literary objects" (Levine 2013: 13), for better or worse: the sonnet and the ballot system, the Viennese Waltz and racial apartheid are all, in whatever different fashion, forms understood as so many "ways of organizing heterogeneous materials" (ibid.: 56), or, in the diction popularized by Jacques Rancière, modes of distributing the sensible: "The distribution of the sensible reveals who can have a share in what is common to the community based on what they do and on the time and space in which this activity is performed" (Rancière 2004b: 12). This contest, which for

Rancière is coterminous with the political as such, is primarily a *struggle over form*, understood as the arrangement – with Levine: the organization, with Kornbluh: the composed relationalities – of bodies and material in social space. Yet no social formation is ever a fully "sutured totality" (Laclau and Mouffe 2001: 105). Hence the "incompletion in the social order" (Kornbluh 2019: 29) remains ineluctable: not as a lack to be bemoaned but as a categorical openness that enables the "political contestability" (ibid.) of each and every established form. If the political, then, is crucially formal, the reverse is also true: the formal is eminently political.

In this scenario, where politics is form and form politics, literature has a particular and privileged role to play. For Levine, Eyers, Rancière and Kornbluh, each of whom operates with a very distinct version of formalism, it offers a space where established social forms, or distributions of the sensible, can not only be affirmatively reproduced in situationally congruent reiterations, but also, often at the same time, critically confronted with hitherto unrealized alternatives in excess of the established given. The politics of form is therefore rarely unequivocal but more often than not suggestive of manifold, frequently contradictory readings. What is specific to literature is not the fact that it is suffused with form: form occurs everywhere and is not restricted to the arts. What *is* specific to the arts (including literature), however, is its unique capacity to play with form: as a prominent field of autopragmatic interdiscursivity, literature has the power to reassemble and reconfigure – to redistribute – available forms on its own terms. Literary forms then may "set forms against one another in disruptive and aleatory ways" (Levine 2013: 40). Within their folds, literary texts can thus accommodate otherwise incompatible forms and thereby symbolically perform what Rancière has discussed as "*dissensus*" (emphasis in the original): the act to "place one world in another" as the effect of a prior "demonstration (*manifestation*) of a gap in the sensible itself" (Rancière 2010: 39; emphasis in the original). In its most basic structural feature – its gappiness – the gutter text demonstrates this gap in the sensible, this incompleteness of the world that alone allows for situationally transcendent projections of other worlds. Dissensus is thus as a key moment of the formal politics of gutter texts.

1.2 Verse novels as gutter texts

The term gutter text is not meant as a genre descriptor but as a name for a textual feature that may occur in a variety of literary formats. This study will restrict itself to one specific form, the verse novel, for several reasons. *Firstly*, in text-immanent terms, the verse novel is arguably amongst those literary forms that are most fundamentally, most radically, constituted on gutter-text features: the tense interrelatedness of separation and connection is inscribed into its very fabric in which segmentivity and sequentiality are inseparably entangled. *Secondly*, the very appellation of the form as 'verse novel' points to the off-centre status of these texts in a largely novel-centred world-literary system. The complicated relation between the verse novel and its normalized dominant contrast foil, the (prose) novel, indeed enables a set of speculations on the hierarchies and preferred articulations of the hegemonic genre system but also the acknowledgment of the actual generic diversity that proliferates below the radar of mainstream publishing circuits and scholarship. *Thirdly*, the verse novel has over the past decades established itself as a highly prolific though largely overlooked literary form especially in postcolonial, diasporic and minoritarian anglophone writing. It is therefore hoped that a form-political theorization of the affordances of verse novels for dissident literary figurations and interventions may offer a meaningful and enriching contribution to the postcolonial conversation.

The formal politics of the verse novel

With regards to the first aspect – the text-immanent dimension – it is important to recall the basic tenets of political formalism and to proceed from the assumption of a social impact of (literary) form. It is true that the contemporary verse novel proliferates and splices into a vast variety of forms from the strictly regular to the apparently amorphous; yet all these multiple manifestations share one basic and defining radical, namely, the presentation of a more or less coherent extensive narrative in versified form. Most basically, the verse novel has been described as a "literary oxymoron […] that uses poetry to compose a type of text that is commonly written in prose" (Abate 2018: v); or in the same vein as "a hybrid of sorts", an "interstitial form" that is capable to "sustain a narrative with a fully developed plot" but at the same time is "introspective in the way lyric poetry might be" (Kroll and Jacobson 2014: 185). The minimal criterion for a verse novel would then comprise the presentation of a more or less coherent extensive narrative in versified form. This in itself may not yet be a satisfactory justification to apply the term 'verse novel' to a book since, as Catherine Addison (2017: 7) remarks,

> To be classified as a verse novel, a text must be both verse and novel. While verse is mostly easy to recognize by its lineation, the novel in its broadest definition is very difficult to pin down, being extremely versatile and ever changing.

The rub, then, lies with the versatility not of 'verse' but of 'novel'. Addison takes her way out of this conundrum by eschewing the thicket of contemporary novel theories and instead basing her own distinction of a verse narrative's status as verse *novel* on the well-worn set of criteria that Ian Watt has long ago defined as paradigmatic for the *realist* novel: therefore, for Addison, a "long narrative poem" may count as a verse novel when it possesses "substantial length, contemporaneity, verisimilitude, dialogism, characters possessing at least a modicum of interiority, a reasonably unified plot and a fictional world containing a redundancy of mundane objects" (ibid.). Of course, to frame the verse novel with such a strong reliance on Watt's criteria for the novel tends to restrict the former to the kind of formal realism that Watt so magisterially presents as defining the eighteenth-century novel in England. More than that, it leaves the inherent Eurocentrism/Anglocentrism of that matrix largely intact. These caveats notwithstanding, Addison's minimal model of the verse novel is among the most productive propositions so far, especially when read as an attempt to distinguish the verse novel not primarily from the (prose) novel but rather the epic. For it is the epic, not the novel, that serves as the implied but constitutive other against which the verse novel, for Addison, gains its profile. Like the verse novel, the epic is a long and often convoluted narrative in verse; but one whose subject matter and personnel are derived from "myth, history, legend" rather than from the everyday "lives of ordinary people" (De Boever 2013: 44–5) that take centre stage in the novel, whether in pose or in verse. Inasmuch as the epic reiterates given narrative material and "traditional plot", it assumes and retrenches a world that is "essentially complete and unchanging" (Watt 1972: 14): the very opposite of the inconclusiveness and incompleteness that the gutter text projects.

In one of the few other extant attempts at a definition, Lars Ole Sauerberg (2004: 447) maintains that

> The late twentieth-century verse novel shares with the prose novel its reliance on a strong narrative drive, mimesis of the world-as-we-know-it, a foregrounding of the subject (human agent) as part of the cast and/or in a narrative stance. To this it adds the formal element of verse, which works its effects by the visual impact of the graphic units of verse and stanza realized as pauses when read aloud, the prosodic emphasis of rhythm, and the semantic configurations arising from rhyme, whether internal or end rhyme.

Sauerberg's definition hinges on a distinction of content and form so that verse novels, as in Addison's model, appear to convey the same subject matter as prose novels but with a significantly different mode of presentation. And it is true: contemporary verse novels cover the same thematic grounds, and often inhabit the same generic fields, that prose novels habitually occupy.[1]

---

[1] In his insightful survey of contemporary verse novels, Adrian Kempton (2018: 129–30) offers a list, by no means comprehensive, that testifies to this: topics and formats range from coming-of-age and bildungsroman narratives to murder mystery and detective fiction, from love stories to historical fiction, from gothic to science fiction, from family sagas to village sketches, national allegories and stylized documentaries.

Given this thematic congruence with the prose novel, for Sauerberg, the appeal, if not raison d'être, of the verse novel is grounded in the sociocultural impact of form, more specifically, in what he perceives as the supremacy of verse over prose. In that understanding, the currency of the verse novel is a symptom of a crisis of prose narrative in late twentieth-century culture. While prose has somehow gone out of sync with present modes of perception, verse participates in the "new synaesthetic formations" of popular culture worldwide – advertisement jingles, pop-music lyrics, the rhythms of rap:

> In response to new synaesthetic formations within global popular cultures, [the verse novel] has the advantage of being able to appeal directly to audiences [...] highly aware of contemporary media forms. The verse novel, especially when performed, combines narrative drive with musical dynamics, a combination found in shorter durations in pop-music ballads. (ibid.: 452)

In this reading, large-format narrative in the form of the verse novel abandons the barrenness of prose and opens up to the performativity of metre and rhythm. Joy Alexander seconds this view when she situates the rise of the contemporary verse novel within the general trends of a cultural dominant in which "our age translates itself back into the oral and auditory modes because of the electronic pressure of simultaneity" (Alexander 2005: 270). A partly similar hypothesis is put forth by Addison for whom, however, the rise of the verse novel entails not so much a *new* turn but rather a *return* to a more natural, less crafted mode of narrativity. Addison puts into question the common-sense assumption that prose is more organic than verse and claims instead that, at least as far as the English language is concerned, it is verse – and for her, this seems to mean: iambic forms – that is 'natural', while "prose passages [...] that consistently avoid iambic rhythms, are perhaps more 'unnatural' and 'crafted' than much iambic poetry – especially blank verse, which does not include the extra formality of rhyme" (Addison 2009: 550).

Sauerberg, Alexander and Addison's positions are fascinating but not entirely unproblematic. Sauerberg emphasizes the performative aspect of verse novels to an extent that makes his argument far less applicable to the scriptural dimension of these texts. Verse novels, however, are not (necessarily) performance poetry, nor are they routinely read aloud. Therefore, they do not participate more intensely than other forms of literature in the rhythmic soundscapes of popular culture. Addison's argument is intriguing in its counterintuitive suggestion of prose's stiltedness; yet if this amounts to a welcome denaturalization of prose as apparent zero-degree style, then the second part of her argument – the claim of an inherent inclination of the English language to iambic patterns – recaptures this move in a re-naturalization of the blank verse as *the* organic Anglophone form: an assumption with a long and problematic tradition that Anthony Easthope has effectively debunked long ago as an ideological construction (Easthope 1983: 64–9). What all these approaches have in common is a tendency to treat form and content as isolated analytic categories. For Sauerberg, the verse dimension is merely 'added' to the novel dimension. But is it really the case that the 'mimesis of the world-as-we-know-it' remains unaffected by the representational apparatus that articulates that mimesis? Put differently, does prose articulate the same world as verse? These questions ripple all through this book.

A second line of argumentation, equally focused on aspects of form, is far more politically inclined and could be labelled as the 'polemics of literary form' position. It is most eloquently presented by Katharine Burkitt in her book-length study of four contemporary verse novels, which she reads as interventions against the "imperialism" of the novel: "These texts harness their generic difference to highlight the shortcomings of contemporary literary forms as they engage in postcolonial critique and underline the political potential of generic subversion" (Burkitt 2012: 28). As for the immanent features of the form, Burkitt is conspicuously agnostic when she asserts that "there is a lack of vocabulary and critical direction available to articulate the position of the verse-novel" (ibid.: 31). And yet her analysis clearly stands in the social formalist tradition of reading form as sedimented political content, culminating in the summary that as far as the contemporary verse novel is concerned, "literary form *is* postcolonial critique" (ibid.: 143; emphasis in the original). My own framing and reading of verse novels are in many ways sympathetic with Burkitt's. However, her analysis appears to be unnecessarily limited to discussing verse novels almost exclusively as interventions into the novel-centred literary field as if they were only concerned with the unhinging of established *literary* hierarchies of genre and style. In that perspective, the critical and creative potentials of verse novels tend to get reduced to their insurgency against the 'imperialistic' prose novel. As I will discuss further on, my own approach, too, is informed by a critique of novel-centrism, so that by and large I heartily second Burkitt's scenario. Yet I would wish to argue that a critique of the hegemony of the novel should not stop short at the denunciation of one literary form's global predominance over all other forms but rather question the impoverishing impact that such an aesthetic and ideological monoculture has on the world-making imaginary at large. The verse novel, in other words, becomes interesting not only as an intervention into world-literary economies but more crucially as a medium to decentre and pluralize worldly imaginaries.

These hypotheses are in themselves fruitful exercises in social formalism, and I will draw on them in my engagements with individual verse novels in the chapters that follow. Yet I argue that a more radical description of the formal specifics of verse novels is needed. Literally, 'radical' affects or relates to the 'roots', the most basal features of something: a dimension where one often seems to engage with the obvious, if not the banal. Such a platitude-prone 'radical' approach to verse novels will attend to the specific tension that this literary form establishes between sequentiality and segmentivity, the former habitually assigned to prose, the latter to poetry. In a reappropriation of Roman Jakobson's structuralist notion of 'the dominant', Rachel Blau DuPlessis emphasizes how poetry foregrounds segmentivity since it can be defined as that kind of writing that is "articulated in sequenced, gapped lines and whose meanings are created by occurring in bounded units, units operating in relation to chosen pause or silence" (DuPlessis 2006: 199). Elsewhere she observes that, while the sequence is the dominant of prose, poetry foregrounds segments: "All the meanings poetry makes are constructed by segmented units of a variety of sizes. The specific force of any individual poem occurs in the intricate interplay among the 'scales' (of size or kind of unit)" (DuPlessis 1996: 51). These distinctions are of course not absolute since poetry is to some extent also sequential and prose to some degree segmentive so that "poetic plots" (Hühn 2010: 21) abound across generic divides. However, the prevalence of either of these two dominants in the two basic modes of literary discourse becomes apparent already at the most immediate encounter with the textual materiality of the printed page, where a piece of prose is primarily marked by the continuity of the running text while poetry's segmentation into lines (and stanzas) suggests a stronger demarcation of the text's units. The effect of this is what Brian McHale (2009: 14) calls a specific "gappiness" of poetry, a spacing of language through the interplay of measure, line and stanzaic structure that makes "gap negotiation" (ibid.) a crucial aspect of the reading process. The dominant of poetry is thus *segmentivity*, that of prose, *sequentiality*, as a mere cursory glance at two pages – one of prose, the other of poetry – makes immediately apparent. A page of prose constitutes the "continuous surface" (Lanham 1993: 74) – an optic equivalent of a "kind of writing that is visually distinct from verse" (Guillory 2017: 61). Moreover, for the modern reader, that kind of visual *and* verbal continuity effect

> is now a commonplace, almost unrecognizable in its familiarity. Unmarked and seemingly unremarkable, the typographic rectangle [of prose] has become so predictable, ubiquitous, and neutral that it now appears, if we notice it at all, as the natural look of language in books. (Dworkin 2020: 21)

In contrast, the arrangement of poetry on the page emphasizes units, or segments, separated by empty spaces, by gaps, and by virtue of that discontinuity supplements typographically the aural effect of poetry as it "disrupts the rhythm of prose" (Shklovsky 2015:14). Jonathan Culler (2015: 252) observes how "the visual delineation of lines and stanzas" disturbs, at the basic level of *opsis*, the continuity effect of prose's typographic rectangle, and instead defines "a set of units that are equivalent but disjoined" (ibid.). More recent developments like erasure poetry or blackout poetry, "where the majority of an original work is erased to leave a new, emergent poem" (Eve 2019: 337), materially transform a given text – often a specimen of unmarked coherent prose – into a pronounced gutter text. These gutter texts, however, are premised on the pre-existence of a 'complete' original and may rather be conceived as conceits since "the source [text] is not on the page, but it remains ever 'present,' in the blanks the poet leaves behind, the white gaps signifying the erasure or loss of text" (Cooney 2014: 18). What erasure poetry foregrounds is therefore the fragmentation of a given surface that, exactly through its decompletion, points to the deletionist intervention and thereby keeps the idea of original wholeness alive, very much like the traces of the censor's redaction work render the incriminated passage illegible but visible under erasure. Proper gutter texts, by contrast, refer to no precedent complete original whatsoever. Where erasure poetry operates on the principle of fragmentation, gutter texts endorse their segmental status as ineluctable in an ever-becoming world of non-continuous and unevenly dense assemblages.

In narrative poetry, of which the contemporary verse novel forms a specific subgenre along with the classical epic or the ballad, poetry's segmentivity is specifically configured with the sequentiality of prose by virtue of the narrative teleology on which these texts are premised (cf. McHale 2010: 50). Unlike in prose narratives, however, the segments are far less subordinated to the sequence: articulation remains markedly incomplete. As a result, a halting narrativity ensues that characterizes the main effect of the verse novel as genre. If genres, with Walter Benjamin, can be understood as "condensed world images" (in Beebee 1994: 251), the verse novel may be seen as articulating the situation, itself essentially discursive and organized by forms, which it then appears to 'reflect': the situation of a particularly heterogeneous space, "a world made up of fragments of many worlds" (McHale 2004: 15–16), or, with Rancière, a dissensus. The verse novel is, in that sense, always on the verge of becoming a *pluri-verse* novel, open to articulate in its form "the practice of a world of many worlds, or [...] a pluriverse: heterogeneous worldings coming together [...], negotiating their difficult being together in heterogeneity" (Blaser and de la Cadena 2018: 4).

Therefore, while attention to form, and the politics of form, *is* extremely important for a project of putting the verse novel in the world, there are other facets that may be even more important than defining the place of the genre on the world-literary map. For instance, attention to the formal and generic specifics of contemporary verse novels might help to not only and primarily trace the form's feud with the 'imperialist' novel but, more interestingly, ask what kind of 'world image' (Benjamin) or 'image-world' (Cassirer) might crystallize in the genre as such. To pursue this speculative path, I will configure McHale's reflections on narrative poetry with Wai

Chee Dimock's theses on world literature as an ecology in the next subsection. From that vantage point, the verse novel will appear as particularly prone to the project of figuring a world neither in terms of abstract globalization nor of isolated singularities, but in terms of a planetarity that attends to the concrete and material specifics of the local but does not deny its embeddedness and participation in manifold translocal dynamics and transactions.

The gutter-text poetics and politics of the verse novel can be exemplified with a cursory glance at a poem which is at the same time a chapter in the little-known verse novel, *Sinking* (1997), which is literally about a gap. In this text the white South African poet Michael Cawood Green relates a disaster that occurred in August 1964 in the Oberholzer mining district (then part of the erstwhile Transvaal province) that holds some 20 per cent of the world's gold resources. A family of five – that of the white mining plumber Johannes Oosthuizen – and their house were swallowed into a sinkhole in the middle of the night, along with four more houses whose inhabitants narrowly escaped the disaster. The chapter titled 'From Event to Structure' relates that catastrophe with a focus on the victims' next-door neighbours who survived at hair's breadth:

> On Sunday evening Dulcie MacMaster boasted to
> Hester, her neighbour just back from the sea, about
> Her strawberries; at two a.m. or thereabouts
> Her strawberries had disappeared – her neighbour too.
> 'Get up, the house is coming down,' screamed Dulcie to
> Her Eric, pumping him awake. He scrambled for
> The back door, yanked it open and found nothing before
> Him. Water burst from walls alive with flames that flew
>
> As tiles popped off around his head. A wind moaned through
> His shreds of dreams, while bundling children, mother-in-law,
> And wife through a window, all doors by now jammed tight.
> Seconds later, all that they owned went down into
> The emptiness. MacMaster screamed at officials he saw:
> 'You said that we were safe. Now you must dig them out!'
> (S 18)

This is no doubt a gripping narrative with a strong linear surge that merges the laconic ('her strawberries had disappeared – her neighbour too') with the vividly expressive ('a wind moaned through | His shreds of dreams'). What difference does it make that the story of the narrow escape of the MacMaster family is presented not in 'normal' prose but instead as a sonnet? It is true that the poem could easily be transcribed into pure linear prose so that a slightly stilted but acceptable text would emerge. In its given form, however, the story appears doubly at odds with itself: as a sonnet, it is conspicuously rigid and strained, as a sequential narrative overly punctured by massive interruptions. Both these 'flaws', however, appear intrinsically motivated by the gaping hole that the poem is centred upon. Indeed, the text gets most copiously unhinged when it approaches that lacuna. The basic metrical pattern of a non-classical hexameter of six iambs per verse gets for the first time seriously out of sync when Eric yanks the back door open 'and found nothing before | Him'; and for the second time, after 'the emptiness' has swallowed 'all that they owned'. The stumbling of metre around these instances of the void is all the more emphasized as the poem performs a marked rhythmic regularity over substantial stretches.

Moreover, especially in the narratively dense, dramatic passages that focus on the escape from the sinking house, the text intensifies the foregrounding of its patterning by adding alliteration to end rhyme: 'Water burst from *w*alls alive *w*ith *f*lames that *flew* || As tiles popped off around his head. A wind moaned *through*'. The end rhyme here countermeasures the text's most conspicuous segmentation, namely the division of the chapter into two stanzas separated by a gap. At closer inspection, these two stanzas reveal a classical sonnet structure of two quatrains (here combined into one stanza) and two tercets (again forming one stanza). These two 'bounded units' are further segmented into lines, in this case rounded off by a somewhat strained but for all that even more foregrounded rhyme scheme (ABBA ACCA ACD ACE). The capital letters at the beginning of the verses also support the line breaks. At all these levels, then, segmentivity and gappiness are enforced, but at the same time, there are other tendencies at work as well, that go against the rigid demarcation of segments. Thus, the most obvious gap – the one between the two stanzas – is doubly bridged by the enjambement of 'flames that flew || As tiles popped off' and by the insistent end rhyme on the phoneme /u:/ that connects not only lines 8 and 9 but indeed the two stanzas, thereby providing a patterned coherence across the whole poem. The text is therefore not only about gaps but also about bridges, however precarious and strained these might be. In this context it cannot escape notice that the last line remains rhymeless and thereby endows the text, as a whole, with a sense of inconclusion that persists beyond the ending: a marker of incompleteness that stands in contrast to the sonnet form with its tradition of "poetic closure" (Smith 1968: 50). This is craftily in tune with the thrust of Eric's vehement demand to the officials which can be understood as a protest against finality: 'dig them out'. And given that this is not simply a poem but a chapter, a segment located in the middle of the larger diegetic arc of *Sinking*, the end of the sonnet marks by no means a proper ending but rather facilitates the transition to the next plot element. The dead, in fact, will be unburied by the historical–political poetic reflections and narrative vignettes that follow. Narrative sequence thus rubs against the terminating impulses of poetic closure. But that sequentiality can only be achieved through the negotiation of the gap that separates the sonnet from its successive chapter. This crucial importance of gutter crossing leads back to Brian McHale's model of narrative poetry. For McHale (2009: 17), poetry establishes "meaningful sequence by the negotiation of gap (line break, stanza break, page space)", that is by way of "countermeasure":

> Poetry is not only measured, but is typically countermeasured: in many, perhaps most instances, measure at one level or scale is played off against measure at another level or scale. [...] All up and down the scale of levels, the 'music of construction' arises from the countermeasuring of one kind of segment against another. (ibid.)

In this way, countermeasure transcends and traverses the gap. At the level of textuality, this begins at the smallest scale where regular metre is transgressed to give way to rhythm, the next scale being that of line jumping (enjambement), followed by the transcending of stanza boundaries and finally, as in the case of *Sinking*, the transition from chapter to chapter. While all these features except the last one apply to all poetry including the lyric, it is specific to narrative poetry (from the ballad to the epic and the verse novel) that narrative syntagms tend to produce further spill-over effects across the gaps between demarcated segments, so that "spacing at one level or scale is played off against spacing at another level or scale" (McHale 2010: 52). Segments separated by gaps are juxtaposed with gap negotiations by way of countermeasure. These give narrative poetry its own kind of sequentiality, which however is by no means linear but ramifies into many directions. All this happens at all levels, and from the perspective of rigid regularity, most of these phenomena would be quirks. More specifically, they are all spill-overs, transgressions of the boundaries between units, producing countermeasures to segmentivity itself while segmentivity remains visibly foregrounded. The segments are not fully dissolved (as in prose) but they are not fully bounded either. Instead, what ensues is a complex interplay among segments of different scales, a relatively loose embedding – neither isolation nor full subsumption – of the individual units into an overarching design that is made coherent by the recurrence of quirky spill-overs at all levels: a kind of fractal geometry of poetry whose ultimate effect, for McHale, is the figuration of "a particularly centrifugal and heterogeneous kind of space – a world made up of fragments of many worlds, a heterotopia" (MacHale 2004: 15–16).

The verse novel in the world

This association with fractal geometry connects McHale's model with Wai Chee Dimock's programme of reading world literature as an ecology in which irregularities and aberrations are omnipresent. In what can safely be dubbed a 'planetary formalism', Dimock envisages world literature not (like Pascale Casanova) in analogy to the world market nor (like Franco Moretti) in terms of world-system theory, but "parallel to anthropology: committed both to a local population and to an unlocal idea of species membership" (in Spivak 2012: 446). The horizon of world literature is no longer the globe of globalization, marked by core-periphery relations and pervasive financialization, but the planet as a site that is produced by the "complex paths of temporal and spatial displacements" (Dimock 2007: 276) that have always connected and disconnected the local with the world at large. In this vein, Dimock develops the notion of literature as an ecology of multiple and tangential interrelations and interdependencies across linguistic and temporal boundaries. Literature therefore is "globalized to be sure, permeated by world-history but also grittily local" at the same time (Dimock 2007: 296). Mathematical set theory and Mandelbrot's fractal geometry serve as epistemological models for this conceptualization of literature as ecology. Mandelbrot's attempt to overcome the abstractions of traditional, Euclidian geometry by the category of scale is specifically helpful in this context. In a famous example, he demonstrates how the length of the coastline of Britain varies dependent on the distance from which it is measured: from a great height, most of its irregularities disappear from view and accordingly from measurement, while from close-up a wide range of nooks and crannies have to be accounted for that do not appear on a school atlas map. However, his is not an argument of absolute relativity but an alternative conceptualization of a spatial coherence that is grounded not in the self-identity of surfaces and bodies but much rather in the omnipresence of irregularities that resurface at each scale of representation and measurement in what Mandelbrot calls 'families of shapes':

> Such irregularities are not limited to just one scale; they are much more deeply transitive. [...] Much more so than cleanness or smoothness, it is the rough weave of the fabric, the bumpy surface of pits and pocks, that is threaded throughout the world, in infinite extension and infinite regress. (Dimock 2006: 77)

For Dimock, this rough weave of the fabric threaded throughout the world cannot be translated into a linear system but into a tangle of relations, so that the planet "counts as a 'system' precisely because its aberrations are systemwide, because pits and bumps come with many loops and layers of filiations" (ibid.: 78). It is therefore not the abstraction of 'purely mathematical space' but the recurrence of quirks and aberrations – the *misfit* – that produces the system's coherence: "A dialectic that makes the global an effect of the grainy" (ibid.: 77) and, by the same token, reveals that the local is "a 'nested' formation, for the local here is not purely indigenous but a 'cradling' of the global within one particular site: a sequence of diffusion, osmosis and readaptation" (Dimock 2007: 277). This approach enables the construal of connectivities across vast temporal and spatial distances and to locate literature within the 'deep time' of the planet: "An analytic frame that reflects, not the life of a single nation, and not the life of a single language, but something like the life of the species as a whole, in all its environments, all its habitats across the planet" (Dimock in Spivak 2012: 445).

In this model, the pervasive quirk establishes some overarching pattern of fractal families of shapes, which reveals itself only when phenomena at all scales are equally acknowledged. This involves a combination of close *and* distant reading. Nothing could be more apt a starting point for such a combination than a focus on the category of genre, which both 'sociologists' (like Moretti) and 'anthropologists' (like Dimock) identify as a privileged object of analysis: while Moretti proposes that the analysis of world literature has to overcome the obsession with the individual text and to concentrate on "genres and systems" instead (Moretti 2000: 57), Dimock introduces genre as a "switch mechanism between a subset of human expression [the individual text] and a species-wide definition of the set [literature as such]" (in Spivak 2012: 446). Planetary criticism in this sense operates within the tension between two leitmotifs of enquiry: on one hand, the focus on the particular rather than the general; on the other, the construction of connections, in 'deep time', by activating the conceptual switch mechanism of genre.

Committed more to the microlevel of textual structures, McHale develops his model of narrative poetry in a strikingly similar way, namely as a model that accounts for 'bumps' and 'pits' and 'pocks' on the allegedly smooth plain of metred verse, the regularities of stanzas and entire poetic forms: countermeasures and spill-overs are 'threaded throughout' poetry at all its scales and levels, or, in Dimock's phrasing, 'in infinite extension and infinite regress'. The most fundamental of all these spill-overs is, in our context, the shading off of poetry into narrative, segmentivity into sequentiality, and vice versa. If for Dimock's planetary formalism, the global is an effect of the grainy, of the quirk, of the grittily local, then for McHale, the precarious coherence of poetic narrative is enabled by the countermeasures of the multiple spill-overs across the separating and connecting gap/bridge of the gutter.

Read this way, the poetics of the gutter text resonate strongly with a planetary approach to world literature as ecology. But ecology, for sure, cannot be thought without politics. Within the 'ecosystem' of world literature, what is the place of the verse novel? What is the effect of its presence in a world-literary space dominated by the well-nigh unquestioned hegemony of the prose novel? In this context, the advent (or resurgence) of the verse novel may be taken as an indicator of how literary texts not only occupy specific positions within the given space of world literature but also actively contribute to the construction of that space. For it could be argued that these texts intervene into the established standards of world literary mapping by way of their formal oddity: they deliberately deviate from the normative genre of the prose novel which not only overshadows all other textual forms in the (world-)literary market (cf. Brouillette 2007: 58) but also consistently enjoys pride of place in literary criticism due to a long tradition of "foregrounding the novel" (Holden 2010: 444) at the expense of alternative modes and forms. Clifford Siskin has polemically dissected this "by now habitual subordination of writing to the novel" as a scholarly myopia that he denounces as *novelism*: "We have so thoroughly conflated the novel with writing that even when we want to separate the two [...] we have trouble pulling them apart" (Siskin 1996: 423). 'Novelism' is surely not restricted to mainstream publishing and criticism but very much part of critical engagements with the (world-) literary field as well. The by far largest part of influential world literature studies centres on the novel as a global player, "a form that is remarkably similar around the world" (Hawas 2019: 7). The diagnosis of novel-centrism holds certainly for most of the debates in anglophone academia on world literature, where the novel has all through the second decade of the 2000s been the privileged object of enquiry in a wide range of studies, many of them excellent in their own ways. Paul Jay's *Global Matters: The Transnational Turn in Literary Studies* (2010) comes to mind along with Caren Irr's *Toward the Geopolitical Novel* (2014), Stefano Ercolino's *The Maximalist Novel* (2014), Rebecca Walkowitz's *Born Translated: The Contemporary Novel in an Age of World Literature* (2015), Debjani Ganguly's *This Thing Called the World: The Contemporary Novel as Global Form* (2016) or Peter Hitchcock's *The Long Space: Transnationalism and Postcolonial Form* (2010), to name a few. Nothing is problematic per se about any of these studies, but in their concerted novel-centrism they contribute to the consolidation of a generic monoculture that, as literary sociologists like Pascale Casanova or Sarah Brouillette have repeatedly delineated, has been effectively spawned, disseminated and entrenched by the agencies of an increasingly streamlined and concentrated global literary market system in which the prose novel – more precisely, its "Anglo-American model" (Casanova 2006: 170) – figures firmly as "the global *forma franca*, the privileged and prestigious form beyond the nation's border" (Julien 2006: 130). Against this backdrop, the novel in its current or emergent avatar routinely appears as the ultimate literary form capable of making the world imaginable: the literary equivalent to the NASA's *Blue Marble* photographs. Echoing Bakhtin's claim of the "novelization of other genres" (Bakhtin 2011: 39), the "novelization of the global" (Siskind 2010: 342) has been introduced as a phrase that firmly lodges the literary articulation of a worldly imaginary with the novel form, however transformed.

Phrased in the connotative domain of ecology, world literature thus appears as a monoculture. But this may perhaps be only the effect of a counterfactual representation. For regardless of the critical overemphasis on the novel, a multitude of alternate forms proliferate, engendering an unacknowledged yet vital biodiversity. One of these alternate forms is the verse novel. As a 'literary misfit' (Burkitt) it deviates from and to some extent unsettles the novelist norm but it all the same has to operate within the literary field as it is: novel-centred. These are not anti-novels but novels with a difference, even if some of these texts (including Bernardine Evaristo's *The Emperor's Babe* or Ana Castillo's *Watercolor Women Opaque Men*) simply parade as 'a novel'. Others come with more capricious paratexts: Dorothy Porter's *The Monkey's Mask* is announced as 'an erotic murder mystery', and Anne Carson's *The Beauty of the Husband* enigmatically as 'a fictional essay in 29 tangos', while Vikram Seth's *The Golden Gate* tongue-in-cheek sports on its title page Gore Vidal's praise as 'The Great Californian Novel'. However, in most cases the formal hybridity of the text is signalled by the paratextual genre designation as 'novel in verse' on the covers of such books as Carson's *Autobiography of Red*, Kathy Oesterle's *Karma*, Fred D'Aguiar's *Bloodlines*, Les Murray's *Fredy Neptune*, Craig Raine's *History: The Home Movie*, Tammi J. Truax's *For to See the Elephant* or Juan Felipe Herrera's *crash.boom.bang*. It is this immediately apparent doubleness in-between verse and novel that leads Jeri Kroll to define the form of the verse novel as an "interstitial entity" (Kroll 2010: 5). The terms that Kroll uses not only evoke the gutter texture at the heart of the verse novel but locate these texts themselves in the gutter: "An interstice, such as a crack in a doorway through which light escapes, is usually empty, but an interstitial entity is caught between two things permanently" (ibid.). The monopoly of the novel, and the concomitant threat of a literary monoculture, are thus held at bay in a formal doubleness that refuses to settle on either of the 'two things' between which it is played out.

The verse novel and postcolonial temporalities

Proliferating underneath the radar, and in spite of hegemonic novelist assumptions, the verse novel thus sets a limit to the ongoing 'novelisation of the global' and imports an alternate mode of narrating *and* versifying. Of course, it is not to be expected (and probably not to be hoped either) that the verse novel is about to supersede the dominant form of the 'normal' novel. It is, however, one of the forms through which the hegemony of the novel is put into question today. In this light, the verse novel deliberately presents itself as a deviation, an oddity, a 'literary misfit' that makes itself felt with increasing insistence. For Katherine Burkitt (2012: 31), the verse novel exemplifies a politics of "generic subversion" through which "literary form comes to stand for ideological positions based on mindful difference and postcolonial critique". Burkitt clearly has a point here for it is not to be denied that the contemporary anglophone verse novel is particularly vibrant in postcolonial and diasporic writing. Since the mid-1980s, in the wake of such works as Vikram Seth's *The Golden Gate* (1986) and especially Derek Walcott's *Omeros* (1990), there has been a boom of books in which big-format narrative comes in versified form. Katherine Addison (2009: 539) actually goes as far as to claim that "English-language verse novels are becoming signature texts of the turn-of-the-millennium period". What makes this phenomenon particularly interesting for the areas of postcolonial studies as well as "world Englishes literary studies" (Varughese 2012: 9) is the circumstance that these new verse novels seem to pop up all over the Anglosphere, but especially in locations that Franco Moretti or Pascale Casanova would call the peripheries or semi-peripheries of world literary space: Australia and New Zealand, Canada, the Caribbean and Oceania and to a lesser extent South Asia, South Africa and East Africa. This is not to say that verse novels were not also produced in Britain or the United States, but even there it is conspicuous that many of their authors are 'ethnically marked' – Bernardine Evaristo, Jackie Kay and Ranjit Bolt in the UK, or Ana Castillo, Guadelupe García McCall and Juan Felipe Herrera in the United States, to name a few. This conspicuous productivity arguably points to a specific suitability of the verse novel for postcolonial or diasporic articulations. All the same, postcolonial literary scholarship has so far largely neglected this phenomenon, and studies like Burkitt's are not only scarce but have moreover met with very little attention. This myopia is plausibly an indicator of the degree to which postcolonial studies are themselves implicated in the novel-centred paradigm that dominates world-literary space. Some critics actually decry "postcolonial scholarship's overemphasis on the novel genre" (Munos and Ledent 2018: 3) and urge for a stronger acknowledgment of the actual pluralism of postcolonial literary forms. A politically formalist theorization of the verse novel enables, I argue, an appropriately nuanced description of the affordances that make that form so specifically suitable for postcolonial projects.

To begin with, there appears to pertain an intimate link between the form of the verse novel and the political temporalities of the postcolonial. For in the smooth space of novelist monoculture, the genre of the verse novel appears as a quirk first and foremost because it disturbs the business-as-usual normalcy of the literary world system by abandoning the claim to contemporaneity in favour of deliberate anachronism. By harking back, as it were, to the 'pre-modern', if not 'extinct' form of the verse epic that the 'rise of the novel' had allegedly left behind for good, the contemporary verse novel overtly "resuscitates a writing practice abandoned long ago and thus felt to belong to the archives of literary history" (Sauerberg 2013: 250). To write (and to read) a verse novel entails, then, an endorsement of the residual in a conscious self-positioning at the temporal margins, at a visible distance from what Pascale Casanova (2006: 97) has dubbed the "Greenwich meridian of literature" where the norm of the contemporary gets defined. This disregard for the status of cutting-edge modernity is in itself a highly political gesture that, from a postcolonial standpoint, enables a stepping-out of the mimetic double-bind of the "outmoded 'writing back' paradigm" (Fasselt 2016: 159) in favour of a far more self-assured and assertive exploration of 'grittily local' indigenous epic resources and archives. 'Epic' here names neither the dominant European tradition of heroic national founding texts in the footsteps of Virgil, Camoes or Spenser, nor, with Bakhtin, the monologic, authoritarian and (thankfully) obsolete predecessor form of the polyvocal modern novel; instead, again proceeding from an observation made by Dimock, I would like to propose that the epic to which the contemporary verse novel refers is much more democratic and pluralistic than its reputation allows. This of course has first and foremost to do with the embeddedness of the epic in orature. In most cases (including the Homeric and the great Indian epics), these texts were "improvisationally composed by rhapsodes, who selectively rearranged the oral epics as they travelled" (Dimock 2015: 127). Mobility is thus constitutive of the epic, imprinting it with what Sneharika Roy (2018: 17) has called a "migratory poetics" that, for obvious reasons, appears most germane to postcolonial, diasporic and minoritarian writing and reading. Dimock assigns the epic form a highly accommodating texture that allows into its folds a multitude of lexical materials and stylistic registers. From Aristotle's *Poetics*, Dimock gleans a programmatic of the epic as "a kind of linguistic sponge" that absorbs "the foreign word" without fully assimilating it:

> Springing up at contact zones, it [the epic] is also superresponsive to its environment, picking up all those non-Greek words that come its way, but not necessarily dissolving them, perhaps keeping them only as alien deposits, grains or lumps that stick. (Dimock 2006: 82)

In a similar way, Roy assigns the epic a decentring effect of weakening normative standards. While Dimock locates this de-standardization at the lexical microlevel, Roy attends to the migratory poetics that informs the epic text in its macrostructure. The migratory constitution of these texts that were "translated, transplanted, transposed through hundreds of tellings" (Roy 2018: 17) engenders a centrifugal poetics specific to the epic: a decentring aesthetic form that in its dominant European variant gets frequently harnessed to "the centripetal politics of the nation", of empire and state foundation (ibid.: 19). Traditional epic, however, retains its genealogy in circuits of orature where, instead of one definitive written standard text, a multiplicity of pliable, interdependent and palimpsestic variants coexist. Drawing on Martin McKinsey, Roy asserts "the absence of 'an established written standard' which in 'the preliterate art of orature' meant that it was impossible to speak of 'variations' or indeed of 'originals'" (ibid.: 152).

Built into the epic is therefore a non-possessive tolerance of equally valued variations none of which is codified as the ultimate text.

It is therefore not only in terms of its immanent structure but also in its pre-copyright, pre-commodity, pre-author-function status that the epic, grasped in terms of its migratory poetics, appears hopelessly incommensurate with a literary system founded on the principle of textual integrity and intellectual property. Standing with one foot on the turf of the novel, with the other on that of the epic, the verse novel blends the contemporaneity of the former with the anachronism of the latter. As a literary hybrid – a "griffin" among the genres (Hearon 2004: 254) – the verse novel thus embodies in its basic generic constitution a warped and palimpsestic temporality that correlates with the complicated and entangled times that Dipesh Chakrabarty (whom I cite here as representative of a whole field of postcolonial critique) has called "time-knots" (Chakrabarty 2000: 243): the overlaps, spill-overs and fusions of temporal stages in heterogeneous time. These overlaps, then, "refer us to the plurality that inheres in the 'now', the lack of totality, the constant fragmentariness, that constitutes one's present" (ibid.). The postcolonial "plurality of heterogeneous temporalities" (West-Pavlov 2013: 166) thus points to the non-wholeness and incompleteness of the present so that, in terms of time, yet another gap in the sensible emerges that leaves established reality principally susceptible to change. It is this time-knot quality that is implied in the verse novel as a form, and it thereby enables a revaluation of norms entrenched in the dominant literary system centred on the Greenwich Meridian of world literature. For anachronism does not have to mean antiquatedness. It can work both ways, naming the residual as well as the pre-emergent, resilient legacies from earlier stages that survive into the present as well as the poetry of the future. And where the ostensibly residual can also simultaneously be the to-come, Eurochronous linear irreversibility gets confused and loops into the complex entanglements of multiple, spliced and spiralled temporalities.

This warped-time politics makes the form of the verse novel particularly germane to articulate modes of worlding alternate to the conventions of the novel both in terms of the figuration of planetarity and of community belonging. With regards to planetarity, verse novels frequently foreground the actual grittiness and irregularity of the earth figured not as a given object but an unfinished, ongoing process whose deep time extends not only into the bottomless well of the past but into the unfathomable future as well. In the next chapter I will read a selection of texts from different locations and situations that address the planet's unfinished processuality through the motif of the volcano that couches in geological materiality the notion of the world as infinitely dynamic. A second focus of verse novels turns out to be the negotiation and refiguration of imagined communities: a preoccupation traditionally associated with the novel that numerous social formalists in the wake of Benedict Anderson's work have routinely described as isomorphous with a particular kind of community: the *nation* (cf. Hawas 2019; Parrinder 2008; Sorensen 2021). In this perspective, the novel as we know it can arguably (but of course not exhaustively) be read as a gratification of what Salman Rushdie (1981: 291) has called "the national longing for form", hence a literary (pre-)figuration of a particular kind of polity that has become problematic in the wake of the transnational impact of globalization, whether in terms of economic deterritorialization, the thickening of technological and communicative networks or demographic shifts ensuing from mass migration on a global scale. These and other dimensions and processes of globalization enforce a revision of the nation-form which, I will argue, ties in with a revision of its literary figuration. Restricting my analysis to texts that focus on present-day Britain, I hope to exemplarily show how the verse novel 'does the job' of the conventional prose novel with a significant difference: like the verse novels that present the planet as open-ended process rather than finished thing, these in-verse figurations of the imagined community generate an inconclusive and heterogeneous assemblage of multiple segments that will not fully integrate into the collective body as which the nation used to be imagined by the novel.

To sum up, with its formal make-up and its peripheral status in the novel-centred world-literary ecology, the verse novel is an oddity, a speed bump that disturbs the dominant novelization of the global and disregards the progressivist evolutionism of a literary history that pivots on invariably occidentocentric norms of contemporaneity. This decentring move occurs at various levels and scales: from the microstructural juxtaposition of the segmentive and the sequential to the generic status of the verse novel in the literary world-system. By virtue of its basic formal features, verse novels figure pluriverses of "'gappy' circuits of connections" (de la Cadena 2015: xvii); and this pluralizing effect spills over into the space of world literature itself where the quirky presence of the verse novel opens a space of alternate modes of literary world-making. Pointing to the gaps in the sensible, the verse novel thus projects a world that is not fixed for good but that always allows for dissensus, the placing of one world in another. Gutter texts in general and the verse novel in particular are thus exemplars of a literature that "points to the opening of other worlds" and is thereby "a real and ongoing process *of* the world, a principle of change immanent to the world" (Cheah 2016: 210; emphasis in the original). These last formulations are cited from Pheng Cheah's attempt to chart a set of criteria for postcolonial projects of "reworlding and remaking the degraded world given to us by commercial intercourse, monetary transactions, and the space-time compression of the global culture industry" (ibid.: 186–7). Literature's mission is therefore to some extent a polemic "counter-worlding", but more than that a constructive opening up of worlds. Whereas capitalist globalization imposes one single reality as given and non-negotiable – an imposition that Cheah decries as 'unworlding' – literature has the vocation "to see the world as a dynamic process with normative practical dimension" (ibid.: 192). Gaps in the sensible, openness and gutters: "As the greatest possible whole of existence, a world must be structurally open. Better yet it must be the endless process of opening itself" (ibid.). All this, no doubt, resonates strongly with my discussion of the gutter text, and it is only consequential that Cheah, too, should identify a special affinity between this kind of literary reworlding and decolonization, which for him is also "precisely an attempt to open up a world [...] that is different from the colonial world" (ibid.: 194). What aligns literature with the anticolonial as such is thus exactly what the gutter text (and hence, the verse novel) figures: a world as process rather than fact. This leads us back to the phenomena of the gappy and the incomplete, and thus to that analytic category that Cheah by and large eschews: the domain of form.

1.3 Gappiness and incompleteness

The gappy fabric of the gutter text lends itself most eagerly to a reading in terms of form-politics, which for Rancière (2010: 37) "before all else, is an intervention in the visible and the sayable". As we have already seen, the gutter text marks a departure from, and an intervention into, hegemonic modes of world-making that posit a complete, closed, hence incontestable and quasi eternal reality into which no other world is meant to be placed. To project as naturally given and unchangeable a single reality without alternatives is the function and effect of any ideology that affirms situational congruence in the service of hegemonic power; a whole tradition of Marxist, feminist, postcolonial, anti-racist and so on ideology critique or discourse analysis points to this basic grammar of domination and its historically specific articulations. For the period in question in this study – the decades around the turn of the millennium – the globally dominant ideological projection has arguably been that of neoliberal capitalism: a formation that needs to be taken "seriously not simply as economics but as world theory" (Gourgouris 2013: 147), that is, as a systematic and elaborate ideological narrative that powerfully informs, and to a large extent delimits, the way in which people imagine their worlds. Addressing the success of the neoliberal 'world theory', Fredric Jameson (2003: 704) posits that "few periods have proved as incapable of framing immediate alternatives for themselves, let alone of imagining those great utopias that have occasionally broken on the status quo like a sunburst". This enforced impoverishment of the imagination is what Pheng Cheah (2016: 193) calls "globalization's unworlding of the world", whose most insistent adage all through the decades around the millennium was the essentially post-political slogan, first 'popularized' by Margaret Thatcher in the 1980s, that 'there is no alternative'.

The term 'post-politics' gives a name to a "condition in which a consensus has been built around the inevitability of neoliberal capitalism as an economic system, parliamentary democracy as the political ideal, humanitarianism and inclusive cosmopolitanism as moral foundations" (Swyngedouw 2009: 609). Thinkers like Slavoj Žižek, Chantal Mouffe or Wendy Brown, among others, have extensively and influentially interrogated this hegemonic condition for its evacuation of the agonistically political. Žižek insistently critiques the supersession of politics proper by the non-conflictual "collaboration of enlightened technocrats" (Žižek 1999: 198); Brown decries the universalization of "the *model of the market* to all domains and activities", effectively rendering "human beings exhaustively as market actors, always, only and everywhere as *homo oeconomicus*" (Brown 2015: 31; emphasis in the original). The critique of the post-political urges for a replacement of the (neo)liberal idyll of compromised consensus by its other – conflict and *dissensus*. This, however, does not mean that it is driven by some irresponsible pleasure in antagonism for its own sake; rather it is energized by the insight that, under the ostensibly seamless veneer of pluralist non-conflictual difference and technocratic proceduralism, conflict has actually never ceased, and that the seemingly smooth space of post-politics is in fact "crisscrossed by so many fault lines that it only *appears* as a continuous, uniform space" (Hardt and Negri 2000: 190, emphasis added). Critics of post-politics therefore urge in the first place for an acknowledgement of the very existence of conflict as such, in other words, of the actual chasms that 'crisscross' the gapless surface of the neoliberal globe. The systematic denial and foreclosure of these chasms will not resolve but simply displace the silenced omnipresence of conflict only for it to resurface in the most ugly and distorted, profoundly depoliticized forms of fascist, racist, sexist, antisemitic, homophobic and so on violence that "bear witness to some underlying antagonism that can no longer be formulated in properly political terms" (Žižek 1999: 243). Especially in the latter half of the 2010s, the protest against post-political hegemony has frequently been articulated in a series of such acts of violence that were carried out by conservative, populist, religious-fundamentalist and/or ethnonationalist coalitions whose ascendancy in multiple and diverse settings from the United Sates to Turkey, the Philippines and India to Brazil and Russia some observers interpret as "the waning days of the neoliberal consensus" (Postero and Elinoff 2019: 15). But that 'waning' occurs in ways not foreseen (and even less, desired) by those who have consistently condemned post-politics for its empty, non-agonistic proceduralism.

For post-politics seems now to be besieged by a new alliance of anti-liberal, often outright authoritarian actors who appropriate the rhetoric of agonism and conflict for an assault not on the neoliberal mode of production but the dwindling residues of its democratic regulation. In fact, "neoliberal projects have increasingly relied on a constellation of legal, administrative and coercive state apparatuses to both legitimize and shield themselves from political and social contestation" (Bruff and Tansel 2019: 239). Thus the post-political idyll of the turn of the millennium gives way to an "authoritarian neoliberalism" (Tansel 2018: 197) that mobilizes the register of agonistic politicization for an even more thorough depoliticization. Admittedly the fusion of the authoritarian and the neoliberal may appear counterintuitive but at a second glance it cannot go unnoticed that "party manifestos and/or actual policies pursued by authoritarian parties often contain ample reference to neoliberal arguments and designs" (Biebricher 2020: 15) while, vice versa, the authoritarian potentials of neoliberal thought "range from calls for a strong state [...] to performative evidence in the form of neoliberal flirtations with actually existing authoritarian/nondemocratic regimes" (ibid.). Wendy Brown describes twenty-first-century right-wing populism as "an 'enraged' form of majority rule (often termed 'populism' by pundits) arising from the society that neoliberals aimed to disintegrate [...] and thus left without common civil norms or commitments" (Brown 2019: 16, 59). With its denunciation of 'the elite' and 'the establishment', the right-wing populism of the 2010s at face value appears to articulate a situationally transcendent desire for some kind of egalitarian redistribution that it, however, effectively cathexes with authoritarianism, market radicalism and the "clear demarcation of those who do not belong to the demos and [...] who (allegedly) threaten the homogeneity of the people" (Mudde and Kaltwasser 2017: 18). Insofar as it claims to act as the immediate expression of some transparent and absolute general will, right-wing populism perpetuates a metaphysics of the self-present substance of 'the people'. Its ideology hinges on the fiction of the continuous self-presence of the people, and it is therefore particularly keen to occlude "the *gap* between the absent presence of the people and the action of representing them" (Arditi 2005: 82; emphasis added).

By contrast, left-wing populism (for Laclau coterminous with politics as such) is concerned with "the increasing *chasm* between the universal communitarian space and the particularism of the actually existing collective wills" (Laclau 2005: 49; emphasis added). At the most, some of these disparate 'collective wills' that coexist and rub against each other in the space of the socius may temporarily articulate "an equivalential chain between a series of social demands in which the equivalential moment prevails over the differential nature of the demands" (ibid.: 43): neither complete nor durable, these populist-political alliances coagulate provisionally around the void of "*tendentially* empty signifiers" (ibid.: 40; emphasis in the original). To sum up, neoliberal authoritarian populism refers to the positive substantiality of 'the people' whom it claims to represent, and it is due to this positivity that it remains stuck in situational congruence. In contrast, properly political populism is "strictly *formal*" (ibid.: 44; emphasis in the original) and, thanks to this intransitiveness, situationally transcendent: grounded in incompleteness and gappiness, it bears strong affinities with the poetics of the gutter text that favours the conflictual over the harmonized, becoming over being, constructed over given, incomplete over whole, contiguous over continuous, temporary over eternal.

I will imply throughout this book that gutter texts, thanks to their gappy incompleteness, are specifically germane to a form-politics in the name of a politicized *Seinstranszendenz*, whose aim "is precisely the opening of a normative horizon that transcends present reality" (Cheah 2016: 31). But this does not mean that they were immune to situational congruence; far from it: at face value, hegemonic reality, too, reproduces itself constantly and increasingly in forms that emphatically partake of the gutter poetics of segmentivity and gappiness, be it in the shape of the president's tweet (often in literal gutter argot), in corporate jingles or in ever more truncated news items both print and broadcast, not to mention the communicative shorthand that permeates much of social media interactivity. Hardly any of those microtexts will raise the suspicion that they might question the status quo. Far from pointing to a 'gap in the sensible', they operate as constant reminders to the invisible continuum of power from which they appear to emanate. The frequency of president tweets confirms to the recipient not only the solidity and seamlessness of "TrumpWorld" but, more fundamentally, of the "Twitter-Sphere" as such (Kellner 2019: 9); likewise, the cookie-enabled personalized online ad – in itself nothing but an isolated bit that pops up only to be deleted – refers back to some long-forgotten random internet search from months, if not years ago, and will remind users that their moves are being archived in an ongoing, cumulating data pool of galactic dimensions suggesting the omnipresence of a whole corporatized world and its increasingly homogenized and streamlined global semiosphere. The proliferation and dissemination of these various genres of splinter messages into the finest capillaries of the socius follows "the tactic of constantly offering novel versions of the fundamentally old and established stories [that] offer no principled objection to the commodifications of culture in the form of the new-made" (Docherty 2006: 151). As a subtone, this strategy reiterates the claustrophobic message that "the system must be eternal" (Jameson 1998: 50). This *basso continuo* consolidates a cultural conformism that can entrench itself as deeply as it does because it interpellates and performatively involves everybody as potential co-author in a host of online forums, service assessment questionnaires and platforms that, in concert, collude to render participants in this recent avatar of the public sphere "monitorial" rather than actively engaged, deliberative subjects (Schudson 2003: 55). All of which, again, does not justify the charge that the form of the segmentive and gappy text were intrinsically 'bad'. Gutter texts may or may not articulate consumptive conformism, just as they may but do not automatically enable situational transcendence. To claim that they are exceptionally prone to this latter operation does not rule out their principal capability, even proclivity for status quo compliance as well.

Given this principal ambiguity, my focus on gutter texts is therefore owed not to the hypothesis that gappiness was inherently oppositional but that situational transcendence, especially in a post-political and/or neoliberally authoritarian situation, has no better form to articulate itself: not although but because the gutter text enacts an incomplete articulation and thereby holds the *potential* for a formal disruption of the coherence-effect that both the post-political idyll and the substantially populist authoritarianism of the twenty-first-century mandate. Already their non-compliance with the normativity of uninterrupted wholeness puts into question the self-defeating "tendency to position neoliberalism as all-encompassing [which] has made it difficult to see already existing alternatives" (Larner 2014: 194). Alternatives, of course, are exactly what dissensus is all about: to demonstrate the world's actual incompleteness ('a gap in the sensible') and thereby open up a given situation to what Alain Badiou calls "the consequence of making an inexistent term exist in it" (Badiou 2006: 286). Badiou's example in this context is the historical event of the 1871 Paris Commune, which, for the first time, brings into existence the theretofore impossible, unthinkable and foreclosed actuality of the working class as self-governing sovereign. In a situation characterized by "the majority conviction that no kind of worker capacity for government exists" (ibid.: 275), there is no vocabulary for the facts that the Commune all the same establishes and thereby "proposes to thought a whole new rule of emancipation" (ibid.: 285). Placing one world in another – making an inexistent term exist: these are operations of a "constructive principle" (Benjamin 1968: 262) that deploys and relies on formal alternatives to the forms that dominate the given situation. These operations are essentially anti-realist and situationally transcendent in their questioning of the givenness of what is. Inconclusiveness, incompleteness and gappiness are among the crucial common features of these alternative forms. This applies to texts in the narrower sense of the term as well as to the social text at large.

In view of literary polemics against the phantasmagoria of a complete and fixed neoliberal world, the very category of articulation blasts that continuum by emphasizing how precarious and temporary all composed relationalities and all identities are due to the principal instability of articulatory chains. In this understanding, the individual literary text (especially the gutter text) engages first of all in the necessarily disaggregating work of *analysis*, here understood as a liberating act of "setting free the constituents of a whole" (Docherty 2006: 4): the kind of work that the *Gendersternchen* does at the level of political semantics. This is a process of unhinging fixed meanings and identities, and of de-hierarchizing the relations between subjects in "democratic indifference" (Rancière 2004b: 35). This, to repeat, is a purely formal precondition for the constructive, dissensual principle of making the inexistent exist in the gaps of the sensible. Literature, then, is to some extent nothing but a manifestation of reality's principal incompleteness, not understood as lack or deficiency but as the inevitable concomitant of its processuality, and the very condition of possibility for newness and, in particular, relationalities to emerge. In this understanding, both individual identities and the sociopolitical scripts from which they spring are inconclusive and processual inasmuch as "the incompletion of subject-formation [is] linked to the democratic contestation over signifiers" (Butler 2000: 12–13) that constitutes the social world. Similarly, Donna Haraway has long argued that decompletion is the precondition for the "partial connection" (Haraway 1988: 586) that underpins the intersubjective epistemologies of situated knowledges where the "knowing self is partial in all its guises, never finished, whole, simply there and original; it is always constructed and stitched together imperfectly, and *therefore* able to join with another" (ibid.; emphasis in the original). Extended to the status of an anthropological category, incompleteness appears as the basic condition of human sociability where non-bounded, non-monadic selves engage with one another on the basis of their 'shared decompletions' (to recall Eyers' notion of non-mimetic relationalities). In this understanding of living socially, "to be is to be composite and a patchwork of conviviality seeking impurities" (Nyamnjoh 2017: 70). As the very foundation of "the ties of sociality and relationships that make one part and parcel of a community" (ibid.),

> incompleteness touches on all aspects of existence or being and becoming, at individual as well as collective levels, and applies to humans and their relationships with non-humans. Its dimensions include relatedness, openness, enrichment, humility and action. It involves seeking out and kindling connectivities. It is predisposed to and predisposes inextricable embeddedness and entanglements. The concept of incompleteness invites reaching out across real or imagined borders to explore ways of thinking, living socially, bridging and networking to make more inclusionary existence possible. (ibid.: 120)

Incompleteness, conceived of in this way, renders subjectivity ineluctably porous to the other and premised on encounters. These encounters do not occur in some power-free vacuum but in arenas always already inscribed with hierarchies, exclusions and marginalizations. Yet the participants have a degree of agency to interrupt, bypass or creatively perform dominant given scripts. Even more important is the principal productivity thanks to which the encounter is "ontologically prior to the question of ontology (the question of the being who encounters)" (Ahmed 2000: 7). In its structure, therefore, the productive encounter unfolds in remarkable similarity to the act of reading in which, as reader-response theories have reiterated ever since Iser and Jauss, text and reader actualize each other in reciprocal co-productivity. We can add now that this co-constitutiveness is premised on the incompleteness of both reader and text.

To conceive of incompleteness as the precondition of an always provisional mutual articulation of instable and impure subjectivities, affinities and coalitions posits selfhood itself as inherently *dialogic*. Both in terms of the process of its constitution or emergence and in its internal structural heterogeneity, then, the incomplete self is formally consonant with gutter textuality. This analogy is familiar from one of the most influential theorems of modern literary theory, namely Bakhtin's notions of heteroglossia and dialogicity: as fundamental features of the social world and its centrifugal tendencies, heterogeneity and communicative intendedness qualify also the literary text down to its most molecular constituents (i.e. the dialogic word) so that the text, far from figuring as a bounded whole, is premised on its constitutive "incompleteness and unfinalizability" (Nikulin 2006: 55). While this notion of the unfinalizable is best known from Bakhtin's work on Dostoevsky, where its formative importance for modern literary poetics gets extrapolated, it is especially in his early writings that Bakhtin, anticipating current theories of performativity, applies the idea of the incomplete and the unfinalizable to individual personhood:

> If I am consummated and my life is consummated, I am no longer capable of living and acting. For in order to live and act, I need to be unconsummated, I need to be open for myself – at least in all the essential moments constituting my life; I have to be, for myself, someone who is axiologically yet-to-be, someone who does not coincide with his already existing makeup. (Bakhtin 2006: 13)

While for Nyamnjoh, completeness spells out 'social death', Bakhtin foreshadows this claim by his assertion that in an 'accomplished and finished' world where all meanings and identities were fixed, "we would find ourselves to be determined, predetermined, bygone, and finished, that is, essentially not living. We would have cast ourselves out of life". (in Renfrew 2015: 36)

1.4 Connexionism and minor cosmopolitanisms

Bakhtin's 'unconsummated' life finds an adequate political counterpart in Laclau and Mouffe's notion of ineluctably incomplete articulation, and in literary terms, in the loosely knit structuration of the gutter text. Incompleteness, however, is not the same as the absolute absence of structure but rather to the contrary the marking of form as never fully realized and hence infinitely emergent. Since the gutter is both a gap and a bridge, it opens up a space that is segmentive but not segregationist. Gutter texts foreground an incompleteness that is the very precondition for sociability. By the same token the flipside of textual gappiness is what I will call connexionism.

The gutter text's aesthetics of incompleteness as connexionism corresponds remarkably with what Leela Gandhi (2014: 2) has discussed as an anticolonial politics of "imperfectionism" that is pitted against the dominant progressivist and ascetic ideals of permanent (self-)optimization. An imperfectionist reconfiguration of ethics and politics, for Gandhi, is the indispensable condition of possibility for democratic being in common, and in terms of aesthetics, it is interestingly something very close to the gutter text that she advocates as most appropriate to facilitate such a project: it is "ongoingly sociable" (ibid.: 165) texts – texts that wear their openness and incompleteness on their sleeves – that uphold a truly situationally transcendent horizon "that is either at odds with its ambient circumstance or that seeks to be circumstance-altering" (ibid.: 166). By way of their loose structuration, these texts invite for the construction or construal of hitherto unthinkable, hence fully surprising connections to and between seemingly unrelated contexts or irrelevant situations. The main impetus of these 'ongoingly sociable' texts is therefore what Mai Al-Nakib (2020: 233) has called the "forging of links" and "commonalities", in short: the making imaginable of the common as such.

I have repeatedly stated that gutter texts foreground the segments that they are made of. Perhaps it is called for to briefly emphasize that a segment is not a fragment in the sense of a fraction, a chip or splinter broken off from some larger ensemble whose wholeness is ruinated by the fracture. The fragment will always recall the fact of the fracture and thereby project *as lost* some past wholeness to which it paradoxically testifies by its incompleteness. The incompleteness of the segment is of an entirely different kind simply because it does not refer to or even evoke some former integrity. The fragment harks back to a lost intactness, the segment is looking forward to potential (though never guaranteed) future articulations with other segments. It is by definition the component part of an assembly to come: not a predetermined specific assembly but rather an open-ended multitude of possible assemblies. Therefore, an intransitive futurity without a teleological trajectory defines the segment and renders it a "project" that "does not operate as a program or prospectus but as the immediate projection of what it nonetheless incompletes" (Lacoue-Labarthe and Nancy 1988: 43): a performativity of the unconsummated. Segmentivity as textual dominant intensifies this performative and highlights "the various different kinds of incompletion, through the gaps of which one might nonetheless glimpse the speculative capacities of form" (Eyers 2017: 186). These capacities, to repeat one last time, enable the speculative insight into the isomorphic relatedness of text, world and reader by virtue of the incompleteness that they have in common: a segmentive instead of a fragmentary incompleteness.

What Eyers calls 'gaps', Anna Kornbluh discusses as 'elisions' that, like Gandhi's 'imperfectionism', make commonality possible. This politics and poetics of commonality by way of gap negotiation is not tied to any one specific historical setting but rather a basic pattern of articulating social formations. For Kornbluh, elisions provide the "common ground of narrative and social formalization: to order relations means to make elisions – remainders of form's installation that become reminders of its incompleteness", more accurately, reminders of the fact that form itself pursues "the ideal of incompletion" (Kornbluh 2019: 125, 140). Kornbluh's main project in her reading of canonical British nineteenth-century realist novels is to reintroduce an interventionist social and political formalism that conceives of literature as a mode of reconfiguring social space premised on the common ground between the literary and the social: formalization as such. Literature has the capacity to reconfigure social space precisely because it has the capacity to form, and thereby to partake of and contribute to the structuration through which social space is generated and reproduced. Text and society are thus, again, speculatively constellated with each other in an "isomorphism that comes into relief via a specific trope: the built form. Architecture appears [...] as metaphor for the modelling of social space, the production of realist aesthetics, and the building up of social forms" (ibid.: 16–17). It is perhaps due to the 'prosaic' poetics of Kornbluh's corpus texts that her conception of built form (whether in architecture, in literary texts or in social spaces at large) privileges "firm standards of integrity" (ibid.: 36) and structured cohesion. But architecture can also serve as a metaphoric vehicle for the segmental gappiness *and* connexiuonism that characterizes the gutter text.

An early articulation of such a poetics can be made out in *Areopagitica* (1644), one of John Milton's most radically republican texts in which the 'house of God' serves as an image for the budding republic on the eve of the English Revolution. The collective act of building the biblical temple serves as a performative antecedent for the creation of a free and egalitarian polity: the "mansion house of liberty" (Milton 1999: 40). What Milton's temple and his republic have in common is their imperfection, their incompleteness and their gappiness. They are both gutter texts, and so is that breathlessly fast-paced 'speech' in which they appear, *Areopagitica*:

> While the temple of the Lord was building, some cutting, some squaring the marble, others hewing the cedars, there should be a sort of irrational men who could not consider there must be many schisms and many dissections made in the quarry and in the timber, ere the house of God can be built. And when every stone is laid artfully together, it cannot be united into a continuity, it can but be contiguous in this world; neither can every piece of the building be of one form. (ibid.: 41)

Instead of wholeness, Milton endorses 'schisms' and 'dissections'; instead of uniformity, "brotherly dissimilitudes" (ibid.); instead of continuous sequentiality, segments at most: 'it cannot be united into a continuity, it can but be contiguous in this world'. Milton's architecture appears to look forward to Donna Haraway's model of the subject that "is always constructed and stitched together imperfectly, and *therefore* able to join with another" (Haraway 1988: 586; emphasis in the original). This programme for a democratic commonwealth is consistently imperfectionist; the self-constitution of the demos as autonomous collective subject will always remain incomplete 'in this world' but in this incomplete inarticulation, the gaps between the 'brotherly dissimilar' segments are simultaneously connectors. In order to give this open futurity a form, Milton resorts to architecture but he draws from that vehicular domain not those tropes of 'structured integrity' that Kornbluh so strongly foregrounds but instead a rich imagery with which to celebrate the ineluctably incomplete articulation of segments that will not yield to complete articulation so that even the 'house of God' stands as a gutter text. This is a modelling of "architecture not as a finished product but as a place that encourages an ongoing search for truth" (Theis 2005: 116): a process rather than a thing. Architecture thus correlates with the open-endedness of a social world that is always in the process of becoming. Not a noun but a verb, the socius emerges immanently from collectively "built social relations 'without origin'" (Kornbluh 2019: 10). The building as vehicle does therefore not correlate to some circumscribed and enumerable imagined community (such as the nation) but much more to an unbounded network of self-governing subjects. Numerous critics have made out a corresponding propensity to openness in the poetics and politics of Milton's writings, where even such traditional forms as the sonnet and the iambic pentameter display "a studied avoidance of finality" and thus manage "to defeat predictability and elude closure" (Creaser 2008: 177).

Milton's architectural imagery helps to enhance an understanding of the radical and constitutive features of gutter texts in general. There is an interplay – perhaps a tension, perhaps a concordance – of the individual building blocks and the overarching structure into which they are inserted. So far, following McHale, I have called the former (the building blocks) the segments, and the latter (the structure) the sequence. Milton and his temple point to a further dimension of this interplay, one that has been metaphorized in a strikingly similar image. I am thinking of Gilles Deleuze's distinction of the molecular and molar, that finds one of its most succinct metaphors in the figure of "a wall of loose, uncemented stones, where every element has a value in itself but also in relation to others" (Deleuze 1997: 86) – surely a revision of Milton's architecture even if neither Deleuze himself nor, as far as I know, any of his followers explicitly draws on that antecedent. In Deleuze's work, as Fredric Jameson (1979: 8) summarizes, the molecular "designates the here-and-now of immediate perception or of local desire [...], the electrifying shock of the individual word or the individual brushstroke, of the regional throb of pain or of pleasure". These 'loose', vibrant and rampant energies and intensities are, then, opposed to the 'mirage' of the molar: "Those large, abstract, mediate, and perhaps even empty and imaginary forms by which we seek to recontain the molecular" (ibid.). Deleuze clearly takes sides for the molecular (the nomadic, the pre-representative, the autonomous and contingent) and, inasmuch as he "opposes order to life" (Kornbluh 2019: 19), appears as an outright enemy of form as such. And yet the fact remains that the image of the wall (however 'loose' that wall may be) is molar as well as molecular. This, at least, appears to be the point of Jacques Rancière's reading of that "last of the great, strong images that Deleuze has left us" (2004a: 161). Rancière sees in that architectural image an oxymoronic figure that organizes a tense union of opposites that is constitutive of literature itself: the holding together of the molecular and the molar, "of autonomy and heteronomy" (ibid.). For Rancière, the fundamental problem of literature consists in the holding-together of formlessness and form: "How to link together in the form of the work the emancipated atoms of thought-matter" (ibid.: 150). In this light, the Deleuze who writes of loose walls may well be of the formalist party without knowing it.

With its tropes of contiguity and becoming, the imagery of architecture enables Milton to envisage the socius of an open future. As "a combination of messy difference and thoughtful arrangement" (Kennedy 2019: 395), Milton's projected building is perfect in its imperfection.

It is only where articulation is incomplete, where the building blocks remain visible, that their connectedness, too, can be seen. Segmentivity, in other words, achieves coherence only partially but therewith foregrounds connectivity: without gap no bridge. This is how the highlighting of separateness puts a limit to what Sianne Ngai, in a different context but very much in 'sisterly dissimilitude' with Gandhi's imperfectionism, Bakhtin's inconsummation and Nyamnjoh's incompleteness, has persuasively critiqued as "connexionism": an "ideological worldview" that is grounded in "a feeling of incompleteness" to which it responds by elaborating connections and "ties between a radically expanded number of actors" (Ngai 2012a: 368, 370). The term 'connexionism' refers back to neoliberal ideology; Ngai derives it from Luc Boltanski and Eve Chiapello's discussion of network capitalism where it gives a name to a distinctly new, post-market ideological set-up of intense deregulation and novel forms of extraction and subsumption.[2] According to Boltanski and Chiapello, in post-1980s management literature the network emerges as "the central paradigm and

---

[2] I am grateful to Benjamin Lewis Robinson who brought the importance of the connection between Boltanski/Chiapello and Ngai to my notice.

concept metaphor of the neoliberal economy" (Wiemann 2022: 216) and establishes a whole "connexionist world" where the most valuable "activity aims to generate *projects*" (Boltanski and Chiapello 2005: 110). Here, the 'worthiest person' is the one who manages to get involved in a maximum of such interactive projects whose main aim it is to generate still more projects, still more connections. To the extent that connectivity gets profiled as a crucial productive force, intersubjectivity and transaction are coopted as modes of value generation. Interestingly, connexionist logic functions on the principle of articulation: "In a connexionist world, links are useful and enriching when they have the power *to change the beings who enter into relations*" (ibid.: 131; emphasis added), or, translated into the terms suggested by Laclau and Mouffe, when elements are transformed into moments. The connexionist world is thus a site of constant articulation, disarticulation and rearticulation; an interminably provisional sphere that Boltanski and Chiapello aptly call the 'projective city'. In terms of its basic grammar, it therefore resonates strongly with the poetics of the gutter text; but as with incompleteness, here too everything depends upon the political horizon within which this poetics is deployed. As Hardt and Negri (2000: 162) propose, on one hand "power can be constituted by a whole series of powers that regulate themselves and arrange themselves in networks"; this only means, however, that on the other hand, counter-power has to establish itself by way of connexionism too: "*It takes a network to fight a network*" (Hardt and Negri 2004: 58; emphasis in the original).

Ngai deploys the term 'connexionism' in a discussion not of network power but of a dominant contemporary narrative strategy grounded in a structure of feeling that strives for pervasive and total interconnectivities of everything with everything else. Ngai thus offers a critique of connexionist narratives as affirmations of network capitalism, and indeed she explicitly frames her argument with extensive references to the critical force with which Boltanski and Chiapello endow the concept of connexionism. Where they focus on the instrumentality of the connexionist logic, its exploitation of encounters and interactions, Ngai lays bare the implicit aesthetic norms "that revolve around connection and information" (Ngai 2012b: 308) and that effectively subtend her reference texts with connexionist utopias of closures in complete articulation. As in the projective city, then, the connexionist text is suffused with a dynamic in which connection is deemed a value for its own sake, and isolation a stigma, coterminous with exclusion. The gutter text, I argue, puts an in-built limitation on this kind of indiscriminate connexionist logic by leaving the flipside of the connector – the gap – foregrounded. And yet it does embrace and endorse the "potential to enhance human connectivity" (Ganguly 2016: 108) and thus enrich intersubjective conviviality. If connexionist narrative buttresses neoliberal networks, gutter textuality attempts to reappropriate the value of connectivity without succumbing to the demands of the projective city.

The persistence of the segmentive ensures that the molecular particularity of the segment will not be stifled in some connexionist molar hyper-inclusivity and yet constellated with neighbouring segments: interconnected but not subsumed, incompletely articulated, segmentive and gappy in a 'loose wall' where (to return to Deleuze one more time) 'every element has a value in itself but also *in relation* to others'.

It is therefore a critical connexionism that is in some ways the optimistic counterpart to the claustrophobic structure of feeling of classical postmodernism where connectedness tends to equate overdetermination, surveillance and control. Distinctly non-paranoid, cautious connexionsim endorses the enriching potentials of that intersubjective conviviality that, for example, Hardt and Negri celebrate in the figure of the multitude. More than that, in its posthuman and new materialist variety, critical connexionism projects and propagates "geoeffective" assemblages that "tend to horizontalize the relations between humans, biota and abiota" (Bennett 2009: 61, 112) and that envisage the overarching ecology of the planet as one vast trans-species family scene where "all earthlings are kin in the deepest sense" (Haraway 2016: 103). This concept of kinship is of course a far cry from the traditional paradigm of consanguinity and filiation that "remains connexionist culture's dominant metaphor" (Ngai 2012a: 387). Present-day posthuman vitalism reappropriates and displaces the very category of kinship by transforming it into a name for a web of planet-wide cooperative networks "with our biotic and abiotic sympoietic collaborators, colaborers" (Haraway 2016: 102): a rhetorical act of displacement that is most vividly captured in the posthumanist slogan, 'make kin not babies'. This revision of kinship structurally resembles the ways in which critical connexionism releases the very notion of connection from its enlistment for network-capitalist ideology and reappropriates it for situationally transcendent projects of alternate world-making. These rhetoric moves of reappropriation find an unexpected precursor in Milton's celebration of 'brotherly dissimilitudes'. Haraway urges us to 'make kin', just as Milton's tract is a plea "to brick oneself into the Temple" (Kennedy 2019: 377). Thus, where new materialism extrapolates subjecthood beyond the confines of the species and invites for an embedding of the self into the linked metabolisms of a multi-layered planet-wide ecosystem, Milton's is a "rudimentary cosmopolitan framework" (Binney 2010: 51) that propagates a republican connectivity far beyond the confines of the nation. In Milton's ideal republic, "people function as self-governing centres and citizens within a larger, higher community [...] without a distinct boundary or circumference" (ibid.). In this "confident intellectual cosmopolitanism" (Worden 2007: 181) the political clearly exceeds the national framework. What emerges is a *major* cosmopolitanism that all too easily, with Milton as well as with many other major cosmopolitans, reverts to an imperialist universalism that, abandoning the egalibertarian potentials of segmentive gappiness and critical connexionism, assumes for itself the authority to "teach other nations how to live" (Milton 1959: 232).

In its republican version, major cosmopolitanism envisages global commonwealths; in its imperialist outlook, global empires; in its more complicated avatars, as in the case of Milton, both at the same time. What I call *minor cosmopolitanisms*, by contrast, proceed from and remain informed by local histories: they are minor *and* cosmopolitan alike insofar as they grasp the local as nested in the planetary and, by the same token, the planet as a web of locales, so that "the local is not purely indigenous but a 'cradling' of the global within one particular site" (Dimock 2007: 277). In this sense, minor cosmopolitanism is a name for a multitude of practices, visions and knowledges through which people construct and construe "links between minor common causes and wider global concerns" (Al-Nakib 2020: 229) by making their imagined worlds in constant interaction and tension with the entrepreneurial vision of the hegemon. Perhaps the most pertinent articulation of minor cosmopolitanism today is the struggle for ecological justice in the Global South, where it is frequently Indigenous communities who commit themselves most intensely to the protection of the biosphere not 'only' within a local horizon but in full cognizance of the planetary dimension of their custodianship of the land. This is simply owed to the fact that their resistance is against a global risk in the precise sense of that term: the violence of land-grabbing, deforestation, extractivism, unrestricted pollution, fracking and surface mining, and so on not only destroy the habitat and sustenance of multitudes of human and non-human inhabitants of, say, the rainforests of Brazil and Ecuador or the archipelagos of Polynesia but also endanger life on earth at large. Cosmopolitanisms, especially in the minor key, have always consistently opposed the dominant dynamic of globalization-as-empire that tends to *make the world a globe*, that is, an abstract and undelimited space of universal equivalence and quantifiability as a smooth playing field for "the global project as such: planetary financialization" (Spivak 1999: 70). In sharp contrast, minor cosmopolitan visions and practices urge for and work towards the reverse aspiration, namely to *make the globe a world* (cf. Spivak 1999: 391): a shared common space of convivial and sustainable co-existence. While projects of (minor) cosmopolitan worlding thus tend to depart from the hegemonic global design of neoliberalism, they are all the same enabled by, even dependent on, the translocalizing tendencies that globalization unleashes.

Constellating "the local, parochial, rooted, culturally specific and demotic" with "the translocal, transnational, transcendent" (Werbner 2018: 278), minor cosmopolitanisms call into question the myopic Eurocentrism and empty formalism of the Kantian universalist vision. All the same, they do not entirely abandon that vision but rather aspire to "carry over some of its valuable elements into a new space" (Raghavan 2017: 5). Among these 'valuable elements' of canonical major cosmopolitanism there is certainly the potential to *situational transcendence*, that is, to "supersede the given, the accepted, the familiar, or the weight of circumstance" (Aboulafia 2013: 3). A minor cosmopolitan standpoint may acknowledge how the insistence on singularity is a corrective of the abstract universalism inherent in major cosmopolitanism; but just as much it will reject self-entrenchment in the singular as a mere identity politics that runs the risk of fetishizing particularity for its own sake and of severely impeding the creation of a shared and common world. In short, minor cosmopolitanisms proceed from and uphold the particular; but with a persistent and keen attention to the ways in which the particular cradles the global in webs of "relations-with and between particularities" that remain commensurate with each other precisely *as* particularities (Hallward 2001: 428 FN81). It is these interconnections and interdependencies – these critically connexionist 'relations-with and between particularities' – through which, perhaps impossibly, the globe may be made a world.

In 1940, Walter Benjamin summed up his critical engagement with Carl Schmitt's political theology by suggesting that "the tradition of the oppressed teaches us that the 'state of emergency' [the German original formulation is *Ausnahmezustand*, i.e., state of exception] in which we live is not the exception but the rule" (Benjamin 2007: 257). The state of exception for Benjamin is clearly structured by the specific relations of class antagonisms: it is 'the oppressed' for whom the emergency has always been the rule, and it is therefore their 'tradition' that 'teaches' 'us', if not in general then at the moment of danger. Benjamin thus grasps his own moment of danger, the historical moment of triumphant fascism, as a situation in which hitherto 'exempt' population groups are stripped of their privileges and coerced into a variant of precisely that state of exception that others had to endure all along. It is a genuinely minor cosmopolitan figure of thought that resonates with much of what present-day minor cosmopolitanisms have to formulate in their invocations of, and appeals to, a global community at risk. Exemplary of this invocation is Achille Mbembe's notion of the "becoming-Black of the world" in the course of the neoliberal "tendency to universalize the Black condition" (Mbembe 2017: 4). This is by no means a complacent liberal humanism of the kind that allows beneficiaries to symbolically identify with the victims of the very same system that ensures their privileges. It is instead the acknowledgment, reflection and – importantly – the attempt to transfigure implication in a situationally transcendent bid for becoming-minor.

Like Benjamin, Mbembe maintains that the generalization of risk in the moment of danger needs to be embraced. It is from the insight of being collectively imperilled, even if in different ways, that solidarities and coalitions may be forged in minor cosmopolitan modes. In this sense,

Mbembe nominates, as a precondition for a "collective resurgence of humanity" in the face of a neoliberal extractivism that is rampant on a planetary scale, the practice of *"a thinking in circulation, a thinking of crossings, a world-thinking"* (ibid.: 179; emphasis in the original): a thinking that is as reminiscent of its obligation to an unredeemed past as Benjamin's class-conscious historians keep their fidelity to the "secret agreement between past generations and the present one" (Benjamin 2007: 254). This awareness of an obligation towards an unredeemed past is today perhaps most vocally articulated in Black theory that posits "a relation and relationship of debt or obligation of spirit owed by later to earlier generations" (Philip 2008: 205) especially with regards to recollections of the Middle Passage and enslavement. It is in this vein that Mbembe enumerates a series of movements and struggles that are both minor *and* cosmopolitan since they combine the grittily local subalternity of the marginalized with a praxis of solidarity that is as world-encompassing as the state of exception that 'our modernity' has inflicted on the planet and its people:

> Like the worker's movements of the nineteenth century and the struggles of women, our modernity has been haunted by the desire for abolition once carried by the slaves. At the beginning of the twentieth century, the dream lived on in the great struggles for decolonization, which from the beginning had a global dimension. Their significance was never only local. It was always universal. Even when anticolonial struggles mobilized local actors, in a circumscribed country or territory, they were always at the origin of solidarities forged on a planetary and transnational scale. It was these struggles that each time allowed for the extension, or rather the universalization, of rights that had previously remained the privilege of a single race. (Mbembe 2017: 172)

This is a long perspective, and very clearly one that does not allow for the cultivation of possessive identities-as-singularities but that instead emphasizes the interconnections and commensurabilities that pertain among and between *particular* subalternized communities. It is important, too, that this long perspective refuses to close in on a coherent and uninterrupted linear narrative. As in Benjamin's discontinuous scenario, Mbembe's story of the Black Man "could be written only from fragments brought together to give an account of an experience that itself was fragmented, that of a pointillist people struggling to define itself" (ibid.: 28–9) in a minor cosmopolitan form. It is this experience of fragmentation that, once endorsed, provides the starting point for what Michael Rothberg (2019: 201) calls "the opening up of the self to others", enabling solidarities across time and space grounded in that existential incompleteness that turns bounded selves into critically connexionist 'patchworks of conviviality'.

1.5 Gappy planet and incomplete nation: Michael Cawood Green's *Sinking*

Verse novels, as we have seen, configure and interrelate the segments they assemble without dissolving or fully subsuming them so that the roughness and gappiness of the texture punctures the illusion of a smooth homogeneous surface. In the phrasing proposed by Gayatri Spivak, the abstract 'globe' gets overwritten by 'the planet' in all its concrete irregularity, upholding the notion of a world that radically departs from the dynamics of sameness. Globalization, construed as the "imposition of the same system of exchange everywhere" (Spivak 2003: 72), gets incessantly interrupted by the resistance of segments that refuse to get entirely dissolved into some overarching sequence of transaction. This structural apparatus proves specifically appropriate for the figuration of two interconnected themes: the sheer materiality of the planet in all its graininess and concrete bumpiness and the complicated and often conflicted communities of human and non-human actors that inhabit that gritty planet – communities whose heterogeneity and openness significantly complicate the traditional nation-form.

A second cursory glance at Cawood Green's *Sinking* may exemplarily demonstrate how the verse novel as a form lends itself to specifically provisional and subjunctive figurations of both these dimensions. Cawood Green projects the 1964 mining disaster as a clash of nature and history, geology and politics, in which the ruthless capitalist pillage of natural resources intersects synergistically with the hyper-exploitation of non-white labour through the violent structures of South Africa's apartheid system. Already in the exposition to the narrative a tense configuration emerges between the planet-as-materiality and a communal 'we' that settles on that surface, which it, however, consistently misconstrues. This community is emphatically not a nation but an exclusive subset of privileged apartheid profiteers enjoying what appears as their natural "share of the wealth | Squeezed out of earth and men | That is due to our | Rank and race" (S 4). Right from the outset, *Sinking* thus postulates that extractivism extends to land and people – 'earth and men' – alike, therewith establishing a nexus in which asymmetries of race and class overwrite the apparent neutrality of geology and ensure that 'nature' is never the sheer other of history but instead always already inscribed as historical nature into the processes of capitalist extraction and "appropriation of planetary work/energy" (Moore 2015: 29). If the speaker and his community of white mining engineers "live to extract a living | Out of that which supports us" (S 5), then they squeeze their 'share of wealth' both out of the very earth on which they build and the Black workforce that they exploit. But *Sinking* is about how the ground itself gives way and swallows what it is deemed to support. With a deliberateness that I will come to in a minute, "the allegory | Becomes rather heavy-handed"

(S 74) as Cawood Green projects a historical nature in which the unreliable, unsupportive earth correlates to the subversive underground labour of the people itself in their anti-apartheid struggle.

As an explicit account of the treacherousness of apparently coherent and stable surfaces, the opening chapter of *Sinking* is at one level a reflection on the disastrous interplay of geology and a history of coercion and extractivism, while on another level offering a metatextual reflection on the quirkiness and porosity of the poetic text. The gaping holes that literally undermine the illusion of solid homogeneous space connect the tectonic with the textual, the ground itself with the spaced and gappy poetry that Cawood Green produces for his rendering of this incident:

> This ridge is here because it is quartz
> And quartzite does not easily erode;
> And the flatness that it embraces
> Is flat because it is yielding dolomite.
> [...]
> This much, more prosaically,
> We knew – even more,
> That the plain face of dolomite,
> The tempting domesticity of its
> Scoured surface smoothness,
> Is eaten out from within by conflicts
> Older than poetry,
> [...]
> Like limestone, *dolomite dissolves in water*,
> So holes,
> Eaten out by water,
> And now filled with water,
> Form in it too *a secret system of caves and conduits*
> That in places (and this we did not know)
> Is all that supports a surface
> Seemingly secure enough
> For the weight of our efforts
> To sink through this
> Mild medium of soft moist stone.
> For us dolomite contained no geology lesson,
> No extended metaphor [...]. (S 5–7)

Two discourse systems are counterpoised here: earth science and poetry. The failure to operate within either of the two is, as it seems, the cause of the catastrophe. Had the speaker and his community 'read' dolomite either in the planetary terms of a geology lesson or in the equally planetary poetic mode as an 'extended metaphor', the disaster would have been avoided. Instead, however, the *modus operandi* is determined by a history of privilege and exploitation that entitles the speaker's community of white mining engineers to "live to extract a living | Out of that which supports us" (S 5): as seen earlier, both earth and Black workforce. By extension, then, if the ground itself refuses to comply with its assigned role as the white man's support, no guarantee is there that the Black majority will continue to do so. As an effect of decades of tunnelling and extraction, the sinkhole becomes an 'extended metaphor' not only of historical nature but of an imminent social and political overhaul presaged in a multitude of acts of anti-apartheid resistance. Tunnelling, after all, has a veritable history of serving as an image of subversion, most memorably in Marx's hailing of the mole as steady underground revolutionary ([1852] 1973: 237); or, more surprisingly perhaps, in Kipling's 'Pict Song', where the racialized indigenous "little folk" work as worms in the wood to ultimately bring the imperial house down (Kipling 1922: 654). In this context it cannot pass unnoticed that Cawood Green's deployment of this vehicular imagery is as strained and out of sync with itself as the poetics of the sonnet discussed earlier. For here it is the exploitative ruling elite, privileged by 'rank and race', that undermines their own basecamp, digging their own grave as it were. Indeed, the concluding section of the novella envisages the overthrow of the apartheid regime as a collective disappearance of its white profiteers into a literal gutter: "Communities, villages, cities | A nation, even, | Pouring out of a broken pipe | Into a hole in history" (S 76).

Looking back on an incident set in the heyday of apartheid, the text cannot but address this historical dimension. It does so, however, in the peculiar mode of restricting itself almost exclusively on the voices of white speakers so that, in effect, a kaleidoscope of implicated subjectivities ensues that makes visible the internal fissures and contradictions of a community of apartheid's beneficiaries, whether perpetrators, bystanders or accomplices. What is conspicuous, and no doubt provocative, is the almost complete exclusion of Black presences from the text where the only discernibly non-white voice is that of the Oosthuizen's domestic servant who identifies herself as "the only ghost | At this funeral" (S 27): a survivor whom the hegemonic reports of the disaster have erroneously counted, along with animals and other property, among the collateral losses of the catastrophe. Yet if the 'ghost' chapter has the unnamed servant speak about her positionality as a part that has no part, then her 'present absence' (S 29) is not at all reserved for the official accounts and the historical archive but extends very resonantly to Cawood Green's own text where the servant/ghost has only this one brief appearance as an unrepresentable blur, "the mist at the margins | Of the soft-edged family portrait" (S 28). For all its polyvocality, *Sinking* thus concedes to be a text with a gaping silence, a lacuna at its centre: not (only) the historical incident of the sinkhole but the racialized and structurally disarticulated subaltern whose silencing forms the constitutive gap around which Cawood

Green assembles a palimpsest of discrepant white voices from whose dis/concert emerges a complicated poetics and politics of white settler self-hatred. In that sense, *Sinking* is a white text energized by a question that Gayatri Spivak posed long ago in a different yet commensurate context, when she addressed her white students' 'chromatist' inhibitions to discuss Black writing: "Why not develop a certain degree of rage against a history that has written such an abject script for you that you are silenced?" (Spivak 1990: 60)

Sinking starts from this insight: that the white writer cannot stop short at the diagnosis of their incapability and illegitimacy to speak (for) the Black, but that they have instead to transform their implication into a 'degree of rage' that is then turned against the historical script. Therefore, what is at issue in Cawood Green's verse novel is the elimination of the grammar of apartheid whose first and most abiding effect it is to have submerged Black speech under an avalanche of white discourse whose excessive proliferation and diversification this verse novel stages ad nauseam – ranging from the aggressively clipped style of Nationalist Party sloganeering in chapter 7 ('A Period of Silence') to the modernist poetic minimalism of 'Premonition' (chapter 2) and 'Johannes's Love Song' (chapter 17); from the heroic couplets of Afrikaans working-class poetry in 'Skagbodem van die Myn en 3.2 Pompstasie' (chapter 18b) to the embedded snippets from geology lectures, newspaper reports and essays on gold mining scattered all over the text. This white noise is significantly amplified by a barrage of bookish paratexts and epigraphs from Joyce, Flaubert, Woolf, Derrida, Auden, Benjamin and so on, and finally a set of appendices in which Cawood Green adopts the personae of forbiddingly erudite fictitious literary critics who offer state-of-the-art dissections of his verse novel. Certainly, this oversaturation with intertextual and intratextual layers indicates the satirical concession of a failure to adequately address a self-set task that is, in itself, already self-defeating, namely to compose an original text (rather than a collage) that would answer to the national longing for form *in the absence of a nation*:

> In South Africa [...] we have not managed to rise above competing nationalisms: lacking the necessary 'confidence of community', we do not have a convincing novel form. Cut off from the free-ranging dialogism available to writers with a guaranteed sense of community provided by a meaningful national identity, South Africans have always and only written 'poetry' in the strict sense defined by Bakhtin; trapped within our fractured and fragmented language, we speak generically unstable monologues which constantly slip back into poetry, regardless of the external features of any form we use. (S 130)

I have quoted this passage at some length for its deeply ironic concession to failure: since there is no nation in South Africa but only the internal separatism of conflicting communal entities, there will be no 'convincing novel form' but isolated enclaves of solipsistic monologism. Hence, instead of the novel proper the "verse-novel" (S 131) as the incomplete and gappy, but precisely for that reason adequate, form to figure a nation of discrepant competing sub-nationalisms. Why is Green writing in 1997 as if apartheid had never been terminated, as if no rainbow nation had ever been inaugurated, as if no Truth and Reconciliation Commissions had ever worked towards the healing of the 'fractures and fragmentations' that beset the traumatized post-apartheid society? Green's rant can arguably be read as a genuine expression of a rage against the script of apartheid that obligates the white writer to constantly rework the excessive heaps of a murderous racist discourse formation that won't go away by decree, and that no sinkhole can swallow. It is this persistence of apartheid, its ongoing vitality, that condemns the Black presence to the status of a non-presence, a blur, a ghost, while the debris of white noise keeps piling up incessantly. Hemmed in the middle as the tenth out of twenty-one chapters, the nameless and faceless 'ghost' of the Black domestic servant takes the place of the gutter that, as discussed in the first section of this book, is both blank and central: "That thing which is not itself a page but makes the page, rather than a mere sheet, possible as such" (Dworkin 2020: 39).

Cawood Green's focus on the white communities around the gold mining districts of the Transvaal and the Far West Rand enables him to unearth a host of internal fissures and hierarchies that complicate the emergence of communal cohesion. Thus, while the Oosthuizen *pater familias* may envisage himself a "king in his way in terms of | Race, class and gender" (S 44), this self-aggrandizement is obviously not available to his wife who is fully aware of "our ordinariness" (S 67). A more analytic perspective of "the big picture" (S 62) reveals apartheid as a racist inflection of welfare-state redistribution whose primary objective "was the creation of a middle class" (ibid.) access to which was at best a project but not (yet) a reality for the white plumber and his family. Like class, gender comes to the fore as a divisive force within the settler community as testified by Hettie Oosthuizen's repulsion at the masculinist glorification of a not-too-distant past where Boer War veterans were given permission to obtain up to four wives (S 65). *Sinking*, in short, signals profusely its acuity to the concrete politics and grammar of apartheid and for this very reason it avoids an undifferentiated homogenizing representation of the in fact internally riven polity of those empowered and entitled by the rampant systematic racism of the state.

And yet does Cawood Green ultimately despecify this precisely circumscribed history by embedding it within the planetary dimension of 'conflicts older than poetry' – conflicts that erupt or implode as the alterity of the planet. It could be argued that Cawood Green thus runs the risk of utterly depoliticizing and naturalizing Black anti-apartheid struggles as virtually telluric. After all, in *Sinking* it is not Black agency but planetary materiality that brings the house down. More than that, there *is* no Black agency. This move could easily be interrogated as evasion on the side of a white South African writer, and Cawood Green seems to have anticipated this critique, as the afterword to *Sinking* indicates. Here he tries to argue that the task of the writer and of the political imaginary in general consists in laying out a counterfactual space where apartheid never happened, because apartheid "can only be transcended if it never existed" (S 112). The rage against the script comes fully into its own when not only the abject utterance (the concrete parole) gets deleted but the script (the langue) itself gets erased, destroyed, sucked into a void. At stake is therefore not a position *against*, *beyond* or *after*, 'anti-' or 'post-' apartheid, but a position in a 'new universe' in which apartheid has always already been completely swallowed whole:

> Apartheid, crashing through the very fabric of our reason, has [...] swallowed more pain than its symphony can sing; there can be no truer way to celebrate its end than to prove that, like the theory of black holes, it existed only in its effects – and that the logic it would take to understand it will take us through a worm-hole to a new universe where it never existed. (S 114)

Narrative poetry with its texture of gaps that may serve as sinkholes, or wormholes, might be the medium for such an endeavour. The 'we' that emerges in the course of this poetic construction of a new universe where apartheid never existed includes Black and white South Africans but it is certainly not the collective of the rainbow nation that post-apartheid reconciliation may once have endeavoured to realize; it is in fact not a collective of the national or any other political framing but a form of community of – with Spivak – planetary creatures. A planet that, in this verse novel, is so gappy that foregrounded spacing appears to be the only way of engaging with it:

> For what is a picture but its frame
> and what are we
> but those folding in on the spaces we've cleared
> planes become depths,
> to swallow us,
> Gatvol. (S 38)

*****

This study cannot possibly do justice to the literary practice of gutter texts at large, and not even to the scope of the contemporary verse novel. It will instead zoom in on two specific domains in which the verse novel takes over the job habitually assigned to the novel: the figuration of worldliness and the negotiation of nationhood. Obviously the novel has a long and veritable history as the most suitable and successful literary apparatus for representing 'world' and 'nation' in relation to individual and collective subjectivities, and it would be capricious to claim that that history were over and the novel no longer capable of giving shape to these experiences. Far from it: the newly-fangled genre of the 'world novel' thrives along with the post-migrant bildungsroman, the multiple formats of 'genre fiction', the experimental novel and not least with that most amazing revenant, the 'state-of-the nation' novel. There is no reason to bemoan (or to celebrate) 'the death of the novel'. What this study aims to weaken, however, is the persistent myth of the novel's exceptional prerogative to figure the present, and it is for this reason that I am trying to show how verse novels operate on the very same turf that is routinely deemed to be novelistic, and how the very basic formal radicals of that gutter-textual form already make a difference to the representation.

The world of the verse novel is not the world of the novel, as the readings in Chapter 2, 'Volcanic Verses: The Planet as a Verb', will demonstrate where a number of verse novels from postcolonial locations across the globe in concert generate a vision of the planet as a process rather than a given. All these texts, whether focusing on the Caribbean (Walcott) or Canada and South America (Carson), Samoa (Wendt) or Hawai'i (Merwin), interestingly gravitate around the central trope of the volcano that introduces a genuinely geological, deep-time dimension in which the planet itself is shown as an unfinished site of constant making and unmaking. The ensuant sense of planetarity, I will argue, is however not posited on the assumption of some raw materiality where the planet appears as "undivided 'natural' space rather than a differentiated political space" (Spivak 2015: 290). To the contrary, in concert these texts figure an always already politically inscribed planet by emphasizing how legacies of colonial, enslavist and heteronormative domination intersect with indigenous forms of rigid social stratification. In such scenarios the imagery of an inherently processual planet establishes as fact the changeability of the world. The dynamism of Earth itself unsettles the ossified stasis of the ostensibly 'eternal' partition of the sensible.

In a similar fashion, the nation of the verse novel is not the nation of the novel. Chapter 3, 'In/verse Britain: The Poetics of the Post-Nation', offers a series of readings of verse novels, all of them written by queer and/or of-colour women authors, that exemplarily re-historicize and re-envisage Britain not so much as an anonymously imagined community in homogeneous empty time but as a jarring conglomerate constituted first and foremost by its heavily policed borders whose function it is to uphold the counterfactual myth of national autarky. Where the verse novels in chapter 2 are spread all over the anglophone world, the four texts under discussion here all focus on Britain, but taken together they produce a vast historical tableau ranging from Roman colonization (Evaristo) and the revamping of Chaucer's multifaceted portraiture of late-medieval budding Englishness (Agbabi) to the radical deconstruction of one of the most shocking documents from the archives of the British slave trade (NourbeSe Philip) and the present-day relocation of the shrinking island in the age of resurgent nationalism (Tempest). In my readings I will try to demonstrate how these texts confront, debunk, ridicule or radically rip apart violently discriminatory discourses: misogyny in *The Emperor's Babe*, antisemitism in *Telling Tales*, enslavism in *Zong!*.

Many other areas could and should have been covered as well: verse novels are highly prolific in young adult literature, in counterfactual/speculative fiction, in diasporic and minority writing including Chicana/o and First Nation writing and in more playful ways, in genre fiction. Dorothy Porter's crime novel-in-verse, *The Monkey's Mask*, was adapted to film, while other verse novels have gone into sequels. To some extent, then, the novelization of the global occurs also as the verse-novelization of the global. Moreover, it is obvious how also the contemporary prose novel is significantly affected by the general tendency to generate gutter texts. Alexander Beecroft's remarks on the macrostructural device of *entrelacement* and multi-strand narrative structures in the current 'plot-of-globalization' novel clearly point to the proclivity to a gappy prose style in fiction today. One of Beecroft's prime examples is David Mitchell's *Cloud Atlas* (2004) with its intricate architecture of elaborately entangled narrative strands; what could be added is that that novel's gutter textuality is not only owed to its global structure of interlacing but goes all the way down to the most molecular microlevel, to the microscopic scale of the lexemes that, in the neo-primitive diction of the narrator of the central 'Sloosha Crossin'' story will be perforated analogous to the segmentation of the entire novel and most of its component units: "Some dusks my kin'n'bros'll wake up the ghost girl jus' to watch her hov'rin'n'shimm'rin'" (Mitchell 2004: 324–5). At this minute lexical scale the normalized smooth flow of continuous articulation and reception is interrupted but not fully disenabled by the gaps that the apostrophe marks, resulting in a resistance of segments to get entirely dissolved into some overarching sequence of transaction. None of this, however, leads to the full suspension of sequentiality: while the gappy structure of the text foregrounds the singularity of the individual units at all levels from the apparently disjoint tributary narratives through their 'chapteroids' to their very graphemes, the fact remains that Mitchell's novel all the more impels its readers to only connect by way of gap negotiation. This may involve the reparation of 'damaged' language (the decoding of, say, 'hov'rin'n'shimm'rin'' as 'hovering and shimmering') or the construction of non-delivered transitions from one story element to the next within the segmented narratives.

It is in this fashion that many contemporary novels are conspicuously marked by the 'gutterization' of prose at the microlevel. Thus Bernardine

Evaristo's 2019 novel, *Girl, Woman, Other*, is over vast stretches written in a metrically patterned English that passes for prose only because of its typographic distribution on the page as a run-on text (cf. Sedlmayr unpubl.).[3] The same holds true for substantial passages of Ali Smith's Seasonal Quartet as a brief reading aloud of only the first few pages of *Autumn* will make clear. Vikram Seth's prose frequently 'reverts' to blank verse (cf. Wiemann 2005: 138), as does that of Michael Ondaatje, Don DeLillo, Jackie Kay or Julian Barnes. As prose gets ever more frequently caught off guard and disrupted by poetry, the novel itself takes on more and more gutter-text features. In this light it might perhaps be more appropriate to assume not a 'novelization of the global' but rather a generic pluralism in which all kinds of literary forms coexist. No doubt, the novel is not just one of these forms but definitely the most prominent and privileged. However, it retains its predominance by turning itself to some extent into a gutter text, too, and by adopting the gappiness, segmentivity and graininess of an incompletely articulated structure that can always be but contiguous in this world – and perhaps exactly thanks to this provide the appropriate form for the making of imagined worlds.

---

[3] I am grateful to Gerold Sedlmayr for bringing this to my notice.

2

Volcanic verses: The planet as verb

The puncture in the continuous surface, the gaping hole, the rendering-visible of segmentivity: in terms of both semantics and morphology, these tropes take centre stage in numerous verse novels throughout the anglophone world. As I will try to delineate in the following readings of exemplary 'volcanic' verse novels, these tropes are frequently articulated in geological, telluric and/or meteorological terms and constitute a lexicon that takes recourse to natural phenomena in order to denaturalize the protocols of the prose of the world, and the world of prose. Arguably this feature makes it more than plausible to discuss the verse novel as a retreat from the hegemonic novel to the epic that, as Hegel and Lukács, Auerbach and Watt agree, has historically been superseded by the modern novel. I will return to that speculative horizon at greater length in my conclusion; at this point it must suffice to note that the current verse novel in many instances displays a highly self-conscious relation to its pre-novel antecedent, as the routine references to Homer, Vergil, Dante and Milton indicate. Nor is this frame of references restricted to the European/Eurocentric tradition but will, especially in Global South verse novels, also include the legacies of other literary ecologies of versified epic narrative: the Ramayana in Daljit Nagra's re-telling as a verse novel; the Hawaiian creation chant Kumulipo in M. S. Merwin's *The Folding Cliffs* (Section 2.4); the legends of the Samoan warrior queen Nafanua in numerous Polynesian verse novels including Tusiata Avia's *Bloodclot*, Penina Taesali's *Sourcing Siapo* and Albert Wendt's *The Adventures of Vela* (Section 2.3); and most recently at the time of writing, Ngugi Wa Thiongo's *The Perfect Nine*, a feminist revision of the Gikuyu founding epic of the nine daughters of Gikuyu and Mumbi, from whom the tribes of the Kenyan Gikuyu people are supposed to derive. Ngugi's own translation into English (2020) of his 2018 Kikuyu verse novel is appended with an acknowledgement to the many interlocutors who supplied him with numerous variants of a story that "has been told and retold as part of the lore of the Gikuyu people" (Ngugi 2020: 228). At least from a provincially European point of view, Jomo Kenyatta's version of that story is the most prominent one among those multiple retellings. Kenyatta opens his auto-ethnographic account of the Gikuyu, *Facing Mount Kenya* (1937), with the story of the founding parents of the nation; that recourse provides a legendary origin for a matrilineal, indeed matriarchal social order that the founding father himself decrees at the beginning of the people's history: it is Gikuyu, not Mumbi, who informs the young suitors of the nine daughters "that if they wished to marry his daughters he could give his consent only if they agreed to live in his homestead under a matriarchal system" (Kenyatta 1961: 5). The feminist outlook is therefore not an innovative move from Ngugi's side but appears to be integral to the Gikuyu and Mumbi tradition. What is specifically striking in *The Perfect Nine*, however, are the strongly foregrounded telluric elements especially in the first passages of the text. What the first parents of the nation have to face is an unformed, unpredictable and perilous world whose dangerousness is primarily captured in the imageries of volcanic eruptions:

> Tremor after tremor raging from the belly of the earth,
> Eruptions breaking the ground around them,
> Making the ridges quake, the earth tremble, as
>
> New hills heaved themselves out of the earth, and
> Others burned, their flames flaring skyward [...]. (Ngugi 2020: 3)

This is a volatile world in the making through unmaking, created through destruction, through the ripping open of continuous surfaces, through upheavals and eruptions. It is a danger zone and as such, the zone of the epic. It is also a generative zone, and as such, too, the zone of the epic. Situated in this duality of epic danger and epic generativity, Ngugi's characters are exposed to the constant threats of a volcanic world with its boiling "rivers of thick red mud moving toward them" and "big red rocks || Hurtling down towards them" (ibid.: 3; 4). Exposed as they are, they emerge as precariously planetary creatures, emblems of a universal state of "vulnerability which cannot simply be overcome" as it is "part of the condition of our embodied being on a dynamic planet" (Clark 2010: 120): a planet whose materiality requires to be rethought as process. This volatility spells out both hazard and opportunity and renders the planet a precarious abode but also an embodiment, and ally, of change itself. In the following sections I will focus on the multiple and divergent topical and formal impacts of the theme of the volcano as a trope that, in numerous verse novels, serves as a pointer to the planet's dynamism.

2.1 Sibylline cures: Derek Walcott's *Omeros*

With its multiple intertwined plot lines, the architecture of Derek Walcott's verse novel *Omeros* (1990), mostly set in the postcolonial Caribbean island of St Lucia, strongly resembles the *entrelacement* structure of the connexionist novel. On closer inspection, however, *Omeros*, all these similarities notwithstanding, turns out to pursue a significantly different trajectory that, as I will argue, is owed not only to its postcolonial locus of enunciation but also to its particularly 'showy' generic and formal specifics as a narrative "composed in the most conspicuously ornate verse forms that strike a reader as existing at the furthest extreme from 'ordinary' prose" (Addison 2012: 89). Walcott's crafty deployment of *terza rima* – canonized as the formal hallmark of Dante's *Divine Comedy* – links the text to the grand tradition of Western epic poetry, as do the many allusions and references to Vergil's *Aeneid*, Milton's *Paradise Lost* and, most prominently, the Homeric epics.

Naming and wounding

Numerous characters in *Omeros* go by epical names that appear directly plucked from the *Iliad*: Hector, Achille, Helen and Philoctete. All these characters are Afro-Caribbean descendants of enslaved ancestors, and this genealogical background persist into the diegetic present where the villagers are members of a Global South working class: fishermen, bus drivers and waitresses. Their seemingly incongruous names do not only serve as internymic devices that link them with Homeric heroes and heroines (even though they do that, too) but also keep visible the history of enslavement by giving "testimony to the colonial practice of naming slaves from mythology or religion" (Van Sickle 1999: 8). Walcott's conspicuous intertextual recourses to canonical epic form and content are thus ineluctably loaded, linked as they are to the traumatic history of slavery: whenever names like 'Hector' or 'Achille' appear in the text, they cathex Homeric heroes to the dehumanizing legacy and persistence of "enslavism" – a term coined by Sabine Broeck as a name for "the continuity between the regimes of Euro-American and Caribbean enslavement and its anti-Black afterlife" into the present and future (Broeck 2018: 6). And yet, as Martin McKinsey (2008: 891) argues,

> Walcott goes some distance in naturalizing these names historically as the legacy of slavery, but at the same time endows them with a symbolic resonance that insists that they be approached Eurocentrically; that is, with reference to their canonical Greek originals.

To be sure, Walcott's stance is not primarily polemic or iconoclastic: far from smashing the marble bust of the white 'Master', Walcott's alter ego narrator recurrently expresses his reverence for Homer, whose very name "meant joy". That 'joy', however, turns out to be somewhat alienated at closer inspection: "Joy in battle, in work, in death" (O 283).

If thus the names of the local protagonists inextricably fuse the mythical with the historical, then this hybridity can be read as a pointer to the text's mixed constitution in-between the epic and the novel. Gregson Davis makes out in *Omeros* a "paradoxical disavowal-cum-assimilation of the epic genre" (Davis 1999: 45 FN6) so that Walcott accommodates both the reappropriation and the supersession of the epic. While Davis does not expand on this point, Charles Lock fleshes it out more fully with reference to the construction of the characters, the bearers of those ambiguous names that are both mythical and (following Ian Watt) quotidian proper names: "Here in *Omeros* we have a world full of Homeric echoes, yet one with a rich and mystifying inwardness: epic and novel combined without 'novelization'" (Lock 2000: 14). The argument is intriguing: what is typically novelistic about Walcott's characters is their rich interiority – their 'roundness' in E. M. Forster's terms – that sets them clearly apart from the flat characters of epic. But if this scenario appears to ooze the triumphalism of literary evolutionism, then Lock elegantly reverses this easy progressivism. The invention of characters' inwardness, far from marking a step 'ahead' toward psychological depth, gets revalued as regression: "The novel is, at the linguistic level, considerably more animistic and primitive than the Homeric epic: access to another's mind – the staple of fiction – is the very condition of animism" (ibid.). Modern fiction, from the eighteenth century epitomized in the dominant form of the novel, is in that perspective not the successor of an allegedly obsolete antecedent but rather a warped return to something even prior to that antecedent: formal realism as magical thinking.

The combination of epic and novel is, however, most visibly signalled by the structuring devices of the text. As Kathrin Härtl observes, *Omeros* "consists of seven books and 64 chapters, thus oscillating between the genre of the novel with regard to its use of chapters and the epic with regard to its stanzaic design" (Härtl 2019: 144). At the macrolevel, *Omeros* highlights the 'anachronistic' dimension of *entrelacement* as a technique that has traditionally been identified with classic and specifically medieval narratives as one of the central "structural foundations of the romance code" (Zatti 2006: 60). Alexander Beecroft (2015: 283) suggests that "multi-strand narration" is typical of the contemporary "plot of globalization": a device that is formative for many of those texts that, like David Mitchell's *Cloud Atlas* or Roberto Bolano's *2666*, are frequently discussed in current criticism as 'world novels'. Beecroft points out that this form of emplotment is in fact a revamping of the narrative composition of

> medieval French romance, and the strategy of moving back and forth between a variety of different narratives, the interconnections between

which drive the narrative of the larger work, is one already familiar to readers and film audiences from numerous works. (ibid.)

This duality neatly corresponds with the epic-novel doubleness of *Omeros* – a text that, as John Van Sickle (1999: 7–9) has delineated, interlaces four major narrative strands. The first of these subplots (dubbed the 'village plot' by Van Sickle) focuses on the rivalry between Hector and Achille, two fishermen, for the love of the local beauty Helen; the second is devoted to the elderly Plunketts, a British expat couple who have retreated to St Lucia after the experience of the Second World War; a third narrative relates the affliction of Philoctete who is suffering from a wound in his shin which is ultimately cured by the local healer, Ma Kilman; a self-referential fourth plotline (Van Sickle's 'narrator's plot') gives room to the reflections of the author-narrator 'Walcott' on his travels to North America and Europe and the difficulties of writing an epic poem from the location of the Global South. It is true that all these subplots are mostly set in the shared chronotope of postcolonial St Lucia and that the various characters meet and interact in the diegetic world of Walcott's verse novel; yet their existential interconnectedness emerges not primarily by way of their narrative contiguity (as in Anderson's model of the imagined community evoked by disparate but synchronic co-activity) but by a set of central tropes – the wound, the gap, the volcano – that the text associates with all of them as a shared commonality. While these shared motifs of injury and disruption activate various traumatic histories from the Black Atlantic to the Second World War, they also extend beyond the cast of characters into the domains of the non-human and even abiotic, thereby embedding the characters in a vast planetary web of life. Ever since Jahan Ramazani's seminal essay on 'the wound of history' (1997), the centrality of the trope of the wound for *Omeros* has been noted recurrently (cf., e.g., Beattie and Bertacco 2017; Benyousky 2019; Hogue 2013). In light of a discussion of gutter texts and their specific capacity of world making premised on incompleteness, the specific deployment of this trope by Walcott must appear particularly intriguing: first in terms of its connexionist impact (where links are paradoxically provided by gaps); second with regards to its scalar distribution across the spatial spectrum that the text evokes from the human body to the entire planet (thus preparing for the obscure 'link between geology and character' that we will re-encounter in Anne Carson's, Albert Wendt's and W. S. Merwin's verse novels); and finally due to the intimate dialectics of affliction and cure where, as it were, the wound can be healed only by the sword that inflicted it.

Jahan Ramazani (1997: 405) has persuasively argued that Walcott "turns the wound into a resonant site of interethnic connection" by way of profiling the variegated cast of his multi-strand verse novel as hybrid intertextual characters that hover between Eurocentric Hellenism and postcolonial *négritude*. Thus the character of the St Lucian fisherman

Philoctete is modelled on the Homeric and Sophoclean hero, Philoctetes, with whom he shares, in a tellingly incomplete manner, the name and, more importantly, the affliction with a piercing and festering wound that won't heal. If this irregular disruption of the body's continuous integrity arguably serves as a powerful intertextual link that holds these two disparate characters together across vast temporal and cultural distances, it is at the same time also the site at which significant differences between these "interfigures" (cf. Müller 1991) come into view. For the Greek hero's affliction is caused by a snakebite (and is hence purely accidental), whereas Walcott's Philoctete conceives of his own incurable wound as embodied history: a corporeal manifestation of the traumatic collective experience of enslavement and the Middle Passage, an inheritance that "came from the chained ankles | of his grandfathers" (O 19). As bearer of that incurable "wound of slavery on his shin [Philoctete] throughout the poem personifies the pain of a history of dispossession" (Melas 2005: 153) and enslavist dehumanization. Such a history cannot be fully articulated and will instead find an incomplete, indeed incommensurable expression in the "agonized O: the scream | of centuries" (O 246), akin to the inarticulate babble of Sophocles' Philoctetes, whose "unintelligible stammerings – literally the discourse of the barbaric – interrupt his Greek when he suffers spasms and pain" (Ramazani 1997: 409). The wound thus engenders interruption and disarticulation both of the body's surface and the form of speech, afflicting them likewise with fissures and gaping holes (of which the 'agonized O' is the ultimate mimic and graphic equivalent) that all the same pervasively operate as connectors. For it is not only Homer's Philoctetes and Walcott's Philoctete who are linked by the wound and the unintelligibility it bestows on them. Philoctete's ailment is not simply an individual's injury but the collective affliction of "a wounded race" (O 299), and as such it is dispersed all across the intricate texture of *Omeros*: from the bleeding cuts that Achille receives from "the shells | with their hard snail-like horns" (O 40) to Hector's "flaming wound that speed alone could not heal" (118); from the Second World War "wound in his head" that is "stitched into Plunkett's character" by the reflexive narrator (O 28) to the "running wound" of plantation slaves driven through "the foam of pods, one arm for an oar || one for the gunny sack" (O 178). This pervasive presence of injury at all levels gets summarily confirmed by the narrator's assertion that "we shared the one wound" (O 295). Yet even if one agrees with Ramazani who observes that "the wound forms the vivid nucleus of this magnum opus" (Ramazani 1997: 409) and functions as a shared connector between disparate actors, it remains to be added that the wound is never only the wound but always also the cure. This gets most impressively articulated in those instances where the motif of the wound extends beyond the domain of the human and appears as a planetary presence at all scales, very much reminiscent of Dimock's notion of quirks 'threaded throughout the world, in infinite extension and infinite regress'.

It is in this vein that, as in Ngugi's verse novel, the planet's destructive and at the same time constructive, injurious and curative volcanism comes into view: in *Omeros*, specifically, as a crucial lexical field through which the notion of the wound gets first projected onto the geological and then re-transferred, as healing, to the domain of the human.

Volcanic wounds – volcanic cures

The island of St Lucia, "whose every cove was a wound" (O 259), is itself an injured entity "split asunder | by a volcanic massif" of the Soufrière, whose "wound closed in smoke, then wind would reopen it" (O 59). The "brittle scab crusting its volcano's sores" (O 289) testifies to the mountain's unceasing interplay of eruption and coagulation. The "signs | of a hidden devastation under the cones | of volcanic gorges" (O 300) overcode the Soufrière as "a place where an ancient fear increased" (O 59). And yet the "volcano, stinking with sulphur || has made it [St Lucia] a place of healing" (O 287). This curative aspect of the volcanic is transferred to the 'self-healing island' of St Lucia as a whole where the "gauze of fine rain" (O 249) soothingly cools off the pulsating intensity of boiling lava and indeed provides a bandage ('gauze') to cover the wound that the island inflicts on itself. If thus the 'wound of history' gets transferred to the geological itself especially through the trope of the volcanic, then, in a kind of feedback loop, the volcanic gets also redirected to the domain of human agency, where its curative force appears even more profiled. Thus the narrator's quest for a postcolonial epic-novel finds its consummation in a nightmarish yet cathartic sojourn to the summit of the Soufrière massif, "a purgative journey through a volcanic entry and into a Dantean Underworld" (Thurston 2009: 130) guided by the bust of Homer that plays Virgil to Walcott-as-Dante. Enveloped in "the foul sulphur of hell in paradise" (O 289), the narrator undergoes a self-conscious re-enactment of the *Inferno*, witnessing and recounting how greedy businessmen and politicos "who had sold out their race" for private profit are punished for their callousness and sentenced forever to boil in the sulphur and lead of the "Pool of Speculation" (O 289). Meanwhile, in an adjacent hellish cavern, the cardinal sin of pride is put on trial as self-indulgent poets proud of their writerly finesse are "condemned in their pit to weep at their own pages" (O 293). Of course, the narrator (as Walcott's fictional alter ego) is here far more involved as in the case of the corrupt politicians and businessmen. After all, the *poètes maudits* and his Homeric guide's stern interrogation confront him with his own shortcomings and vanities, his predisposition to what in Dante's world is a deadly sin: "Pride in my craft. | Elevating myself" (O 293). The lesson to be learned from the volcano, therefore, is modesty, and this insight occurs as cathartic remedy, as an exorcism of the demon of self-aggrandizement: "I was an ant on the forehead of an atlas | the stroke of one spidery palm on a cloud's page |

an asterisk only" (O 294). Numerous critics have voiced their impatience with Walcott's Dante act as "an embarrassing gaffe at the poem's very summit: even when drawn with the utmost tact, parallels among oneself, Dante, and Homer must appear absurdly pretentious" (Martin 1992, 204). In this light, it is precisely by claiming to abstain from such deadly sins as 'pride' and 'self-elevation' that, in the garb of hyperbolically exaggerated modesty, elitist and 'absurdly pretentious' assumptions proliferate. But why not read the narrator's Soufrière tour as a figure for the author's voyage in, and hence a postcolonial claim to partake of a canon that has been traditionally made inaccessible from the position of the Global South. Such a partaking surely involves a decentring of that canon, as an earlier scene of literary initiation in *Omeros* indicates. Here, the narrator remembers how, as a young boy in 1950s (still) colonial St Lucia, he initiated himself into world literature. Back there/then, a visit to the neighbourhood barber, who happens to be "the town anarchist" (O71), amounted to an act of familiarization not only with 'the world's events' but also with the corpus of 'the *World's Great Classics*'. In the anarchist barbershop,

> toga'd, in a pinned sheet,
>
> the curled hairs fell like commas. On their varnished rack,
> *The World's Great Classics* read backwards in his mirrors
> Where he doubled as my chamberlain. I was known
>
> For quoting from them as he was for his scissors
> I bequeath you that clean sheet and empty throne. (O 71)

It is to be assumed that 'the *World's Great Classics*' will be biased constructions, most likely a number of exemplars from the fifty-volumes series edited from 1899 to 1901 by Timothy Dwight and Julian Hawthorne from the Colonial Press in New York, spanning European and North American writing from Homer (vol. 1) to Alexis de Tocqueville and John Stuart Mill (vol. 50), with heavy doses of Dante, Cervantes, Shakespeare, Milton, Racine, Goethe and Pushkin in between. For the colonial subject in the Caribbean periphery, all this is accessible only at a skewed angle, in reverse, and through a glass darkly, as it were: 'Read backwards in his mirrors.' Even so, however, "the classics in the barbershop are instantly recognizable for the ambition, aspiration, and cultural perfectibility they synecdochally signify" (Mukherjee 2014: 91). But at the same time, as the reverse optics suggests, their reception in the barbershop occurs against the grain of established standards, so that their claim to universal validity gets contested in the act of such inverted reading in a markedly 'inappropriate' setting. Their appeal, then, is somewhat "countercultural, as the association with the anarchist barber suggests" (ibid.).

Accordingly, if the barbershop scene, like all initiations, engenders a transformation of the speaker, then this transformation does not take place as a full submission of the speaker to the authority of World Literature as unquestioned norm; it rather enables a dissident participation in the sense of what Edward Said has described as a "voyage in" in which the colonized subject assumes for themselves "the same areas of experience, culture, history, and tradition hitherto commanded unilaterally by the metropolitan centre. [...] No longer does the logos dwell exclusively, as it were, in London and Paris" (Said 1994: 295). In the barber's mirror, the speaker imagines himself as agent of world-literary achievements, in other words, as metropolitan subject. Thus the barber's sheet becomes a toga, the chair a throne and the hairdresser himself the chamberlain to the speaker who must have incorporated much of the mirrored canon of World Literature: 'I was known for quoting from them' at apparent ease. Given the solemn diction and slightly antiquated semantics, readers are misled to assume that the last verse of the quoted passage ("I bequeath you that clean sheet and empty throne") must in fact be one of those citations lifted from the *Great Classics* that the speaker as a child recited to the rhythm of the barber's scissors. However, this is neither Shakespeare nor Tennyson but Walcott himself, whose magnum opus, *Omeros*, is, among other things, a long meditation about the poetics and politics of postcolonial quotation as well as a text that owes its very existence to the technique of creative recycling. None of this, to be sure, can fully defuse the charge of pretentiousness with regards to the narrator's self-fashioning as Dante regarding the pain of others in a volcanic vision. It can, however, help to explain that for Walcott – writing from the position of the postcolonial South and from the fact of Blackness – there is no access to that relaxed relation to the canon that we will encounter, in the next section, in a metropolitan writer like Anne Carson.

Less contentious than the autoreferential episode of sulphurous 'self-healing' from the hazards of pride on the volcano's summit is certainly the equally volcanic healing of Philoctete at the hands of the Obeah woman, Ma Kilman, who undertakes a "sibylline cure" (O 235) by bathing the persistent wound in a boiling concoction of seawater and sulphur that soon transforms into "gurgling lava" (O 247). Ma Kilman is repeatedly identified as a sibyl and thus associated with those "female prophets of the ancient Greek and Roman world" who were traditionally revered as oracles and healers but at the same time marginalized as celibate hermits whose cave dwellings were frequently believed to be the "entrance to hell" (Montroso 2020: 92). Ma Kilman's improvised practice is in that sense a quasi-sibylline location at the back of a rum shop where "the heat was hellish" (O 306). Consistent with this, her therapy is as ambiguous as the figure of the sibyl herself who, especially in medieval receptions of Virgil's *Aeneid*, oscillates between the curative and the infernal, and whose cavernous abode of "tuff from hell" (Kroonenberg 2011: 51) yet functions as "a therapeutic spa" (Clark 1995: 157). This tense interplay of the poisonous and the curative repeats itself, as it were, in Ma Kilman's 'sibylline' sulphurous concoction that proves effective against all expectations. The wound will close as Philoctete repeats the island's 'self-healing process' by rain: "The tears trickled down his face | like rainwater" (O 248). It is noteworthy in this context that the cauldron of this sibylline cure is a residue from the old sugar mill which is, historically, associated with the slave economy of the plantation complex. Thus the whole scene configures not only the geologically toxic and curative but likewise transforms "the tools of slavery into instruments of healing" (Benyousky 2019: 9). Moreover, the 'gurgling lava' cure rehashes the cathartic purgation of the narrator in the toxic vapours of the sulphurous pools of the Soufrière volcano.

What remains to be added, however, is that Ma Kilman is not only *associated with* the volcanic but that she herself gets subtly *identified as* a volcano – a feature that is in a similarly inconspicuous way ascribed to the character of Helen the village beauty, who causes the rivalry between Hector and Achille that sets in motion the 'village plot'. Helen's eyes with their "vertiginous irises" appear as shafts through which some alluring and seductive interior surfaces: they "could not help their work | any more than the earth's fascination with fire ‖ as it left the earth": "All I had heard | flamed in that look" (O 264) from those singeing eyes that unwittingly pierce a 'gap' or 'chasm' into the funeral service for Maud Plunkett. If Helen's volcanic interiority 'cannot help' but show visually, Ma Kilman's geotropic corporeality manifests as sound. Walcott draws on the traditional assumption that the body of the sibyl is "coextensive with the toxic volcanic ecology of the underworld" (Montroso 2020: 93). In this vein, *Omeros* endows Ma Kilman with volcanic corporeal features when she emits "one of those cavernous sighs | that came from the bowels of the earth" (O 306): an utterance that is as telluric as it is inarticulate, and to which no human interlocutor but only the volcano's proper element, fire, can respond as "the candle peaked | and the flame bent" from the 'oracle's' cavernous exhalation (O 306). Sibylline figures as the Pythia, the Delphic oracle, were traditionally deemed to be inspired "by the divine afflatus which at least the later ages believed to ascend in vapour from a fissure in the ground" (Farnell [1907] qu. in Compton 1994: 217). The sibyl can perform only over a geological gap that, gutter-like, simultaneously serves as a connector – here between the known world above ground and the hidden subterranean realm whose miasmas emerge through the indispensable fissure that interrupts the plain surface. It was believed that the inhalation of these volcanic vapours transported the sibyl into a state of trance-like ecstasy in which she produced wild utterances whose 'correct' interpretation was the prerogative of the initiated. Like the Sophoclean Philoctetes with his spasmodic stuttering, the sibyl is then a figure of incomplete articulation or, perhaps, complete disarticulation whose unformed noises remain unintelligible unless experts transform them into proper speech.

And yet, despite all these disarticulating tendencies, the sibylline Ma Kilman is at the same time interfigurally positioned as the summary epic narrator, a composite plebeian embodiment of the great 'masters' that Walcott's text nods to. After all, in Virgil's *Aeneid*, it is the Sibyl of Cumae who guides the errant Trojan survivor through the underworld where she elaborately "describes a selection of the torments in Tartarus" (Gowers 2005: 171) more to the reader's than her co-witnessing travelling companion's benefit. In her function as tour guide through hell, she thus prefigures Dante's Virgil, but in her role of verbose reporter of the tortuous punishments witnessed there, she resembles Dante himself. By the same token, Walcott's Omeros on the volcano's summit performs the tour-guide part of both Virgil's Sibyl of Cumae and of Dante's Virgil, whereas the narrator/'Walcott', as the one who is guided by an expert, reiterates the positions of Virgil's Aeneas and the *Inferno*'s 'Dante'. All these speakers re-enact, partially or in toto, the performance of Virgil's sibyl as guide through and/or reporter of hell. In that sense Ma Kilman, in her capacity as the village sibyl in the diegetic world of *Omeros*, takes the place of all these figures – from Homer and Virgil to Dante and 'Walcott' – while at the same time clearly overwriting this grandiose canonized pantheon with the abiding character traits of an Obeah healer who produces 'gurgling lava' concoctions in volcanic cauldrons and speaks in island patois or else broken English: "What is wrong wif you, Philoctete? [...] give the foot a lickle rest" (O 18, 19).

It is perhaps exactly this incompletely articulated language that ultimately emerges as the medium of postcolonial epic narrative poetry. Not that Walcott ever resorted to a language or style as irreverently and iconoclastically deviant as the poetics of say Kamau Brathwaite or even Wilson Harris; what he arrives at, however, after the narrator's katabatic and cathartic volcano trip, is a revision of the epic: namely, as an oceanic blank/et, a "wide page without metaphors" (O 296) enshrouding all myth and history in oblivious anonymity. To the cured narrator, the sea is "an epic where every line was erased || yet freshly written in sheets of exploding surf | in that blind violence with which one crest replaced | another with a trench" (O 296). Clearly the ceaseless ebb and tide of erasure and rewriting articulates articulation itself: a process in which meaning "will always be made, unmade and remade" (Clifford 2001: 479). Moreover, the inconclusiveness of ceaseless opening, closing, re-opening and re-closing of wounds is common to the volcanic and the aquatic alike, and at the same time shared by the textual, thus extending the figure of endless destruction and renewal where wound and cure coincide to yet another domain, "as if the sea kept alive some underground intercourse with the volcano's hidden fire" (Glissant 1990: 121). Just as the volcanic eruptions that rip open the surface of St Lucia are the precondition for the "process, the proof of a self-healing island" (O 249), so does the continuous erasure of epic lines prepare the necessary ground for the (re)writing of 'explosive' new verses. The ceaseless 'epic' of the sea holds 'no metaphors' precisely because it evades the totalizing force with which, in Jakobson's terms, metaphor arrests the flow of metonymic contiguity. As David Lodge succinctly puts it, "When we interpret it [the literary text], when we uncover its 'unity' [...] we make it into a total metaphor: the text is the vehicle, the world is the tenor" (Lodge 1977: 109). And the text is as closed, as 'consummated' as life after life, as imagined by the young Bakhtin. It can of course not be denied that the sea serves very much as a metaphor in Walcott's scenario, but it is ironically a metaphor of metonymy: an image of incessant flux and reflux in which 'crests' and 'troughs' take their turns ad infinitum. The tenor of this vehicle is, therefore, the interminable principle of metonymic exchange itself that Walcott's text strives to keep operative and open beyond its material end. In this light, the very last verse of this verbose verse novel – "When he left the beach the sea was still going on" (O 325) – appears as one last metatextual device: the reader exits the text just like Achille leaves the empty nocturnal beach, but just as the sea will 'go on' (doing what?) regardless of the presence of an observer, so will the text continue its interminable work of metonymic combination even after the book has been closed, a process that Lodge (albeit in an entirely different context) has aptly called a "deluge" (Lodge 1977: 111), and for which Julia Kristeva has suggested the term *signifiance*, understood as "a structuring and de-structuring practice" that unleashes an "unlimited and unbounded generating process, this unceasing operation of the drives toward, in and through language" (Kristeva 1984: 17).

Given *Omeros*'s overt saturation with epic, this metonymic movement of ceaseless doing and undoing will also hark back to Homer's *Odyssey*, more specifically Penelope's play for time by unravelling every night the shroud that she had woven by day. This endless withholding of closure enables an inconclusive textility and textuality very much in line with the dynamic stasis of Walcott's constantly self-effacing and self-rewriting ocean-as-epic, "our last resort as much as yours, Omeros" (O 296). The 'Omeros' addressed here is not only the legendary bard of the *Iliad* and the *Odyssey* but also his modernist revenant: "Mr. Joyce" who "led us all" (O 201), "our age's Omeros, undimmed Master" (O 200). The culmination of Joyce's version of the *Odyssey* in the apparently incomplete articulation of Molly Bloom's "flowing, unpunctuated sentences" (Lawrence 1990: 253) has often been discussed as the consummation of *Ulysses*'s journey into female speech. In this understanding, the 'Penelope' chapter enacts a "movement beyond form" (Brivic 1991: 23) towards an alleged *écriture féminine* that Stuart Gilbert, in his influential 1930 study of *Ulysses*, has authoritatively declared to be "unmistakeably earthy" and indeed volcanic: "She speaks with the voice of the Earth: 'I feel all fire inside me'" (Gilbert 1958: 400; see also Henke 1978: 235, who dubs Molly "a primordial Earth-Mother"). This no doubt deeply problematic tendency to read 'Penelope' in terms of raw nature continues into the present with critics claiming to have made out an "oceanic" flux and reflux gestalt in Molly's monologue (see e.g. Bleikasten 1995: 82; Paul 2014: 37). Naturalizing readings like these fix Joyce's Molly as an embodiment of those volcanic, aquatic and textual processes of ceaseless metonymic doing and undoing that Walcott distributes all through the diegetic world of *Omeros*, without localizing them in some chimeric 'female principle'.

Moreover, while pivoting on the planetary materiality of the human body or the physical island, as well as the interminability of the text, the nexus of doing and undoing, of cure and injury, is at the same time intensely invested with another, far more devastating kind of unspeakable: the political history of the genocides perpetrated by the *conquistadores*, the atrocities of the Atlantic slave trade and the displacements of colonial and postcolonial rule. The infliction of wounds and their healing thus epitomizes "a wider sense of renewal and creativity in the aftermath of empire, which is what motivates Walcott to reveal how the individual stories of St Lucians and of the island embody an 'epical splendour' of survival and re-creation" (Woodcock 2001: 554). One of the main symbols of this work of re-creation, and a major agent of connexionist worlding, is the sea-swift, a migratory bird that crosses the Atlantic Ocean and thereby stitches together the "two worlds", Old and New, that imperialism has created as two distinct and incompatible spheres:

> I followed a sea-swift to both sides of this text;
> her hyphen stitched its seam, like the interlocking
> basins of a globe in which one half fits the next
>
> into an equator, both shores neatly clicking
> into a globe; except that its meridian
> was not North and South but East and West. One the New
>
> World, made exactly like the Old, halves of one brain,
> or the beat of both hands rowing that bear the two
> vessels of the heart with balance, weight, and design. (O 319)

Like the sulphurous 'lava' in Ma Kilman's cauldron from the slave-operated sugar mill, stitching involves both violence (the piercing of the text/ile) and healing (the suturing of what is disparate). This ambivalent movement is enacted here on the globe as well as the human body, whose hands, brain and heart are all held together in (spite of) their essential duality by the stitching swift. More than that, as 'hyphen' the bird becomes a metatextual conceit that crosses not only the ocean but also the text, where it indeed serves as the constant leitmotif of a connexionist mediator between worlds. *Omeros* thus ends on a self-referential note in which this prominent piece of postcolonial world literature reflects upon its own status as a text whose "language carries its own cure, its radiant affliction" (O 323). In the motif of stitching as a movement of piercing and suture, wounding and healing, the basic doubleness of the gutter as gap and bridge finds an apt imagery, and to the extent that stitching serves as a metatextual self-reference, *Omeros* arguably identifies itself as a gutter text. This hypothesis finds some support in an observation made by Gregson Davis, who reads the vast and intricate tapestry that Maud Plunkett embroiders as "a partial emblem of the poem as a whole" (Davis 1990: 47). Maud's needlework here serves as textual autoreference precisely because of the gappy structure that her "immense quilt" (O 88) shares with the verse novel. For figural embroidery combines the segmentivity of a pointillist mosaic structure with a visual mimesis that allows for the coherent representation of sujets. Unlike the Blue Marble pictures, embroidery thus does not suppress but highlights its gutter textuality by leaving the gaps between the individual stitches visible. By that token, Walcott renders Maud Plunkett's quilt – and along with it, the text as a whole – an emulation of the starry sky, that overarching ur-gutter text looked at from the gutter. For embroidery and verse novel alike take their cues, as it were, from the stars: "Needlepoint constellations | on a clear night had prompted this intricate thing" (O 88).

2.2 'Links between geology and character': Anne Carson's *Autobiography of Red*

The volcanic 'essences' of Walcott's Ma Kilman and Helen surface as telluric sighs or fiery flashes from 'vertiginous irises': instances where some deep core interiority reveals itself but won't become legible. A gutter is thus introduced as a major communicative gulf between inside and outside, whose epic model, as we have seen, is the ambiguous figure of the sybil. In sharp contrast to Walcott's magma women, the cast of Anne Carson's verse novel, *Autobiography of Red* (1998), is mainly made up of lava men. This holds true especially for the protagonist Geryon, whom the text follows through a series of rather quotidian but formative episodes from early childhood to adulthood. The loosely configured chapters of this bildungsroman-in-verse show Geryon as bullied schoolboy, gay adolescent, semi-professional photographer, student of philosophy, hobby anthropologist and not least autobiographer. In each of the chapters, Geryon learns something, be it "about justice" (R 23), how to distinguish between himself and the world (R 29), how to give a sad story a happy ending (R 38), how to take a photograph (R 41), and so on. Oddly, and in striking contradiction to the relative everydayness of Geryon's story of education, he is also introduced as a "strange red winged monster" (R 5). Many readers (among them, the most insightful ones) perceive this protagonist as "the epitome for monstrous otherness" (Neumann and Rippl: 2020) or else as a "metaphor for debates about social and cultural difference" (Burkitt 2012: 107), yet it appears at least one-sided to overemphasize Geryon's monstrosity or reduce that fictional character to the status of a representational type standing in as 'epitome' or 'metaphor' for ousted alterity. Not that this were not the case but only besides the dominant quotidian streaks of Geryon. The most striking feature of Carson's handling of 'monstrosity' – after all a rather spectacular character trait – is precisely its de-exoticization, the cool naturalness and deliberate understatement with which Geryon's otherness is woven into the text. Yet of course the fact remains that Geryon *is* a monster, and this is not so much due to the way he is treated as other by others in Carson's text but because of the cascades of intertextual resonances of his name.

Exorcizing epic masters

Like Achille, Hector, Helen and Philoctete, the name Geryon comes a long way that reaches back to Dante and beyond to Greek antiquity; not to Homer but to writers like Hesiod, Apollodorus and a somewhat obscure epic poet named Stesichoros. It is through these intertextual echoes that Geryon 'achieves' his monstrosity, and a forceful resonance with Walcott's volcanism: "The most Dantean episode in *Omeros*" (Austenfeld 2006: 20), namely the cathartic visit to the Soufrière massif, can be quite accurately located intertextually as a sojourn to Dante's eighth circle of Hell, that region where according to the *Inferno* the monster Geryon as embodiment of treachery and fraudulence is doomed forever to stand guard over the steaming trenches of the Malebolge. Walcott's sulphurous 'Pool of Speculation' borrows its name, 'the Malebolge', from that pit where according to the first lines of *Inferno* XVIII liars and "sin-divided traitors" (Alighieri 1928: 75) are being punished for eternity and a day. Made up of ten concentrically arranged moats that encircle a central abyss, Dante's Malebolge is itself located inside a steep crater whose perpendicular walls frustrate any attempt to reach the pit on foot. The descent to the otherwise inaccessible Malebolge is possible only with the help of "the unclean monster" Geryon, a hybrid of "reptile", "beaver" and "scorpion" with "hairy paws" but a human face fraudulently displaying "a glance benign" (ibid.: 70). Though expressly introduced by Dante as "wingless" (ibid.), Geryon has the power or skill to "swim" through the "fetid air" around the malodorous and venomous trenches of the Malebolge, and gets recruited by Virgil to act as vehicle for the descent to "the utter depths of Hell" (ibid.: 73). Geryon is thus at once an abject "beast of guile" (ibid.) *and* in Proppian terms a necessary helper enlisted by Virgil, the master, to serve as hovercraft. Structurally, the figure of the servant who is at the same time a monster is easily recognizable as the traditional trope of abjecting the exploited *while* exploiting them: women, proletarians, Blacks,

Dalits – Caliban being the most recognisable example (cf. Federici 2004: 11; Linebaugh and Rediker 2000: 58). One crucial leitmotif of such hegemonic constructions has always been to deny those 'things of darkness' the status of full humanity by subjecting them to oppressive powerful structures and dynamics of reification/commodification, thingification or enslavism that consolidate the representation of the other as "black semblance" of "white presence" (Bhabha 1994: 90). It is therefore not by accident that, for Dante, Geryon's most fraudulent feature is the human face that grotesquely sits on his reptile body as token of a futile attempt at passing for human. Dante obviously stands on the side of the hegemon in his revulsion at the "filthy image of fraud" (Alighieri 1928: 72) that is Geryon.

As more expert readings of the *Divine Comedy* have persuasively pointed out, the Geryon canto is the one passage in the *Inferno* in which the problem of veracity becomes thematic since it is here "that Dante staked the truth claim of the *Commedia* on the truth of the monster Geryon. Dante's claims for the ethical authority of his poetic vision are accordingly evoked at the heart of fraud" (Cachey 2010: 340). He repeatedly insists here, as if in a witness's testimony, that he has in fact seen with his own eyes what he knows to be utterly unbelievable for any reader: the flying monster on whose broad shoulders the narrator and his masterful tour guide make their descent to the Malebolge. It is when Geryon makes his appearance as "a shape" (Alighieri 1928: 70) that Dante launches a volley of pre-emptive concessions to the reader's anticipated incredulity, concessions that make these passages appear as "the most exposed weapons in a massive and unrelenting campaign to coerce our suspension of disbelief" (Barolini 1992: 41). The strategy is twofold: it rests on an excessive display of authorial honesty ('I am aware that this must sound extremely implausible but …'), and on the delinking of the improbable literal textual surface from the truthful actual underlying message. The tension if not rift between these two textual levels clears a space – a gutter – for the acknowledgment that

> the discourse that undertakes to represent that incredible beast is [...] a 'truth that has the face of a lie.' In other words, although a *comedia* may at times, as when representing Geryon, have the 'face of a lie' – give the appearance of lying – it is intractably always truth. (Barolini 1992: 38)

In short, the ostensible unmasking of the monster concealed behind the 'benign' human face can itself be read as fraud: an act that camouflages the violence of abjecting the servant body as a seeing through the monster's pathetic masquerade.

It is telling that Walcott, while so conspicuously inscribing himself with his terza rima stanzas into the footsteps of Dante, omits Geryon altogether: no 'vehicle', no monstrous abjected helper is required for the narrator's and Omeros's ascent to the Malebolge and the volcanic catharsis. This arguably has everything to do with Walcott's locus of enunciation: as one who speaks from the position of, and on behalf of, the descendants of the enslaved, colonized and dehumanized, his narrator is himself a 'Geryon' that now, however, claims for himself the place of Dante. It is equally telling that Anne Carson, a white settler Canadian, conspicuously revisits and revises Walcott's volcanic imagination but, for her part, omits Dante altogether while profiling Homer as an embodiment of stifling traditionalism. No authoritative poet claiming truth for power is needed for her novel in verse that, instead, puts Geryon at the centre in a project that sets out to speak truth to power. If Walcott writes (himself) from the margin into the very heart of the "hypercanon" (Damrosch 2006: 46) – Homer, Dante, Joyce – Carson performs the inverse move as a writer who speaks from the centre but explores and obviously prefers the obscured, eccentric and peripheral. It is in this vein that she construes and constructs the central intertextual reference point of *Autobiography of Red* as a discernibly marginal voice: instead of the better-known Geryon texts by Hesiod or Apollodorus, it is the pre-classical Greek poet Stesichoros whose fragmentary epic functions as the fundamental pretext for Carson's verse novel. Even though canonized as one of the elevated 'eight poets' of Greek antiquity, Stesichoros occupies a precarious position that makes him appear, in Carson's text, as an ideal exponent of minor literature: "Born about 650 B.C. on the north coast of Sicily in a city called Himera, he lived among refugees who spoke a mixed dialect of Chalcidian and Doric" (R 3). What Carson draws on in particular for her novel in verse is Stesichoros's *Geryoneis*, an epic account of Herakles's raid of the cattle of Geryon and the ensuing fight between the antagonists in which the cattle thief kills the cattle owner. Readers of the classics will recall that the raid on the cattle of Geryon is the tenth of Herakles's 'labours', adding the cowherd to a series of victims of the hypermasculine demigod including, among others, the Hydra, the Nemean lion or the Cretan bull: monsters all of them from the perspective of the victors. Notably, Geryon appears in most extant accounts as an embodiment of *entrelacement*: a three-headed giant with three torsos and three pairs of legs connected at the waist, in some versions winged, and a veritable sparring partner, perhaps even a perilous opponent to the itinerant superhero. Time has reduced Stesichoros's epic poem to a gutter-text materiality as only "some eighty-four papyrus fragments and a half-dozen citations survive" (R 5). Carson takes these fragments as a springboard for her own multi-layered and fragmented gutter text, a perforated and gappy late-twentieth-century *Geryoneis* that consists of seven loosely constellated sections that Ian Rae has succinctly summarized as follows:

> A 'proemium' or preface on the Greek poet Stesichoros, translated fragments of Stesichoros's *Geryoneis*, three appendices on the blinding of Stesichoros by Helen, a long romance-in-verse recasting Stesichoros's

Geryoneis as a contemporary gay love affair, and a mock-interview with the 'choir-master' [Stesichoros] – each with its own style and story to tell. (Rae 2000: 17)

Of particular interest for the problematic of the gutter text and the tension of separateness and connexionism is the first of these tributaries, the proemium: a mock-philological essay on the place of Stesichoros in literary history, where he figures as a writer who "came after Homer and before Gertrude Stein, a difficult interval for a poet" (R 3). What at first glance appears to be nothing but a playful quip soon turns into a substantial historicization of the little-known Greek lyricist. Carson's introductory essay presents Stesichoros as a rigorous modernizer who punctures the conventionalism and fixed order of the Homeric worldview, where "being is stable and particularity is set fast in tradition" (R 4). Stesichoros, in Carson's reading, interrupts "the still surface of this code" by undoing the "latches" that hitherto had regulated the economy of value ascription. Unsettling the Homeric epithet, Stesichoros invents, as it were, the free-floating adjective that from now on is no longer irrevocably fixed for good to the thing it qualifies. With that gesture, he turns a whole worldview upside down and transforms the world from givenness to becoming: as he 'released being' from its confinement in the ossified diction of the Homeric code, "all the substances in the world went floating up" (R 5). To 'release being', the fixed linguistic/idiomatic ties have to be severed that in concert produce and reproduce a stifling *ordo* that keeps things in their proper place, a hierarchical division of the sensible whose most binding authority, for Carson, is the very same figure that Walcott's text so reverentially elevates to the status of unsurpassable 'master': Homer. Stesichoros's innovative usage of non-conventionalized combinations of adjectives and nouns, qualities and substances, is thus a liberating act that starts with the undoing of traditional ties so that new, fresh and specific connections can be invented. This is especially true for a highly tattered and fragmented text like Stesichoros's *Geryoneis*. It is, in a different way, also true for *Autobiography of Red* itself. For Carson, too, gives her text a significant porosity and gappiness all the way down to the minute close-up of its peculiarly asymmetric form of alternating very short and very long lines that give the text "a rapid and elliptical momentum" in which "prosaic" and "lyrical" tendencies "conjoin (and jostle at the same time)" (Bundschuh 2015: 222):

Herakles standing at the window staring out on the dark before dawn.
When they made love
Geryon liked to touch in slow succession each of the bones of Herakles' back
as it arched away from him into
   who knows what dark dream of its own, running both hands all the way
     down

from the base of the neck
to the end of the spine which he can cause to shiver like a root in the rain.
Herakles makes
a low sound and moves his head on the pillow, slowly opens his eyes.
He starts.
Geryon what's wrong? Jesus I hate it when you cry. What is it?
Geryon thinks hard. (R 141)

If this form of versification in fact creates some oxymoronic hybridity of the prosaic and the lyrical at the formal microlevel, then a similar collation of discrepant elements reoccurs at the overall structure of the book, where the text presents itself as a loose collation of numerous jarring segments. The text about the monster is thus itself a monster in the canonical Victorian understanding of that term as a "composite beast" (O'Connor 2012: 497), and indeed have readers of Carson's verse novel made out a virtual identity of monstrous protagonist and monstrous text: "Just as *Autobiography of Red* is an assemblage of disparate genres, Carson's monster Geryon is a composite pieced together from fragments which originate elsewhere" (Tschofen 2004: 34). The monster, conceived in this way, is of course closely affiliated to the gutter text and its segmentivity, its incompleteness, its visible form as 'composed relationality'. It is, qua gutter text as well as qua monster, a structured assemblage of segments whose connectedness requires their separateness: "Boundaries [...] actually function to increase connection with others" (Barthold 2016: 141). The monstrous text is a connexionist device that brings relatedness to the fore precisely by the withholding of full articulation and continuity: it can but be contiguous in this world.

In this vein, Carson proceeds from (but by no means fills) the gaping lacunae between the extant fragments of Stesichoros's *Geryoneis*, from which the possibility for an alternative take on the Geryon/Herakles story appears to emerge. Instead of producing a conventional, pro-Herakles "thrilling account of the victory of culture over monstrosity" (R 6), Carson's Stesichoros empathizes with the "strange red winged monster who lived on an island called Erytheia (which is an adjective meaning simply 'The Red Place') quietly tending a herd of magical red cattle, until one day the hero Herakles came across the sea and killed him to get the cattle" (R 5). Aggressor and victim are clearly identifiable from this reading. Carson thus turns the value assignments upside down that prevail in hegemonic versions of the Geryon story by fundamentally redefining the very notion of 'monster'; yet she is "not content with a simple reversal of value judgements" (Rae 2000: 29). In her laconic summary of Stesichoros's lost epic, Geryon is not restored to humanity: he explicitly remains a 'monster' but one that, somewhat a-typically for a monster, 'quietly tends a herd of cattle' and falls prey to a pillaging invader whom the text wryly calls a 'hero'. Gentle, pacific monstrosity thus gets annihilated by aggressive and predatory heroism. Moreover, the fact that Geryon's 'strangeness' is conspicuously tied to complexion – the prominent trope of "racial epidermal schemas" (Fanon 1986: 84) – arguably allows for a boldly anachronistic reading from which (Carson's) Stesichoros emerges not only as anti-imperialist but decisively anti-racist. As Catherine Hall conjectures, Carson's version of Stesichoros's Geryon figures as

> a sign of ethnic alterity [...] whose red skin and wings mark him out as different [...]. Although no such connection is ever explicitly drawn, the implicit ethnic associations of 'red skin' in North American and Canadian culture lurk just beneath the poem's surface. (Hall 2009: 220–1)

What dominant narratives stigmatize as monstrosity (and will later blow up to six-legged, three-torsoed and three-headed grotesquery, not to mention Dante's meticulous description of the monster's 'unclean shape') can thus be reduced to – indigeneity: First Nation American in Hall's reading, perhaps also Guanche (i.e. aboriginal Canary Islanders) when following Jan Schoo who speculates from Hesiod's and Apollodoros's accounts of Herakles's battle with Geryon that the many-limbed giant, whose name translates as "roarer" (Schoo 1969: 86), may have been a displaced personification of the Teide volcano on the Canary Island of Tenerife (see also Ulbrich 1992: 67; Stafford 2012: 45).

Psychogeology

I will come back to this fascinating speculation further down; suffice it for now to assume that an indigenous face, whether Native American or Guanche, 'lurks' behind the monstrous mask as much as 'beneath the poem's surface', and whatever lurks beneath the surface will tend to break through and 'come out': as volcanic eruption in geological terms; as dreamwork, as the uncanny (if things go bad) or as psychosis (if things go really bad) in psychological terms; as figurative or anagogic meaning in reconstructive hermeneutics of the text's political unconscious. The continuity of these – and probably more – entangled levels of the geological, the psychic and the textual is explicitly stated in Carson's verse novel when Geryon muses how he

> liked to plan
> his autobiography, in that blurred state
> between awake and asleep when too many intake valves are open in the soul.
> Like the terrestrial crust of the earth
> Which is proportionally ten times thinner than an eggshell, the skin of the soul
> is a miracle of mutual pressures. (R 60)

There is then, as Stesichoros himself puts it in the mock interview at the end of the verse novel, "a link between geology and character" (R 149), even if the exact nature of that link remains to some extent opaque: "I: What is this link | S: I have often wondered" (ibid.). The link can be grasped formally in terms of the composed relationality that connects the soul (that both Plato and Freud called 'psyche') and the planet by virtue of one common feature, namely the mediating surfaces – the 'crust' of the planet, "the medium of the *Pcpt.-Cs.*" of the psyche (Freud 1984: 363; emphasis in the original) – that serve as organs with which they attempt to uphold the equilibrium of external and internal 'mutual pressures'. The same holds true for the text of Geryon's autobiography and by extension for Carson's book as a whole, that now can be read as experiments, not in pschogeography, but indeed in psychogeology. Carson's verse novel derives its title from that intradiegetic work with which it may or may not be identical: Geryon's autobiography, as memoir psychogeologically premised on the "difference | between outside and inside" (R 29). Geryon discovers and explores this distinction at an early age: "Inside is mine, he thought" (ibid.). If one follows the clues that the text itself offers, Carson's *Geryoneis* is about monstrous life writing as psychogeology, a run-on account of that which 'lurks beneath the surface': the eponymous autobiography is a 'work' in which, from the age of seven onwards, "Geryon set down all inside things" and "coolly omitted | all outside things" (ibid.). Of course, at the moment they are 'set down', all 'inside things' become outside things. Framed this way, the autobiography would best be grasped as an ongoing externalization of interiority, the bringing to the surface of what is underneath: in Freudian terms, the making manifest of what is latent; in geological terms, a series of gentle eruptions. The volcano is, in this understanding, an outlet valve that will be activated once the internal terrestrial pressure gets too high: "Volcanic processes mediate between the Earth's forbidding interior and the lively envelope around the planet's surface" (Clark, Gormally and Tuffen 2018: 273–94). Likewise, according to Freudian scripture, psychic energies get discharged by various modes of organizing outward release – some uninhibited (as in sexual intercourse), some blocked (as in psychosis), some sublimated (as in such artistic creativity as Geryon's autobiography). But what is underneath, latent or 'inside' if not that which the soul's 'intake valves' have allowed to enter? Both the planet and the psyche involve complex processes of mediated trafficking between the 'forbidding interior' and the 'lively envelope'. As far as the psyche is concerned, Carson can take convenient recourse to Freud himself, who projects a permeability of inside and outside that makes the membrane in-between these domains the interface and crucial mediator of contrary forces. For Freud, this mediating function is the task of the "poor ego" hemmed in between the superior force of "the external world" on the one hand and the "claims and demands" of the inner "harsh masters", the ego-ideal/superego and the id (Freud 1989: 85; also 1984: 397).

So far, a web of analogies between the geological and the psychic has emerged; what remains to be established is how language, and writing in particular, are included in this web. In this regard, Carson's text takes recourse, one more time, to *Omeros*, more specifically to a short passage where Walcott's text likens the beginning of the lunch break in the St Lucian harbour town of Gros Islet to a volcanic eruption that stifles all life. The drone of the church bells descends like volcanic refuse – "the ash of the Angelus" (O 121) – and transforms Gros Islet into a virtual "Pompeii" as "each citizen ‖ stood paralyzed as the bell counted the hours" of high noon (O 120). While the reference to Pompeii reiterates Walcott's strategy of superimposing European antiquity onto the Caribbean, the more elaborate comparison is with the harbour town of St Pierre (Martinique) that was destroyed in the devastating 1902 eruption of Mt Pelée. The magnitude of the event – some 30,000 inhabitants were killed within a couple of minutes – "inspired divine interpretation: a boiling, three-hundred-degree cloud of gas, steam, dust, ash, and pumice formed within the mountain and then burst forth" (Agard-Jones 2012: 329). According to Walcott's verses, the "only survivor had been a prisoner | who watched the volcano's powder mottle the air" (O 121) from the window of his cell. With regards to historical veracity, this is almost but not quite accurate: the prisoner in question (a Black, Creole-speaking workingman named Louis-Auguste Sylbaris popularly known, Walcott-style, as Sanson) could survive the devastation only because his cell had no window.[1] On the night before the eruption, Sylbaris had been incarcerated for rowdyism, most likely on grounds of racist profiling, and put into solitary confinement in a crypt-like construction that ironically turned out to be the only halfway safe location in town. In that bunker he endured for four days after the volcanic gas cloud struck and wiped out all life in Saint Pierre. A group of disaster tourists accidentally detected and rescued him, heavily burned but alive. Later on, he made a career as "an exhibit in a famous American circus. [...] Posters described him as

---

[1] It is noteworthy yet somewhat marginal to the main argument of this chapter that within the sparse space of two verses Walcott renders the prison cell a room with a view, thus adding a dimension of visuality that is strikingly absent from the recorded history of Sylbaris: whereas in *Omeros* it is emphasized that the prisoner "*watched* the volcano's powder mottle the air | *across the channel*" (emphasis added), Sylbaris's surviving testimony pivots on the disorienting experience of completely blocked sight and the concomitant dependence on the sense of hearing:

> It was eight o'clock, and they hadn't yet brought my rations for the day, when all of a sudden there was a terrifying noise. Everyone was shouting "Help, I'm burning! I'm dying!" Five minutes later, no-one was shouting any more, except me. Then a cloud of smoke gushed through the little opening above my door. For the next quarter of an hour, this smoke was burning me so much that I had to jump left and right, up and down, anywhere and everywhere, to get out of its way. An awful silence fell when it was over. I kept listening and shouting for someone to come and save me. No-one answered. So, I decided that all Saint-Pierre must have been crushed under an earthquake, in the fire. (Scarth 2002: 186)

'Ludger Sylbaris. The only living object [*sic*] that survived in the Silent City of Death'" (Scarth 2002: 189).

Carson weaves the same incident into her verse novel, but whereas Walcott's text refers to this extraordinary incident only in passing, Carson puts the figure of the "Lava Man" – the "prisoner in the local jail" (R 47) who alone survives the volcanic eruption – centre stage. It is true that, as in *Omeros*, the proper name of Sylbaris is never mentioned in *Autobiography of Red*. Yet as the 'Lava Man' he serves multiple crucial purposes: as a veritable double of Geryon and more crucially as an important allegory of a volcanic speech that, unlike Ma Kilman's telluric sighs, is highly articulate. With "volcano blood" running in his veins (R 59), Lava Man literally embodies geology, but he does so in a culturally and politically specific way. For the equation of the body with a volcano is far from innocent but instead loaded with a long history of demonization and containment. In his seminal study, *Male Fantasies*, Klaus Theweleit demonstrates how pre- and proto-fascist masculinism rests on the construction of a fortified male, white and non-proletarian soldier identity whose constantly looming dissolution is forcefully held at a distance through the "body armour that 'bottles up' [one's] own seething interior" (Theweleit 1992: 242). The 'enemy' of this militarized subject is therefore not only the many-headed hydra of the multiple others 'out there' (Bolsheviks, women, Blacks, Jews, homosexuals etc.) but just as much all "the 'floods' and 'lava' that are capable of erupting from within soldier males" (ibid.: 256). In this light the queerness of Carson's Lava Man comes to the fore: while ideal soldier males "freeze up, and become icicles" (ibid.: 244), Lava Man proudly declares his hotness: "I am molten matter" (R 59). At the Barnum Circus, his most spectacular stunt is to prick his thumb and to "press out ochre-coloured drops that sizzled when they hit the plate" (ibid.). He thus literalizes the paramilitary proto-fascist fear with the unformed interior that 'lurks beneath' the body armour, but significantly endorses and enacts precisely that intimation which masculinism tries to suppress, namely that "every vessel is a potential volcano, particularly the human body" (Theweleit 1992: 244). And of course the very name by which Sylbaris goes in Carson's verse novel associates the very opposite of that which Theweleit's soldier males stand for: 'Lava Man' sounds like 'lover man' and thus links Carson's Sylbaris with all the eroticism that fortified, pleasure-phobic masculinity attempts to contain in the cage of the body armour.

As a human volcano, Lava Man doubles Geryon perfectly, who after all bears the name of that very 'monster' from Greek mythology that, as some critics argue, "personifies the volcano El Teide on the Canary Island of Tenerife" (Rae 2000: 32; for philological support, see Davies and Finglass 2014: 288, who point out that the term κορυφη that Stesichoros uses for one of Geryon's heads literally denotes the top of a mountain). This association of Carson's protagonist with the volcanic (and hence with Lava Man) intensifies in the course of the narrative when Geryon at times "could feel something like tons of black magma boiling up | from the deeper regions of him" (R 105), and when introspection equates the "pondering of the cracks and fissures | of his inner life" (ibid.). Even more importantly, Lava Man/Sylbaris functions as a messenger returned from the bowels of the earth. It is in this capacity that he emerges as the representative of a particular language use that stands in close affinity with the volcanic and the psychic. For this, Carson rewrites Sylbaris's sojourn with the Barnum Circus not so much as a sensationalist *melée* with the survivor as spectacle (even if that is naturally also the case) but rather as a concrete enactment of "what Freud would have called [...] | unconscious metaphysics" (R 59), and the Stesichoros of the 'Interview' appendix, 'a link between geology and character': Lava Man introduces himself as "molten matter returned from the core of the earth to tell you of interior things" (ibid.). Obviously this telling of hitherto untold 'interior things' echoes the young Geryon's discovery of the preciousness of 'inside things' to be brought into language in his autobiography. Lava Man thus refers back to the beginning of Geryon's project; but not only that, he likewise proleptically anticipates the much later identification of Geryon with the (fictitious) Peruvian myth of the "*Yazcol Yazcamac*" – a Quechua word meaning "the Ones Who Went and Saw and Came Back" (R 128):

> Yes. People who saw the inside of the volcano.
> And came back.
> Yes.
> How did they come back?
> Wings.
> Wings? Yes that's what they say the Yazcamac return as red people with wings.
> (R 128–9)

Lava Man, 'returned from the core of the earth' with tales to tell of 'interior things', thus finds his peers in these legendary volcano visitors whose outer appearance exactly coincides with Geryon's: 'red people with wings'. Monstrosity here gives way to giftedness: the *Yazcol Yazcamac* are "wise ones. | Holy men" (R 128) revered by the communities of the volcanic regions of the High Andes. As a collection of articulations of 'inside things', then, Geryon's autobiography is in league with the testimonies of the miraculously saved Lava Man, the sole survivor of St Pierre and the reports of the mythical Andean volcano travellers.

Light writing – life writing

Volcanic and psychoanalytic resonances aside, the emphasis on the f/act of Geryon's *writing* strongly refers to a tradition of seeing, as in German

Romanticism, language as the mediator between outside and inside: the medium that, for Jean Paul Richter (very much in consonance with the poetics of Carson's Geryon), enables the "equilibration of inner and outer world" (Richter 1990: 57; my translation). However, this essentially expressivist understanding of language has long since been complicated by multiple metalinguistic and metapoetic investigations of the many layers that give language – the soul's 'outer world' – an interiority all its own, for which the young Peter Handke, in a 1974 poetry collection, has coined the intriguing formula of "the innerworld of the outerworld of the innerworld". If I propose to read *Autobiography of Red* as an exploration precisely of this interiority of language, then such a focus is emphatically not meant to sideline the more overt anti-hegemonic political themes of Carson's text that numerous readers like Catherine Hall, Katharine Burkitt or Birgit Neuman and Gabriele Rippl have persuasively pointed to, but rather to emphasize how Carson deploys form itself for a politics of radical revaluation. In this perspective a largely overlooked dynamics of Carson's text comes into view, namely, the extrapolation of doubleness. Thus, the volcano/psyche/writing complex is not only expressive and eruptive but just as much impressive and imbibing: the volcano in verse is also a volcano inverse. Even if the work-in-progress autobiography is clearly an 'output' of what is 'inside', it is important to add that much if not all that is inside has been absorbed from the outside. The soul is virtually a camera whose 'intake valves' will at times be tightly closed, at other times as wide open as the shutters of the camera that another gay autobiographer, Christopher Isherwood, famously claims to 'be': "I am a camera" (Isherwood 2001: 3). No wonder therefore that the code Geryon deploys for his autobiography gradually moves from verbal to visual, from writing to photography. In chapter VIII, the adolescent Geryon is first seen with the camera that will, from then on, be his constant prop and writing tool. At this stage in his life, the visual has already fully replaced the verbal: "He had recently relinquished speech" (R 40), giving up utterance and expression in favour of exposure and impression: "*A photograph is just a bunch of light | hitting a plate*" (R 71; emphasis in the original), muses Geryon's lover Herakles. 'Hitting a plate': an odd enough phrase that stands out and recalls a different context, where the drops of Lava Man's 'volcano blood' 'sizzled when they hit the plate', producing a controlled minor volcanic eruption that is now readable as analogous to a photograph.

"Click", the chapter's title, indicates that Geryon in his early stages as autobiographer deploys the technique of instantaneous and short exposure. During the course of his autodidactic explorations of the medium, however, he increasingly develops a preference for slow-shutter photography which he first encounters in a picture taken by Herakles's grandmother. The photograph shows the eruption of a volcano captured with

> a fifteen minute exposure that recorded both the general shape of the cone with its surroundings (best seen by day)
>
> and the rain of incandescent bombs tossed into the air and rolling down its slopes
>
> (visible in the dark). (R 51)

Thanks to the extremely long exposure time, the photograph "has compressed | on its motionless surface | fifteen different moments of time, nine hundred seconds of bombs moving up | and ash going down | and pines in the kill process" (ibid.). Blending the spatial ('motionless surface') with the temporal ('fifteen different moments of time'), the photograph becomes a crystallized film or, more accurately, a narrative painting that – like the Armada Portrait of Elizabeth I or Poussin's *Gathering of Manna* – shows various consecutive story elements within one frame. And yet the iconic turn that Geryon appears to take and that makes his autobiography ostensibly a photo essay rather than a verbal account of himself is not actually enacted by *Autobiography of Red*: unlike other Carson texts, this one remains strictly non-pictorial. Starting with the grandmother's volcano photograph, all the images in the book are *described*, not *presented*. This ekphrastic dimension becomes especially pertinent in the last seven (but one) chapters that are paratextually advertized by their titles as 'photographs', and that all begin with the announcement, "It is a photograph of". These chapters then offer a glimpse of the photographic autobiography that Geryon has been working on ever since his adolescence. These verbal photographs 'show' strictly quotidian material with subjects ranging from "four people sitting around a table with hands in front of them" (R 136) to "Geryon's left pant leg just below the knee" (R 137) and "a man's naked back, long and bluish" (R 141). If the opening line of each of these chapters identifies the object of the photograph, then it thereby arguably encourages the expectation of an ekphrastic rendition of that object in the subsequent verses: a *verbal* evocation of what is introduced as a *visual* subject. What transpires, however, is not ekphrasis proper but narrative proper – not in the sense of some enfolding of the subject into a narrative vignette, but in the form of a reconstruction of the moment of taking the picture in question. The close-up of Geryon's jeans below his knees, for instance, is owed to the intervention of a co-passenger who prevents Geryon from pointing his camera at a bunch of soldiers who stop the car in which Geryon and his friends are travelling: "Geryon is focusing | the camera on their guns | when Ancash's mother slides her left hand over the shutter and gently forces it | out of sight between Geryon's knees" (R 137). This is not ekphrasis but narrative, not *nature morte* but anecdote trying to reconstruct the precise moment of taking the picture. But that moment, following Jacques Derrida, cannot be easily identified because it falls apart into a giddying, vertiginous multitude of moments:

> When, exactly, does a shot [*prise de vue*] take place? When, exactly, is it taken? And thus, where? Given the workings of a delay mechanism, given the 'time lag' or 'time difference', if I can put it this way, is the photograph taken when the photographer takes the thing in view and focuses on it, when he adjusts the diaphragm and sets the timing mechanism, or else when the click signals the capture and the impression? Or later still, at the moment of development? And should we give in to the vertigo of this metonymy and this infinite mirroring when they draw us into the folds of an endless reflexivity? (Derrida 2010: 25)

Photography as metonymy, then, is a chain of moments leading one to the next without the arrival at a resting point or closure, whether in a subsuming metaphor or in the achieved spatiality of ekphrasis. Announcing but not actually 'delivering' ekphrasis, Carson's text appears firmly in league with this typically Derridean gesture of deferral and delay. By stirring up the 'motionless surface' of the picture into the dynamic mobility of narrative, the text repeats and updates the very gesture that it ascribes to its pretext, Stesichoros, who, according to the proemium, also disrupted a 'still surface' – that of the conventionalized Homeric code – and 'released being' by puncturing a closed worldview, opening fissures and gutters through which 'all the substances in the world went floating up'. The vertigo of metonymy is then owed to the bottomlessness that is revealed through the cracks and fissures in the surface once words and things have been unlatched from one another. From then on, metonymy energizes the ceaseless search for some stable meaning, some transcendental signifier, some re-closing of the fissured surface. Carson's own Stesichoros act lies in the extension of this unlatching of writing from verbal language by releasing it into the gutter of a poetics that shuttles between the verbal and the visual: after all, photography literally is "the writing of light" (Derrida 2010: 19). One of the first insights that Geryon obtains in his self-*bildung* is a grasp on the disaggregating force of this shift from verbal to visual that engenders a radicalized version of Stesichoros's unhinging of the fixed universe of Homeric epithets. What Geryon experiences is a re-segmentation at the most basic level of writing, a severing of the most 'natural' ties of articulation: "A word [...] | when he stared at it, would disassemble itself into separate letters and go" (R 26), as its organic continuity gives way to its segmentivity.

The framing, all through the book, of photography (light writing) as autobiography (life writing), now makes the overlap of the psyche with its intake valves and the camera with its shutters well-nigh ineluctable. Writing (as photography) and psychic processes (as the capture and 'development' of initially unconscious impressions in the Freudian "photographic apparatus"; Kofman 1998: 22) are thus isomorphic, and this isomorphism extends in a crucial twist toward the very end of the verse novel to the planet itself via the volcano. Not only the soul but also the volcano is a camera, and this isomorphism enforces the notion of some 'link between geology and character'. The verse novel part of the book ends with an ascent of the peak of the Peruvian volcano Icchantikas where Geryon

> peers down
>
> at the earth heart of Icchantikas dumping all its photons out her ancient eye and he
>
> smiles for
>
> the camera. (R 145)

The gaze into the crater engenders not just a mirror image but leads to a final inversion in which the bearer of the gaze becomes its object as the photographer has his "picture taken by 'her ancient eye'" (Rae 2000: 34). The volcano-camera thus appears as the ultimate light writer ('dumping its photons') into whose open shutter the monstrous-yet-human life-writer/light-writer 'smiles'. Peering into the 'vertiginous iris' of the crater, Geryon repeats the gesture of his first photographic subject, his mother's "gazing down the sight line into his lens" (R 40) so that his status as object, not subject of this concluding photograph, gets emphasized: the photographer gets photographed, the writer gets written in a constellation of *"confusing subject and object"* (R 52, emphasis in the original.). This last picture of the autobiography is introduced as "a photograph he never took, no one here took it" (R 145), and it is titled '# 1748' after the Emily Dickinson poem that serves for an epigraph to the verse novel.[2] The full title of the chapter – 'XLVI. Photographs: # 1748' – literalizes and enacts the traditional and canonical understanding of ekphrasis, *ut pictura poesis* (as in painting, so in poetry) by introducing the chapter as simultaneously a fictitious picture *and* an actual poem, whose penultimate verse closes the 'photograph': "'The Only Secret People Keep'" (R 145). Who is speaking here in the guise of Dickinson? Is it Geryon, citing that gnomic poem of the 'reticent volcano' while peering into the 'earth heart of Icchantikas'? Is it the volcano itself that, as we have seen, acts as the camera that took the 'photograph' that now bears the title of (and hence somehow *is*) Dickinson' poem? Or is it Carson, whose masterful and at the same time playful reshuffling of pretextual matter is so constitutive for the entire book? Like photography according to Derrida, the multi-layered paratextual and intertextual composition of this chapter and the book of which it is a part seems to 'draw us into the folds of an endless reflexivity' that re-enacts the act of unlatching, of dissolving

---

[2] The reticent volcano keeps | His never slumbering plan – | Confided are his projects pink | To no precarious man. || If nature will not tell the tale | Jehovah told to her | Can human nature not survive | Without a listener? || Admonished by her buckled lips | Let every babbler be | The only secret people keep | Is immortality. (Dickinson in R 22)

fixities, that Carson ascribes to Stesichoros. It is this releasing gesture that *Autobiography of Red* appears to also extend to one of its most important pretexts, Walcott's *Omeros*, whose high-epic ambitions it so obviously opposes. Walcott's concluding line – "When he left the beach the sea was still going on" – reappears in Carson's liberal translation of Stesichoros. The final fragment of Stesichoros's *Geryoneis* according to Carson tells of Geryon's death at the hands of Herakles, and her version of this fragment subtly but insistently echoes Walcott's idea of a continuity of the world (and the text) independent of a contemplating or experiencing subject: "The red world And corresponding red breezes | Went on Geryon did not" (R 14). Stesichoros' and Walcott's texts, then, converge in the similarity of their non-endings – a non-ending that Geryon, obliged to compose a school essay, adopts almost verbatim in his own readaptation of the Herakles-Geryon story: "New ending. | All over the world the beautiful red breezes went on blowing hand | in hand" (R 38). Given this intertextual resonance that Carson possibly establishes (forges?) between Geryon's essay, Stesichoros's *Geryoneis* and Walcott's *Omeros*, the latter text now appears not only as an endorsement of the grand style of Homer, Virgil and Dante that it so conspicuously rehearses, but also as an affirmative recourse to the anti-Homeric tradition of a minor literature that Stesichoros in Carson's framing embodies. What Carson and Walcott have most profoundly in common is thus the projection of an *ongoing* world that (as in Dickinson's poem) 'survives without a listener'; more crucially, in order to be capable to 'go on', it has to be processual instead of inert. It is a world that defies consummation and closure, a verb rather than a noun. The formal affordances of the gutter text with its emphasis on the incomplete and the interminable process of gap negotiation prove exceptionally germane to an imaginary that figures such a malleable, unfinished, open world.

2.3 The space that connects: Albert Wendt's *The Adventures of Vela*

As we have seen, *Autobiography of Red* is framed as the radical updating of a classic myth, more precisely, of a very particular, counterhegemonic version of that myth that only survives in a couple of disconnected fragments. Carson's text definitely does not restore these disparate leftovers from Stesichoros to some kind of wholeness by filling the lacunae and constructing narrative continuity; to the contrary, *Autobiography of Red* adopts the massive gappiness of its fragmented pretext for its own gutter textuality. And yet, the very notion of the fragment suggests a prior integrity that got lost: "The fragments of the *Geryoneis* itself read as if Stesichoros had composed a substantial narrative poem then ripped it to pieces" (R 6). Even if it is beyond repair and retrieval, the lost totality of the original whole remains visible under erasure and defines a normativity even when asserted as irrevocably out of reach. Carson's reconstructive work, then, becomes readable as a deliberate endorsement and celebration of incompleteness that is yet premised on the notion of wholeness. This is most evident when the text zooms in on processes of intersubjectivity, where the inevitable "failure of communication" (R 105) is perceived as a gap, an existential "separation of consciousness" that dispels an original naïve belief "in an undivided being between us" (ibid.). As soon as this belief proves counterfactual, space becomes the fundamental site of separation and solipsistic imprisonment: "The terrifying | spaces of the universe hemming me in" (R 91). Waking up in the middle of the night in a strange house full of unknown sleepers, Geryon perceives how a "mantle of silence stretches between them | like geothermal pressure" (R 48). Space, in short, is here mostly a medium of social distancing at times blown up to terrestrial dimensions ('geothermal pressure', 'spaces of the universe'). True, the erotic encounter with "a magnetic person" (R 54) can momentarily suspend this distance, but space will all the more appear as separating after the magnetic allure has withered. In Carson's text, it is only art that can sustain composed relationalities, and photography – a "way of playing with perceptual relationships" (R 65) – proves the ideal medium as it allows for an aesthetic of imaginatively *constellating* what is categorically held separate in/by the Euclidian, thermodynamic space of Carson's volcanic world. For the photograph establishes a two-dimensional space that connects: a kind of space-experience which in other modes of worlding may extend far beyond the boundaries of the frame.

For this I turn to indigenous Samoan writer Albert Wendt in whose verse novel, *The Adventures of Vela* (2009), the notion of space as separating gives way to the assumption of space as essentially relational and connective. The verse novel's main speaker, Alapati, is a poet and translator who, like Walcott's narrator in *Omeros*, figures to some extent as the alter ego of the author himself, whose first name, Albert, is the anglicized version of the Samoan Alapati. As Jean Pierre Durix notes, "Wendt mixes the most personal material with the wildest forms of fantasy" by interspersing his sweeping magic realist saga of precolonial Samoa and South Pacific cosmologies not only with "stories in the dimension of tall tales and sci-fi" (V 224), but also with readily identifiable autobiographical detail including "reference […] to the painful break-up of his marriage, as well as to his three children, who appear under their real names" (Durix 2016: 175).

The story begins in what the narrator wryly calls "the 'real' world" (V 224): as a patient recovering from an ulcer surgery, Alapati happens to share a hospital room with the ancient and emaciated Vela, whom he describes as "Mahatma Gandhi's physical reincarnation", and immediately associates with volcanism: "A mythical creature polished to lava hardness" (V 4), who bears his name Vela (Samoan for 'cooked') because, very much like Carson's Geryon, he "looked red and hot" (V 11) already at birth. To

Alapati's (and the reader's) puzzlement, Vela turns out to be a centuries-old "songmaker" (V 9), a virtuoso of Samoan orature, a living archive of South Pacific islanders' precolonial and early colonial knowledge and, most importantly, the "most honoured confidante" and "chronicler" (V 96) of the legendary precolonial Samoan queen and war goddess Nafanua, the "undefeated uniter of our islands" (V 9). Unlike Vela, who is all Wendt's creation, Nafanua is a vibrant presence in Samoa at large where she figures as a historical icon, whose military and political achievements form the kernel of a multi-faceted mythology. According to the key elements that reoccur in most versions of her story, Nafanua succeeded in conquering and uniting Samoa, "cemented the four paramount pāpā [chiefdom] titles and prophesied the coming of Christianity to Samoa" (Anae 2017: 203). The "enduring narrative power of Nafanua's legacy" (Lesuma 2019: 272) is amply demonstrated by numerous rewritings of that legendary heroine's life and exploits in contemporary Samoan and diasporic literature, not least narrative poetry and verse novels that "function as written extensions of the chants, songs, and poems about Nafanua that have been passed down orally for generations" (ibid.: 261). This status of the contemporary literary text as written extension of a sophisticated and venerated oratorial tradition is inscribed into Wendt's verse novel as the quasi-contractual relation between Alapati the chronicler and Vela the songmaker.

A red-skinned and "ugly" oddity that "everyone | stared at [...] wherever we went" (V 223), Vela (in this respect again like Geryon) personifies an alterity that defies normalization but does not preclude participation in the everyday altogether. In one of Alapati's metafictional asides, this ambiguous status of Vela in-between magic and realism, the marvellous and the mundane, gets explicated:

> Can we believe he's over 300 years old   an anachronism
> who's totally out-of-it? [...]
>
> Let me assure you   Vela is in the 'real' world
> and knows it more complexly than us because he's lived
> the longest and travelled the world over   For instance
> he knows a latte from a cappuccino from a flat white
> a chardonnay from a merlot from a Coke from a Vailima
> a Sears from a Wal Mart from the Kremlin from the White House.
> (V 224)

At the beginning of their decades-long friendship, Vela the royal biographer/hagiographer appoints Alapati as "*his* chronicler | in the written script of the Albinos" (V 6; emphasis added). All through the reading of *The Adventures of Vela*, most of the book accordingly appears to be a translation of Vela's indigenous Samoan orature into Alapati/Wendt's modern anglophone literature. This fictional transaction, in which orature gets transmediated to literature, points to the question, both philological and political, that has riddled the systematic study of Polynesian poetics from late nineteenth-century German scholarship to the present, namely how "to evaluate the fidelity of the published text to oral performance and the extent of the subsequent editing process" (Charlot 1990: 416). Through the lens of a self-interrogating reflexive anthropology, this framing of the text as a transliteration of the spoken word may be read as a self-conscious staging of the text as what James Clifford, in a different context, has called the "allegory of salvage" (Clifford 1986: 113), that is, a mode of representation in which the vestiges of vanishing cultures are symbolically preserved in their textual representation on condition of their actual disappearance. As Clifford remarks, "'Salvage' ethnography'" works on the principle that "the other is lost, in disintegrating time and space, but saved in the text" (ibid.: 112). Implicitly applying this critique to the working dynamics of an ever more monocultural, anglocentric literary world system, Emily Apter observes that "World Literature [...] increasingly resembles the global museum in its practice of curatorial salvage" (Apter 2013: 326). Salvage writing, whether ethnographic or literary, is thus an antiquarian business underpinned by a subtext that *demands* that the other be lost so that the text becomes indispensable as the quasi-museal shrine in which alone that vanishing other is preserved. It is true that much in Wendt's text apparently complies with this strategy. For the story of Vela is inextricably tied in with the destruction of Nafanua's queendom, the indigenous Samoan polity, through European colonization and Christianization with "firesticks and Book" (V 49), that is military supremacy and enforced religious conversion. The devastating repercussions of that conquest can be felt in the diegetic present when Alapati and Vela visit Samoa and the narrative turns into a straight rehearsal of what Clifford problematizes as "the theme of the vanishing primitive, of the end of traditional society" (Clifford 1986: 112).

For indeed, all traces of "Nafanua's world" (V 229) seem to have been erased from the present; instead "the Palagi world I was the inescapable reality" with its "tarsealed road and traffic", "the large American timber mill denuding the rainforest" and, not least, "the numerous churches like warships" (ibid.). Yet even if the text appears to pit a cherished but irretrievable past against an impoverished and outright destructive present, it by no means subscribes to the nostalgic poetics and politics of salvage. Instead, it complicates these in at least four respects: firstly, it *refuses to idealize* precolonial Samoa as some paradise lost; secondly it *deflates essentialist or nativist fantasies* that would project precolonial indigenous formations as homogeneous and pristinely not-modern; thirdly it does not portray or render precolonial Samoan culture as entirely erased but rather as a resilient and *secretly vital force* in the present; and it fourthly, at a metatextual level, rejects any status as shrine to a romanticized vanished culture but instead aims to operate as a subversive device to *intervene into the present*. A closer look at these four distinct moves that Wendt's verse novel enacts will, I hope, illustrate how the text draws on the gutter to significantly complicate Eurochrony, to decentre modernity into a multiplicity of minor cosmopolitan genealogies and futurities and to bring forth plural 'worlds' that are each premised on the acknowledgement of their ineluctable volcanic incompleteness. This incompleteness infects both space (in the endorsement of an archipelagic poetics as a particular version of gappiness) and time (by pointing to the fundamental unfinishedness of the planet).

The appealing/appalling precolony

Wendt's writing, in *The Adventures of Vela* as in much of his earlier literary or scholarly output, follows a genuinely postcolonial agenda that "espouses indigenous rights to land and cultural self-determination while refusing a limiting view of tradition that would insulate local identity from the complex interactions of global modernity" (Sharrad 2003: vii). Moreover, his construction of Samoan cultural formations is decisively realistic and probably deeply informed by his formal training in history, culminating in his PhD thesis on the Mau resistance movement in Samoa, "an interest sparked by the involvement of his grandfather Tuaopepe Tauilo" (Sharrad 2002: 109). In *Vela*, a thoroughly unromantic attitude towards indigenous Samoa prevails as Wendt rejects not only the missionary myth of precolonial Islander 'savagery' but also the equally stereotypic idealization of some Edenic pre-*papalagi* times allegedly terminated by Western colonization:

> There was no Fall, no sun-tanned Noble Savages existing in South Sea paradises, no Golden Age, except in Hollywood films, in the insanely romantic literature and art by outsiders about the Pacific, in the breathless sermons of our elite vampires, and in the fevered imaginations of our self-styled romantic revolutionaries. [...] I do not advocate a return to an imaginary pre-*papalagi* Golden Age or utopian womb. (Wendt 2019: 389–90)

Wendt's effort to "subvert the tendency [...] to idealize mythic pasts in relation to a presumably debased cultural present" (Henderson 2010: 293) is thus not restricted to *Vela*. As Bill Ashcroft suggests, the unceremonial, anti-nostalgic perspective of Samoa is indeed a hallmark of Wendt's works, and often comes across as a deliberate sassy juiciness that has earned him the reputation of either bawd or nest polluter; in any case a troublemaker who takes delight in provoking "the objections of some ('older Samoans') to perceived crudity, and (from others), of 'disloyalty' to Samoa" (Ashcroft 2018: 186). To be sure, *Vela* abounds not only with a remarkable catalogue of unusual sexual practices involving all sorts and numbers of human and animal participants, but also with gory cruelties including the extraction of every single bone from a living body, and a keen interest in courtly love poetry that takes its inspiration from rather abject olfactory stimuli: "My love is like the malodorous scents | of red meat melting in the breeze" (V 167). In this vein the later orator's own sexual initiation occurs during his stint as an adolescent pigherd and finds its repetitious climax in Vela "shooting his gift" "into | the hot clutch of slippery pig" after having been pleasurably turned on by "sniffing wetnoses of pig nudging his crevices" (V 15).[3]

However, what I have called an unceremonial rendition of Samoa is not primarily based on these graphic descriptions of "bodily concerns" (White in Ashcroft 2018: 186); it is much more the rather unappealing portrayal of precolonial social and political structures and dynamics that makes *Vela* thoroughly unidealizing. For what emerges from Vela's orature is the re-construction of an absurdly hierarchical society characterized by the unbridgeable gulf between a "divine aristocratic class" (V 90) given to excessive conspicuous consumption resulting in the "beautiful feature" of "a blossoming obesity" (ibid.) and a vast majority of exploited and rightless commoners whose lot it is to feed and worship their betters. As Alapati suggests in one of his asides, Vela himself is deeply complicit with this bizarre system from which he substantially benefits in his elevated status as the deified queen Nafanua's prime orator and chronicler. The immense prestige of what in a European context would have been a court poet (that group of upstarts whose precarious social mobility Stephen Greenblatt describes in *Renaissance Self-Fashioning*) illustrates with what extraordinary value orature was/is endowed in South Pacific contexts: it is "one of the most important elements of Polynesian culture [...] and is considered a prestigious social accomplishment" (Charlot 1990: 416). As a member of the 'divine aristocratic class',

> Vela's feet never touched the common ground (literally):
> to protect his sacredness the ground had to be first covered
> with siapo and sprinkled with fresh coconut milk
> And whenever he accompanied the Lady Invisible (to mortals that is) [...]
> all humans were forbidden from looking up at him. (V 87–8)

---

[3]No wonder such passages were not exactly conducive to reconciling Samoan cultural nationalists to Wendt's poetry, as the outraged response by Tupuola Terry Tavita, the editor-in-chief of *Savali*, a government-run Samoan newspaper, exemplifies. Tavita decries Wendt's novel in verse as wallowing in "the graphically obscene, the perversely sadistic and the profane" (Tavita 2010). Ironically, Tavita was convicted for sexualized violence, attempted rape and assault in five cases in June 2015.

Through most of the narrative, Vela remains an unapologetic beneficiary and propagandist of this rigidly stratified social edifice that may at first glance invite for a reading in terms of the excessive "baroque" theatricality that Achille Mbembe assigns the postcolony (2001: 115). But what is actually in operation here is a rather rational fundamental ideologeme – hierarchy – that Vela nonchalantly generalizes as the defining marker of any society's accomplishment: "All civilized societies are ordered in classes" (V 126). By the same token, then, all classless societies are savage. Notably, however, the category of class as distinct from 'rank' or 'caste' names a thoroughly relational, hence ontologically groundless, positionality as each class constitutes itself (including its 'consciousness') by way of defining itself as not its other. As a consequence, class (consciousness) is never pure but riddled with the spectral presence of the respective counterclass: "Each of the opposing classes necessarily carries the other around in its head and is internally torn and conflicted by a foreign body it cannot exorcize" (Jameson 1999: 49). In Vela's world, the "divine appointment of chiefs and commoners" already gives way to the meritocratic principle of rewarding "heroic action" (V 144), introducing a genuinely modern but entirely autochthonous dynamics of social mobility. Vela himself is after all an upstart with more than modest origins, part of a "litter of six brothers and five sisters" born to a "ringwormed father" and a mother who "bred heirs in obstinate silence and was always hungry for pork" (V 7). Moreover, being "punily unheroic" (V 8), Vela does not even answer to the criteria of his own chart of the order of things in a 'civilized society', where it is '*heroic* action' that qualifies for upward social mobility. Vela's excellence, next to a way with words, rests certainly not in "the Way of the Weapons" (V 52) but in his extraordinary capacity to insinuate himself into the minds of others. In this respect, Wendt constructs a nexus between social mobility and empathy that comes most eerily to the fore, and in fact fully into its own for the first time, in the colonial contact zone. Readers of Stephen Greenblatt will here be reminded of the interpretation of Shakespeare's Iago as a displaced personification of the kind of improvisation of power that characterized not only the schemes and intrigues of Tudor courtiers but, to more devastating effects, the early modern conquest of the Americas. As a capacity of strategically knowing the Other, empathy figures as a form of reconnaissance that gets rarefied in the process of conquest itself. Greenblatt suggests that what we call "'empathy,' Shakespeare calls 'Iago'" (Greenblatt 1980: 225): less cryptically, what passes for "sympathetic appreciation of the situation of the other fellow" (ibid.) is in fact inextricably entangled, as power/knowledge, in colonial trafficking. Consequently, Greenblatt frames his reading of *Othello* as a paradigmatic dramatization of Renaissance self-fashioning with an apparently misplaced account of 'empathy' wielded as a political weapon of the *conquista*. His example is the luring of the indigenous population of the Lucayas (now called the Bahamas) into slavery in the goldmines of Hispaniola by the promise to lead them into the 'paradise' projected in their own eschatological system. Only inasmuch as the Spaniards refine their skills in anticipating the position of the Other – the Amerindian systems of values and beliefs – do they gain those strategic advantages that make conquest and enslavement possible. Improvisation and dissimulation thus form the crucial elements of "the Europeans' ability again and again to insinuate themselves into the preexisting political, religious, even psychic structures of the natives and to turn those structures to their advantage" (Greenblatt 1980: 227).[4] A similar point is made by Tzvetan Todorov in his *The Conquest of America*, where he laconically summarizes the Spanish take-over of Aztec empire as an instance of an "understanding-that-kills" (Todorov 1984: 127).

This is precisely the pattern that Vela himself reiterates in his own colonial/civilizing mission on the remote island of Nei, where he happens to end up as a castaway after being "canoewrecked" (V 123) in a storm at sea. The first encounter with the islanders immediately transforms the panicky Vela, who is convinced to have fallen into the hands of "ferocious maneaters" (ibid.), into a comically pathetic volcano: "My fear was liquid fire that I burst out of arsehole and dribbled" (ibid.). Even if Vela soon discovers the peaceful and hospitable character of the islanders, he remains severely appalled by the complete absence of hierarchy and hence 'civilization' in the Nei society whose non-progressive cyclic worldview projects "a cosmos content I with its richness" (V 138): a lack of lack that rules out any stimulus for expansion, 'improvement' or modernization. Such a static cosmology holds "no choice for individuals to pursue separate I destinies to excel to innovate civilisation further II For the unchanging circle was perfection to be I as it was always admitting no deviance" (V 129). More precisely, the world of Nei, to Vela's utter horror and disgust, is a world without separate individuals, a seamless social continuity and complete articulation that precludes individuation as such: Nei is a world where "each creature object and relationship I [was] satisfied with its placing in the Circle I of Intelligence in the Unity's Dreaming" (V 138). This stasis persist until Vela launches his mission "to civilise I [his] hosts in the Samoan image" (ibid.) and convert them to an approximation of what he deems proper humanity. Vela "reduced Nei to [his] Samoan reflection" (V 157) very much in the ways in which European nineteenth-century colonial discourse produces the other as incomplete semblance. Both introduce the concept of the self in Cartesian style as a consequence of the primary and foundational causal

---

[4]It is tempting to pursue this further by reading Greenblatt's discussion of empathy in tandem with Chris Lock's notion of modern fiction since the 'rise of the novel' and the device of character interiority as animism qua 'access to the consciousness of the other'; cf. the discussion of Lock in the *Omeros* section of this chapter.

principle: hierarchy. As Vela puts it, first "I introduced | the civilized concept of chiefs and commoners" and only then

> one night I told them they too
> were individual identities [...]
>
> They were puzzled so I quoted my example:
> I am   I am separate   I am Vela
> You   you are separate   you are individuals. (V 144)

What ensues from this original separation is the breaking-up of the circle, the introduction not only of rank, hierarchy, exploitation and other epiphenomena of 'civilization' but more than that a murderous contest for supremacy among various groups and crews within Nei society, culminating in the almost complete self-extinction of the islanders in a civil war that "spilled | like an epidemic over all of Nei territory | breaking forever the eternal circle which had | guaranteed peace and abundance for every creature" (V 157). At the point of telling this story that hovers between Crusoe's robust imperialism and Gulliver's misanthropic scepticism, Vela regrets his pursuit of the civilizing mission and judges the 'conversion' of the Tagata-Nei "an unforgivable crime" (V 140). This insight comes, however, as "hindsight's wisdom" (ibid.): too late to save the day but wisdom all the same. It is this kind of belated wisdom that Vela shares with his queen Nafanua at the moment of the invasion of Catholic missionaries. Their destruction of the pre-Christian island culture and Nafanua's relatively peaceful rule is an exact rerun of Vela's conversion of Nei, and of Nafanua's own conquest of the various minor kingdoms of the Samoan islands:

> Because they're human   like us   they're capable of limitless violence and
> in their mission to 'save us' for their God   are willing to even kill us
> Sounds familiar to you   songmaker?   She asks   He nods slowly
> Yes   Nafanua   Auva'a and Tupa'i established their religion the same way. (V 270)

In their capacity and propensity to conquer and colonize, then, pre-palagi South Pacific cultures are far from innocent but instead remarkably similar to European imperialist forces. Precolonial Samoa thus appears by no means as a pristine Eden polluted and destroyed by Western take-over; none of this however belittles the fact that that take-over remains – very much like Vela's conversion of Nei – an unforgivable crime whose memory a repentant Vela wishes to "bequeath to you" as a cautionary tale so that "the planet over Nei shall become our common heritage" (V 158) in which the desire to colonize would ultimately be overcome.

We have never been not modern

Wendt's debunking of the myth of a golden age before Western influence allows him to focus not only on the 'appalling' facets of Samoa's precolonial history but also on its inherent modernity. In *Vela*, the past is constitutively shot through with the present, most obviously in the resonances of Western pop music that anachronistically resounds in Nafanua's world. When the queen herself deigns to recite to Vela bits of her own poetry, it is slightly modified song lyrics from The Doors ("C'mon baby lick my fire", V 65) or The Beatles:

> He loves you yes yes yes
> He loves you yes yes yes
> He loves you yes yes yes
> He loves you yes yes yes! (V 60–1)

That Vela (in secret) dismisses such poetry from the future as "very forgettable compositions" (V 60) confirms his profile as a cultural snob but cannot do away with the effect these "samples" (ibid.) have: to unsettle the dictates of homogeneous empty time in favour of a heterotemporality that allows for all those con-fusions of past, present and future – the "time-knots" and "the plurality that inheres in the 'now'" (Chakrabarty 2000: 243) – that postcolonial writing from magic realism to speculative fiction has endorsed in defiance of Western historicism, progressivism and irreversible clock-time. In the context of South Pacific indigeneity, conceptualizations of time tend to be more specifically associated with the notion of "a complex spiral temporality which allows for the simultaneity […] of diverse experiences of time" (DeLoughrey 1999: 64). The still centre of the temporal spiral is the permanent *nunc stans* of a "now-time [that] simply reaches out in any direction towards outer circles named "past" and "future" only for our convenience" (Grace in Gabbard 2018: 35). In the spatial image of the spiral, the cyclic/repetitive and the linear/progressive are inextricably merged so that a move forward is simultaneously a return, though never (as in a circle that shapes the temporality of Nei) a full return but rather a repetition with a difference. In this respect the spiral is specifically apt to conceptualize the complexities of a time that is not only multi-layered but multidirectional, moving "back even as it progresses forward, hence embracing the common Polynesian adage: 'We face the future with our backs'" (Marsh 1999: 340). If this temporality allows for the presence of the "past within […] the spiral of the ever-moving present" (Va'ai 1999: 69), then the reverse is just as true inasmuch as the present emphatically becomes a part of the past. It is yet another indicator of Wendt's cheeky unceremoniality that he refuses to endow this notion of spiral time with "the aura of a time which is not yet historical, still sacred" (During 1990: 30) but instead exemplifies the bleeding of the past into the present and vice versa primarily with pop cultural recourses. On the spiral of time, Nafanua is not only quoting but also anticipating Lennon/McCartney and Robbie Krieger so that 'She Loves You' or 'Light My Fire', oddly enough, appear as Nafanua covers. What follows from this is "the notion of a recurrent but transformative (and transformable) past" (Ashcroft 2018: 189) that is both subject *to* and *of* change.

All his disdain for Nafanua's 'forgettable compositions' notwithstanding is Vela himself the most spectacular embodiment of this kind of spiralled pop temporality. His elective affinity and partial identification with the flyingfox (a South Pacific variety of bat) is readable at once in terms of indigenous totemism *and* of contemporary fandom, a pop cultural appetite feeding on "all the stories about Dracula Batman and Batwoman who from then | on he referred to as his 'revered cousins'" (V 5). This fusion of vernacular and globalized cultural resources comes fully into its own in "The Contest" (V 23–33), first published in 1986 as a self-standing narrative poem and much later inserted as chapter 4 into *The Adventures of Vela*. In this new context its function for the overall plot is to relate how Vela's rise to the stature and position of a master orator is contingent on his capacity to integrate late-twentieth-century hip hop and rap idioms into the traditional normative poetics of Samoan oratory. Vela's career leap hinges on his victory over Alopese, the hitherto undisputed laureate of all Samoan spoken-word artists, in an oratory contest that is in truth a duel fought to the death: according to convention, such a contest "was run until one [of the contenders] | was empty of artifice | then the winner could demand | anything of the vanquished" (V 25). On an earlier occasion Alopese had challenged and triumphed over Vela's lover Mulialofa, and as a trophy demanded every bone from the body of the defeated. To avenge his deboned partner, Vela spends ten years of training trying to no avail to turn himself into a viable opponent on par with Alopese. He achieves a decisive, indeed undefeatable advantage only when he steps out of Alopese's turf – the conventions of song making compliant with codified rules – and instead introduces an unheard-of "brand new beat" (V 30) that transforms the traditional ritual of the oratory contest into the 'modern' ritual of the hip hop battle. To do this, Vela has to shuttle on time's spiral in the "gifted flow of dream" (V 29) into a wholly other and yet commensurate world, where he finds himself circling in the shape of a flyingfox above what he perceives as "a strange reef of cloudhigh dwellings | with millions of eyes and fissured | with deep chasms like dry riverbeds" (V 28): a setting that the reader will readily decipher as a contemporary (probably US American) metropolitan city whose grooves and skyscrapers the speaker translates, in a well-worn display of inverting the Western anthropological gaze, into the lexicon of his own oceanic world. It is "in one of the chasms" of the 'strange reef' that Vela observes with fascination how

> black youths in exotic hides gyrated
> to a black singing box
>   to a beat I'd never heard
> like the rapid shatter of rain
> or branches breaking in strong wind
>   to a voice chanting an imagery
> both savage and hypnotically direct
> muscled like jabbing spear arms. (V 29)

This ode to the raw irresistible energy of hip hop's 'beat' and 'imagery' not only inserts the breakdancing 'Black youths' into the spiral but indicates how they are themselves generating it through their *gyrating* locomotion. This creative worldmaking force of Black urban culture reveals entirely new options of self-fashioning to the 'gifted dreamer', who will transfer hip hop's hypnotic directness into his own "pre-Christian, pre-Newtonian, pre-*papalagi* world" (Wendt 1986: 153): not as anachronism but as a brand new beat, a gift and "inspiration from the non-Pacific present that invigorates a mythic Pacific past" (Henderson 2010: 293). Thanks to this gift, Vela prevails over Alopese. He styles himself as "a holy rock 'n' roller" (V 31) rapping to his own, unheard-of 'brand new beat' that Alopese cannot counter: "He tried and tried | but my beat wasn't in his knowing in | his air or in his future" (ibid.). By introducing a present-day Afro-American (now global) cultural idiom into a pre-Christian Samoan setting, Vela as an actor inside the diegetic world as well as Wendt at the authorial level insert that "epichoric literary ecology" (Beecroft 2015: 33) into a web of minor cosmopolitan crosspollinations and thereby instigate a hybridization that Vela's purist antagonist cannot respond to.

Vela's initiatory dream vision finds its powerful equivalent number in the "final revelations" (V 255) with which the narrative comes to its unexpected closure in a similar demonstration of how the apparently archaic has always been modern all along. Set in the 'real world' of present-day Samoa, the final chapter relates how Vela and Alapati (re)visit the deserted lava cave that, in Nafanua's time, had housed the sanctum sanctorum of the warrior queen/goddess who, since the Christianization of the islands in the 1830s, had been ousted as a dangerous pagan idol "of the Darkness" (V 229). With the rising of the full moon, the cave surprisingly turns into a natural cinema hall as the rays entering through the narrow entrance as if through the shutter of a film projector form "an arrow cutting | across the glistening Cave dome" (V 246). It is then that Nafanua actually appears on the scene as a hideous "bundle" that immediately triggers a cascade of cinematic associations – from "*The Mummy Returns*" (V 251) to "the witches in Kurosawa's *Throne of Blood*" (ibid.): "Was this for real or was it a horror flick heavily influenced by | *Jeepers Creepers Blade* and Coppola's *Dracula?*" (V 252) With the intensifying force of the moonlight, the projection ray gets ever more "clear | and as mesmerizing as the cinematography in *Kill Bill*" (V 253) so that finally "onto the Cave's dome in the Moon's golden passage was *born* | a film which as it unfolded I titled *The Final Revelations*" (ibid.). What Nafanua's 'film' shows is her and her last loyal followers' final stand against the invasion of the "missionary Albinos" (V 255): not as re-enactment with a cast of present-day players but as if captured, documentary style, on location and while it happened. The climactic scene of this "audio-visual experience" (ibid.) is the disclosure of Vela's betrayal of his queen as he and the vast majority of Nafanua's aristocracy change sides and succumb to the Christian invaders. The final take shows Nafanua, ready to depart into exile, addressing the sleeping Vela with what he will interpret as both curse and promise, and Alapati as yet another appointment to a new chronicler's post:

One day you will return to the Cave of Prophecies and face my wrath
for your betrayal but   for now   Vela   you'll roam the world training

chroniclers who'll write down my life in their different languages
out of them you'll select one who will return with you to be
my chronicler in an even more terrible future   Only then will I release
you from your immortality. (V 272–3)

I will come back to the metatextual implications of this construction in the last section of this chapter; to the question at stake here – namely Wendt's positing of Samoa as always already hybrid in spiral time – the film in the Cave of Prophecies adds yet another layer of transculturation as it inserts both trash and *auteur* Hollywood as well as 'world cinema' into the cultural register of a discarded Samoan deity and thereby again disproves the notion of epichoric insulation of the ostensibly insular. Like Western pop music, then, international cinema appears as a cultural resource that is not simply imported but just as well autochthonous to a spiral-time Samoa that in this understanding has never been *not* modern. Wendt refers to both pop music and film as "forms of oral culture with the power to reshape, reinvigorate, revive Oceania. The marriage of words with beats [and words with images] potently stirs pools of possibility, destroying, creating, and remixing the old world to spin it anew" (Henderson 2010: 304). Where Walcott takes recourse to the hypercanonical figures of Homer, Vergil and Dante to engage the ongoing work of signifiance, and where the even more erudite Carson uncovers the obscure, eccentric discards of canon-formation, Wendt embraces the popular head-on to energize his project of continuous articulation, disarticulation and rearticulation.

The Va

When Alapati and Vela visit present Samoa in the last sections of the narrative, they end up in a locale where all vestiges of 'Nafanua's world' seem to have been superseded by an imposed monolithic modernity. Inserted as it is into the dynamics of transnational extractivism (cf. "the large American timber mill denuding the rainforest"; V 229), Samoa is revealed as very much part of "a planet teethed | with silver dollars and ruled by aitu of various fang shapes" (V 3), a predatory ('fang shapes') capitalist global totality that allows for no outside or exemption. Yet even while it emphasizes the inescapability of ruthless capitalist subsumption and the coercion into the iron cage of a streamlined modernity, already this exposition belies the assumption of the 'vanishing primitive' s problematized by Clifford, by making manifest the 'traditional' society's "refusal to become nothing" (V 275) even at the lexical level: without the active participation of the indigenous and vernacular, no critique of the financialization of the globe can be articulated. For notably it is not big financiers, CEOs, nor even politicos who rule this monetarized planet but – *aitu*. This Samoan word for 'god' (Pratt 2009: 121) is the first of a plethora of Polynesian/Moanan lexemes that proliferate all through the text.

No doubt, these "speed bumps of untranslatability" (Apter 2013: 3) puncture the anglophony of Wendt's verse novel and render it substantially opaque for the transnationally illiterate reader (whom they in other words confront with their provincial transnational illiteracy). Note the tongue-in-cheek nod to Dante that differs widely from the reverence of *Omeros* or the learned understatement of *Autobiography of Red*: "As Vela has sung: ‖ All streets lead to the Fale of Terror | Above its front door is this question | WHAT'S ALOFA GOT TO DO WITH MONEY?" (V 3) As author of this recourse to the *Inferno*'s inscription above the portal to hell, Vela is yet another Dante revenant: one who right at the opening of the text identifies hell with an all-encompassing capitalism, thereby recalling not so much Walcott's Dante allusions but rather Patrick Bateman, the manic narrator in Brett Easton Ellis's *American Psycho*. That novel opens with the welcoming Dante citation, "Abandon all hope ye who enter here" (Ellis 1991: 3), and culminates in the non-closure statement that "this is not an exit" (ibid.: 432). *American Psycho* is in many ways the opposite of a gutter text as it is composed as a virtually unstoppable "endless litany" of "deadening prose"[5]

---

[5]Cf. Ellis 1991, 3:

> ABANDON ALL HOPE YE WHO ENTER HERE is scrawled in blood red lettering on the side of the Chemical Bank near the corner of Eleventh and First and is in print large enough to be seen from the backseat of the cab as it lurches forward in the traffic leaving Wall Street and just as Timothy Price notices the words a bus pulls up, the advertisement for Les Misérables on its side blocking his view, but Price who is with Pierce & Pierce and twenty-six doesn't seem to care because he tells the driver he will give him five dollars to turn up the radio, "Be My Baby" on WYNN, and the driver, black, not American, does so.

(Eldridge 2008: 22), a nearly unpunctuated cascade that formally evokes the claustrophobia of precisely that seamless, hence inescapable continuity of capital-as-hell that Ellis sets out to register. By contrast, Wendt's text is, as a verse novel, conspicuously gappy and by that token rather averse to the figuration of a closed world without egress. To the contrary, as we will see, the text closes on an emphatic 'exit': the ascension of Nafanua and Vela. But even right at the outset it is obvious that Vela (unlike Bateman) does not faithfully quote Dante but rather playfully alludes to the inscription above hell's gate in a way that once again demonstrates the versality of spiral time and Wendt's propensity to fuse high literary and pop references. For here the hypotext of the forbidding inscription is not taken from the *Inferno* but from Tina Turner's 1980s commercial soul-pop hit 'What's Love Got to Do with It', co-written by Graham Lyle and Terry Britten. This, however, is complicated with segments of a vernacular lexicon and a concomitant mode of worlding that will not get fully integrated and dissolved in the anglophone text. The persistence of such 'untranslatables' as *fale* and *alofa* certainly points to the limits of "the efficacy of translation" (Mufti 2016: 92), but for all that does by no means simply affirm some Herder-derived insistence on cultures' incommensurability that allegedly manifests in "the stubbornly ineffable and untranslatable in language" (ibid.). True, 'love' is not likely to be a nearly adequate translation of *alofa* (even a standard dictionary like Pratt's lists 'compassion', 'present' and 'gift' as three further English equivalents), and yet does the superimposition of this Samoan term upon the formulaic title of the well-known 1980s pop hit suggest exactly that: where Tina Turner says 'love', Vela says 'alofa', postulating that the two terms are identical and different simultaneously. He therewith does neither confirm nor negate the fiction of some unproblematic interchangeability and exchange between languages even as the foreignness of the non-English word in its anglophone context emphasizes its displaced, heterotopic opacity. That the (non-Samoan speaking) reader can nevertheless guess what the term means is simply owed to the relative readability of the phrase as a whole thanks to the widely known pretext from the stock of American mainstream pop (where, to do some justice to Tina Turner's Britten and Lyle, the concept of 'love' also splices into a multiplicity of meanings, including that of a soddy 'second-hand emotion'). But there's more to this as Vela not only replaces *love* by *alofa* but also *it* by *money*. This is of course not a translation but, technically speaking, an intralingual paradigmatic substitution (of 'money' for Turner's forever indeterminate 'it') that specifies Vela's notion of hell: the 'fale of terror' to which all roads lead is then a fully financialized globe run by "merchants with bible-black eyes and smiles | as bright as new coins" who

> assess   in orderly litanies   the various cuts
> decide on weights and prices
> the profit and sources of supply

and at their meetings echo the refrain
What's alofa got to do with money?
What's alofa got to do with a person's price? (V 3)

Even as a material signifier (let alone as a concept), *alofa* appears lost and out of place in this otherwise monolingual environment that corresponds to a (still) largely anglophone 'planet teethed with silver dollars' whose thoroughly "apoetical" lingua franca, "Anglo-American, is a persistent threat for everyone and [...], in turn, risks being transformed into a technical salesman's Esperanto, a perfunctory containerization of expression" (Glissant 1990: 112). Against this money-driven monoculture Wendt's text rallies the power of a polyglot impurity that signals the persistence of the vernacular both linguistically and epistemologically: "The Lulu Aitu of his aiga swept in at his birth | and perched on the fale rafters | gazing down | [...] | until he was agaga in Tagaloa's reflection | leaping up into Saveasi'uleo's inventive mouth | to survive each shade of Po" (V 9). If nothing else, such passages declare a secession from Anglocentrism and inaugurate an orgy of opacity: both in Glissant's understanding of that term as the endorsement of the non-transparent particularity of "human cultures in their solid materiality" (Glissant 1990: 111), as well as Greenblatt's distinction of opacity as what demands to be recognized as "the independence and integrity of [the other's] construction of reality" (Greenblatt 1990: 31) which shows first and foremost in the other's undecipherable articulations – acknowledged as such and not dismissed as noise. With only one exception, Wendt's text operates precisely on the principle of not introducing, not translating, not defining non-English terms, thereby demanding from the non-Samoan reader the readiness to acknowledge and live with opacity. The only Samoan word for which the text offers a definition is the concept of the Va,[6] that finally brings us back to the problematic of the gutter text, the aesthetics of incompleteness and the connexionist desire.

The very first song that Vela creates is his birth cry: "Va-Va-Va-Va-aaah!" (V 10). For Alapati the chronicler this is not an inarticulate scream but instead a cosmological hymn to the all-encompassing ur-principle:

His first song is of the Va   the Space between all things
like the birth fluid holding all in the Unity-that-is-All
Va   the relationships that must be nursed and nurtured
Va   the Harmony in which we are one: stone   bird   fire
air   fish   atua   blood   bone   shit   sound   colour   cloud
tree   smoke   eye   lizard   turtle   shark. (ibid.)

---

[6]Spelling of this Samoan term varies from source to source. I will use the non-diacritic upper-case variant 'Va' that Wendt uses in *Vela*, but will of course leave other spellings unchanged in citations.

In (spite of) the bawdy and debunking diction of this book, the Va, I argue, is sacred – not as a mystifying or auratic shibboleth but as the vital and vibrant underlying principle of an essentially relational world order that (like the spiral re/generated by the gyrating breakdancers in Vela's visionary hip hop dream) is not statically given but contingent on human 'nursing and nurturing'. As l'uogafa Tuagalu explains, the Va is a web of relations that are "socially defined" but always also "divinely sanctioned", and that bind "participants in va relations together by threads of cause and effect. The spiritual connections are fundamental and seem to underlie and act as foundation to all permutations of va relations between people" (Tuagalu 2008: 117). The term literally refers to the "relationship (*va*) between man and all things, animate and inanimate, sentient and insentient" on the premise that all things are *genealogically* connected to a "life force (*mauli*)" (Tui Atua 2009: 135); hence "relations between all things extend in the Samoan indigenous reference to all things living or dead, where a genealogical relationship can be traced" (ibid.). Vela's first song as chronicled by Alapati is in that sense an enumeration of who 'we' are: a probably incomplete list of human, animal, vegetable, divine, abiotic and purely conceptual members of an assemblage that invites for a reading in terms of contemporary post-anthropocentric ecocritical theory, where the Va would probably figure as both the matrix and the outcome of the continuous labour of "making kin" with a whole world of "biotic and abiotic sympoietic collaborators, colaborers" who cooperate on the ground that "all earthlings are kin in the deepest sense" (Haraway 2016: 102). Arguably neither Vela nor Alapati nor Wendt would find fault with such an enlarged notion of kinship nor with the 'translation' of the notion of the Va into the terms of a Western theory of interspecies collaboration[7]; in fact, a number of indigenous South Pacific scholars have developed cross-locational transfers to bring the Va into conversation with germane concepts from elsewhere, including Western academic traditions. For instance, in view of its dynamic, interactive and generative dimensions, the Va has been seen to resonate with such notions as Henri Lefebvre's "lived space" that is "alive, qualitative, fluid and dynamic [and] thus points to some aspects of the Samoan idea of vā" (Lilomaiava-Dokter 2009: 4). Caroline Sinavaiana Gabbard points to the compatibility with assemblage theory in the wake of Deleuze inasmuch as "the vā is essentially kinetic, a transactional field of space open to negotiation between things and/or entities framed within its permeable boundaries" (Gabbard 2018: 34). For Wendt himself, the Va appears to epitomize connexionism as such when he posits that "the vā is not empty space, but space that relates

---

[7]In turn, Donna Haraway would probably have been more than delighted had Wendt allowed Vela to further hybridize Nafanua's world with a sprinkle of tentacular sympoietic kinmaking in one of his 'solos' as an act of intertextual hospitality.

and binds entities together [...], not space that separates but space that relates, that holds separate entities and things together" (Wendt in Tuagalu 2008: 110). If the Va is a void, then it certainly is not an empty abyss. Rather, it is an unevenly dense space constituted by and constitutive of connections. In *Vela*, it can at the most profane level denote the distance between two bodies intended towards each other even in a fight to the death ("Ten paces was the Va between them", V 24), but also, as a fundamental paradigm, it can be identified as the seat of the vital force as such: "For us love is stored | in the Va between your heart and lungs" (V 159). This notion of a space that relates and binds reoccurs time and again in *Vela*, for example, when Alapati refers to "all the spaces | that linked us" (V 251), or to "the apt connectedness of things and the objects around you'" (V 214), or to "the Unity that weaves | winner and loser conjurer and conjured artifice and reality illusion and fact" (V 32). But it is crucial that in order to bind entities together, these entities must first be separate from each other: connexionism can only work on and with segments, not with always already fully articulated seamless wholes. This appreciation of a gappy and yet interconnected world finds its most obvious formal articulation in the conspicuous spacing technique that Wendt deploys. Instead of commas, enlarged spacing between words; instead of full stops, enlarged spacing and capitalization of the first word of the new sentence. Space, thus, perforates the continuity of the run-on line and infiltrates even the interior of the verse with segmentivity; yet like the gutter between panels of graphic narrative, the space that is cleared in this way does not merely separate but also mediates between and connects segments thanks to the ongoing sequentializing countermeasure of rhythm, verse, sentence and narrative unit. In that sense the gappiness of Wendt's verses posits reading as a co-creative act in which the reader repeats the writer's performance of spinning the "cord | that stretches across the abyss" (V 23), rendering the gap a gutter, the void a Va.

Given the crucial importance of the gap, it would be an ideological distortion to reduce or simplify the Va to a collectivist orthodoxy: "The ontological premise of being-for-the-collective is not a transparent reflection of how Samoans always actually are; it is rather the story that Samoans tell themselves (and others) about themselves" (Henderson 2016: 323). This sheds a new light on Vela's abhorrence of the non-individuated unity of the Nei people who, being fully integrated into their collective consciousness, their "group mind" (V132), retain no residue of separateness and hence cannot enter into any relationships in the sense of the Va. In Nei's self-content static cosmos, "each creature object and relationship | [is] satisfied with its placing in the Circle | of Intelligence in the Unity's dreaming" (V 138). For precisely this reason, they cannot engage in the active, dynamic, mutable and at times perhaps antagonistic relations of "conjurers and conjured" embedded in the Va that "holds every thing in balance" (V 276): 'every thing', unlike 'everything', names a composite of distinct units, not a seamless unified whole (with David Mitchell, a multitude of drops, not an ocean). Balance, however, can tip and unlike the fixed cyclic order of Nei, the Va is not only deeply antifoundational but premised on "the constitutive gap in all relationships and the void at the heart of creation" (Sharrad 2003: 111); as such it posits worlding rather than world, becoming rather than being, dynamic intersubjectivity rather than fixed identity, every thing rather than everything.

As a set of relationships that must be nursed and nurtured, the Va is never guaranteed and its maintenance and sustenance, for Wendt, is the obligation of the "communal culture" (in Tuagalu 2008: 110) that is, in return, maintained and sustained by the Va. This relation of reciprocal mutuality achieves cosmic dimensions in Alapati's account of a night outing with Vela, where the self and the world become one another's texts and readers at the same time: "We would share our food and read the stars as they in turn | observed and read us into existence" (V 243). In such a framework of worldly mutuality, relations are chiasms: I read the stars, the stars read me. Paul de Man asserts that as a trope "chiasmus [...] can only come into being as the result of a void, of a lack" that serves as the hinge that enables the "crossing that reverses the attributes of things and words" (de Man 1979, 38, 49). In light of Wendt's adoption of the Va, the void at the heart of chiasmus is not exactly, as de Man claims, a 'lack' but rather a connector or, to stay with deconstruction for a minute more, a copula that in specular terms structures "a self-mirroring in the other" (Spivak 2006: 45). The copula par excellence, also for the trope of chiasmus, is the verb 'to be' which can serve the function of copular verb best when it is devoid of intension or signifying force. Thus, Aristotle holds that 'to be' as a copular verb "did not actually signify anything, that it operated simply as a synthesis" (Benveniste in Derrida 1976: 552). 'To be' in this view has zero intension and therefore, by implication, "extends infinitely" (Derrida 1976: 553) as a void that connects ('operates simply as a synthesis') even what appears to be mutually exclusive. As the "grammatical mark of equivalence" (ibid.: 558) the copula as void, whether explicitly actualized in the verb 'to be' or not, establishes relations that connect the gazer and the stars in a mutuality that is always open to reversal, and that stands as an alternative to the Cartesian subject-object opposition of the Kantian sublime, where the contemplation of the "starry sky above" (Kant 2002: 203) serves the ulterior goal to demonstrate the mind's supremacy over the res extensa: an assumption that "elevates infinitely my worth as that of an *intelligence* by my personality, in which the moral law reveals to me a life independent of animality and even of the entire world of sense" (ibid.; emphasis in the original). Nothing could be further removed from the reciprocity of both the chiasmus and the Va. Where humans and stars read each other there can be no exit from 'the entire world of sense', and no place for the supremacist anthropocentrism that speaks from a position 'independent of animality'. In Wendt's verse novel, that sort of anthropocentrism and logocentrism is associated firmly with the Christian missionaries in Samoa. It is their 'unforgivable crime' to introduce that worldview, to propagate it from 'churches like warships', to narrow down kin to species and therewith to spell out "the breakdown of va relationality caused by modernity" (Gabbard 2018: 47). Christianity as "the religion that preached | humans' divine right to dominate everything and | dismissed as superstition the tapu that connected all things in the Va-Atoa" (V 231) is thus finally revealed as the ultimate ideological antagonist against which the whole text rallies its immense energy. What remains to be clarified is the question of the poetics with which that politics is pursued. In other words, with what 'brand new beat' do Vela, Alapati and Wendt combat their powerful opponent?

The gospel according to Vela/Alapati/Wendt

Perhaps it is not by accident that the novel's very first verse begins with a flexion of the copular verb 'to be' that engages the speaker, Alapati, with his interlocutor in a relation of reciprocal mirroring similar to that in the 'starry night' scene: "Is Vela of my dreaming? Or am I the object of his?" (V 3). This opening introduces the chiasmic reversal of subject and object in the form of a question not only about the ontological status of Alapati and Vela but also about that of the text: who is the writer and who the written here? Has Alapati made up Vela to pose as his 'chronicler', or has Vela invented Alapati as his amanuensis? The question is moot in the transactional web of Va relations where identity boundaries are permeable and negotiable, and yet it resurfaces time and again through the book. In one of Vela's most renowned nature poems the same reciprocity reappears, now defining the Va relation between the speaker and the mountains he sings about: "I am of their dreaming | and they of mine" (V 43). Notably, these lines are lifted directly from Wendt's 1986 poem, '*The Mountains of Ta'u*',[8] and this intertextual entanglement adds yet another layer to the palimpsest of aliases. If what the verse novel explicitly introduces as a poem by Vela turns out to be a poem by Wendt himself, then not only the distinction between Vela and Alapati (his intradiegetic chronicler) but also that between Vela and Wendt (his empirical author) gets blurred. The ensuant confusion of degrees of fictionality and facticity enlarges and thickens the web of fluid chiasms and transactional reciprocities in the medium of the Va. Also, the friendship that ties Vela to Alapati and vice versa is a relation that rotates around such reversals. Thus the moment of 'adoption' in the hospital ward, when Vela appoints Alapati as his scribe,

---

[8] I am grateful to Lars Eckstein for bringing this intertextual entanglement to my notice. Wendt's poem is documented in Sharrad and Peacock (2003: 386).

appears like an ensnarement with Alapati "trapped in the sieve of his [Vela's] breathing" (V 6), but at a much later point it is exactly the other way around:

> Now it's winter and I fish again for Vela
> in the Tokelauan manner of short handline
> pearl-shell hook   slow moving canoe   hand tug-tugging   teasing
> the fish like the heart beating   across a lagoon that's
> a page of anae swarming: (V 122)

The 'fish' that Alapati teases out of the lagoon is not exactly Vela himself but one of his adventure stories, in this case the Nei episode that sets in immediately after the colon as an embedded narrative. Vela, then, *is* his stories, as one of Alapati's numerous self-referential asides conveniently confirms: "The chronicler *is* the chronicle | the teller is the tale" (V 85) – and in the case of the long-lived and far-travelled Vela, Alapati has to concede that "he's an epic" (V 224), not just a story. But what is true for the agent of enunciation holds just as well for the enounced: "He's an epic and I'm writing it down". In this vein, Vela's standing in the coterie of Queen Nafanua hinges crucially on the circumstance that it is in the stories, chronicles and songs he makes about her that she takes place at all – a relation so obvious that the copular verb 'to be' is not even required here: "Her future | my versions of her" (V 96). If therefore the role of the chronicler is to write his/her object into existence, then this is also exactly what Alapati does for Vela. "Storying" (V 211) is in that sense a constituent, world-making power, explaining the high status of the skilled songmaker in Nafanua's world. After all, this is a world that, according to its own myth of origin, was created (in that respect similar to the biblical cosmos) by divine speech when the supreme god "Tagaloa whispered the first Word into Vanimonimo" (V 177), the ultimate Va of the outer heavens. Unlike the bible god, however, Tagaloa remains in some ways a songmaker, the first in a long line of orators ridden with the problem of how to produce a ripping yarn that still can be plausible: "For every stroyteller since Tagaloa invented the first Word the constant | challenge is how to tell your tale so your audience reader viewer | will believe it" (V 249). The eschatology of the divine omnific word is thus conflated with a radical constructivism in which the world is Tagaloa's story, and we are what we tell (or what is told about us). Accordingly, "we don't inherit the past | but a creation" of it (V 23), and the version of the past that is remembered is the one that has been 'storied' the best. Vela's is a worded world of worlding words: a consistent and solid cosmos, but a cosmos that is aware of its limits since 'storying' implies beginnings and endings. Hence the minor cosmopolitan acknowledgment of the simultaneous co-existence of other worlds "outside the world as we conceived it" (V 100). Even Tagaloa concedes that there are worlds "out-of-reach | way-beyond the Va and

Heavens He'd created" (V 104), and Nafanua impatiently awaits the arrival of visitors from such other worlds. When the missionaries actually make a first landing, she is eager to receive them, "to come | forward and embrace them [...] | utterly convinced that they will love her" (V 256). Predictably this hospitable pluralistic cosmopolitanism runs aground on the hard rocks of the arrivals' monocultural universalism that is articulated almost exclusively in theological crudities: "We believe in One God one Church one Pope who is infallible!" (V 258). Christianity obviously allows for no coexistence with other creeds but even after its victory over Nafanua's religion it can be relativized through the lens of the constructivism of a mode of worlding that has always been aware of its limits. In this light, even triumphant Catholicism is just one among many modes of storying that "come and go depending on | their mana to provide what people desire and fulfil their dreams | of the ideal afterlife" (V 272). Once subjected to that story-centred episteme, in which it turns out to be only one delimited story among many others, Christianity loses its self-enclosed absolutism and becomes vulnerable to the subversive tactics of the vanquished who "to survive It [...] must join It and conquer It from within" (ibid.). Resistance therefore has to adopt a politics of patient intertextuality-as-infiltration, and it comes to fruition by the end of the narrative when Alapati and Vela meet a Catholic priest in contemporary Samoa who is at the same time a secret follower of the precolonial Nafanua cult that apparently has survived in certain underground pockets. The ultimate monument to this subversive hybridization of Christianity is, of course, *The Adventures of Vela* itself – finally revealed as a counter-book to 'the Book' that the missionaries wielded as their most effective weapon in the conversion of Samoa. At the end, Alapati's chronicle claims for itself the status of a new testament.

After the strange screening of 'The Final Revelations' in the moonlit cave, Nafanua appoints Alapati as her new chronicler and releases Vela and Auva'a (another survivor from her former entourage also present on the scene) from the curse of immortality. As a "pagan trinity" these three then have their own "holy ascension" on the wings of a torrent of flyingfoxes (V 276), leaving the stunned Alapati alone to his task of concluding his chronicle, which given the last twist of the plot should be centred on Nafanua, not Vela. But whose book is it anyway? As the concluding stanza, titled 'The Resurrection' reflects,

> 'The Adventures of Vela' has been accepted for publication
> I don't think I *lied* to Nafanua not telling her the title of *our* book
> I'm certain that   because She can *see* everything   including the future
> She *knew* what I was going to do while we collaborated on her biography
> I also know She'll forgive me when She reads the book and realises

it is Her and Vela's and Auva'a's resurrection grander even than that of Jesus. (ibid.)

Our book, a collective effort of actors embedded in Va relations, is now revealed to be Nafanua's biography, but the title of that biography bears the name of another. More than anything, however, it is a gospel in its own right giving testimony to a 'holy ascension'. In this capacity the book itself ascends to the beatific status of scripture that not only relates but really *is* the resurrection. And yet it is not a revealed text but the output of the collaborative effort that the whole book narrates. If both Nafanua's resurrection and the text that makes it happen are 'grander even than that of Jesus' (arguably another vague John Lennon reference here), then for sure the 'pagan trinity' finally outshines the Christian one, but on top of that, *The Adventures of Vela* is revealed as a holy rock 'n' roller's brand new testament that challenges the Christian bible just as the young Vela had challenged the arrogant Alopese.

An ongoing planet

In a frequently quoted passage, Jorge Luis Borges adopts Edward Gibbon's observation that

> in the Koran, there are no camels; I believe if there were any doubt as to the authenticity of the Koran, this absence of camels would be sufficient to prove it is an Arabian work. It was written by Mohammed, and [...] for him they were a part of reality, he had no reason to emphasize them. (Borges 2007: 174)

The fact that Gibbon was wrong about the absence of camels in the Koran does not invalidate Borges's point that the ubiquitous requires no foregrounding, and that "only a falsifier, a tourist, an Arab nationalist would [...] have a surfeit of camels, a caravan of camels on every page" (ibid.). Extending this argument to *Vela*, an 'authentic' Samoan text written from a chain of islands spectacularly shaped by volcanism will not foreground volcanoes but treat them as camels and imply and presuppose their presence as 'part of reality'.[9] And in fact, *The Adventures of Vela* is dotted with references that subtly but continuously evoke a volcanic everyday, a landscape of "lava tunnels" (V 48,

---

[9]The same could be said for the naturalness with which Nafanua's subjects navigate vast distances across the South Pacific; it is only a few nonchalant references to such faraway places as Fiji or Tonga (along with Vela's sojourns to Nei and Olfac "near the atua-less Equator", V 159) that evoke a whole network of aquatic wayfinding across Polynesia and beyond; for "narrative geographic" knowledge and long-distance voyaging in the precolonial South Pacific, see Eckstein and Schwarz 2019, 34.

142, 243), "lava channels" (V 9), "obsidian channels" (V 11), "lava caves" (V 140, 179, 245) and "lava fields" (V 213), and a deified queen seated on a "lava throne" (V 246). But most of the time the volcanic is simply implied as a pervasive presence and as a constituent partner in the nursing and nurturing of the space that connects. The mountains with which Vela bonds in a Va relation of reciprocal mirroring ('I am of their dreaming | and they of mine') are "the mountains of Taʻu" (V 43) that are among the most spectacular volcanic formations of the Samoan island chain. Vela articulates himself to these mountains by way of a chiasmic transfer pivoting on a poetics of equivalence and exchange across vast conceptual distances so that humans and volcanoes can easily be confused. In this logic, characters in *Vela* may at any point take on volcanic features or perform volcanic acts. Though only a "whisper", Vela's very first utterance in the hospital ward equates an eruption that "blew the mountain skywards" (V 6), while in one of the more 'bodily interested' sections of the verse novel, Nafanua describes how sexual arousal "almost got me blowing my top" (V 65). As an aside it may be noted here that Nafanua actually *is* a volcano in 'the real world' since a newly risen, 300 meters tall cone discovered by a 2005 expedition inside the crater of the submarine Vailuluʻu volcano located to the west of American Samoa was named after the queen. Nafanua is supposed to have grown "from the 1,000-m-deep crater floor in <4 years and could reach the sea surface within decades": evidence of the ongoing reshaping and creative/destructive rearticulation of a planet that is far from finished but instead "vigorously active and unpredictable, like Nafanua, the Samoan goddess of war, the namesake for this most recent volcanic construct in [Vailuluʻu's] crater" (Staudigel et al. 2006).

As in Carson, there is clearly a 'link between geology and character' in Wendt's book – a link that extends to actual geology if only thanks to the arbitrary naming of an underwater volcanic cone, but that has its fundament in the relational space of the Va that provides a paradigm of dynamic connexionism not available to Carson. That connection is deeply engrained in the Samoan language. While he was revising the final drafts of *The Adventures of Vela*, Wendt occupied himself more extensively with visual arts. During a sojourn as visiting professor at the University of Hawaiʻi he started working on a number of paintings exploring the Hawaiʻian volcano deity Pele. In a commentary on what he called his 'Pele series' he elaborates how the basic semantics of Samoan captures and maintains an inextricable link between the planet and the animate organism by coupling lava and blood. What ensues is one more chiasmic interchange, now between the bleeding body and the erupting volcano. In these paintings,

> the basic colors are black, the color of lava, and red, the color of molten lava and blood. In the Pele series I use the color red as if it's blood, which is basically what it is. Molten lava is molten earth. Our words for blood in Samoan are *toto*, *eleele* for earth, and *palapala* for mud. When someone is

bleeding, we use *eleele* and *palapala*, as if the person is bleeding earth. Thus every time I see molten lava I see blood [...]. (Wendt in Hereniko 2006: 67)

2.4 The planet as praxis: W. S. Merwin's *The Folding Cliffs*

Fredric Jameson (2013: 308) has described *Cloud Atlas* as a glimpse of the future form the historical novel might take; the following reading of W. S. Merwin's *The Folding Cliffs* (1998) is underpinned by the implicit claim that Merwin's verse novel – a retelling of incidents around the overthrow of the Hawai'i monarchy in the 1890s – offers the historical novel yet another, truly alternative future in verse. Merwin deploys a form of "long lines of alternate lengths, loosely derived and alluding to the classical Greek and Latin elegies" (Merwin 2013: 649) without following any one traditional pattern or prescription. The text's obvious stylization becomes immediately apparent not so much through metric regularity or a pervasive superior tone but primarily, as in Carson's verse novel, by way of typographic arrangement, here through the distribution of differently indented long lines and the concomitant visual foregrounding of both gaps (line-breaks) and gap negotiation (enjambement). As one critic remarks, the graphic dimension of Merwin's text on the page takes on a significance in its own right as "the dancelike sashaying of clauses around line-breaks and subtle zigzagging of alternate line indents may seem to articulate the characters' physical moves in nature even more vividly than the verbal content" (Lieberman 2012: 41). Despite all these formalities, *The Folding Cliffs* over long stretches evokes a sense of simplicity, sincerity and *Volkstümlichkeit* that indeed recalls Lukács's distinction of the historical novel in its democratic avatar. In this vein, Merwin's protagonist Ko'olau can be seen as what Lukács has called a "popular character" (Lukács 1989: 283) – the democratic and plebeian heir to the "world-historical individual" at the centre of the bourgeois historical novel of the nineteenth century. For Lukács, both types of literary character emerge not so much as fictional 'personality' but as "embodiment[s] of the important tendencies of an important transition in popular life" (ibid.: 310–11). Crucially, the world-historical individual's centrality is not necessarily acknowledged in the diegetic world but at the level of the diegesis, where that figure functions less as a singular individual but as an indispensable "centre of force in which the social forces of a crisis are united" (ibid.: 311). Therefore, Lukács's notion of the world-historical individual is as fundamentally anti-individualistic as his whole normative theory of the historical novel, which is polemically pitted against the "popularity of the biographical form in the present-day historical novel" (ibid.: 301) that, for Lukács, denigrates the genre to a mere celebrity cult. The world-historical individual, in short, can only exist in a deep 'organic' embeddedness in the popular, which for Lukács at the time of writing his treatise in the mid-1930s, necessarily implies a further de-individualization towards the common and plebeian. In a situation of anti-fascist and anti-capitalist politicization, it is 'popular characters' (rather than the outstanding 'world-historical individual') that "express plastically and convincingly all that is best in the popular forces" (ibid.: 342).

Merwin blends that historical–materialist aesthetic tradition of the popular with the entirely different repertoire of an indigenous communitarianism that, like the Va, assumes a similar organic embeddedness, albeit not in the dialectic juxtaposition of historical forces but in "the interrelationship of all things in an everlasting continuum" (Kanahele 1997: 2). This continuum includes human and animal, biotic and abiotic partners alike, and in Merwin's text this immediately manifests in the fact that his central 'popular character', Ko'olau, like Wendt's Nafanua (arguably a Polynesian 'world-historical individual'), shares his name with a local volcano. To the extent that *The Folding Cliffs* marks an approximation to a non-Western mode of worlding, the whole book might describe the inverse *voyage in* of a continental US Caucasian poet writing himself out of settler-colonial subjecthood by crossing over into an indigenous epistemology and cosmology.

Both the events and the characters in Merwin's text are historically documented, albeit somewhat marginally so. The crucial crisis on which the narrative pivots is the implementation of a highly restrictive and discriminatory politics of epidemic containment targeting patients afflicted with Hansen's disease. In the proto-colonial context of late-nineteenth-century Hawai'i, such containment policies were never neutral, especially as the disease – "according to European tradition the most repugnant of all maladies" (Crosby 1992: 191) – hit the native Hawai'ian population particularly hard while resident foreigners remained by and large unaffected. This uneven distribution of contractions and casualties provided "one more excuse for *haole* racism" (ibid.) as the vulnerability of Native Hawai'ians was interpreted as both symptomatic of racial inferiority and (concomitant) incapacity to contain the disease by way of the observance of basic hygiene:

> After the outbreak of leprosy in Hawai'i in the late nineteenth century, Native Hawaiians did not initially follow Western standards of quarantining those with leprosy, or Hansen's disease. These things shocked and mobilized Western missionaries, and similar concerns were translated into scientific literature through eugenics, where breaking such taboos became the cause of Native Hawaiian racial degeneration. (Arvin 2019: 74–5)

This construction of Hawai'ians as incapable of protecting themselves against Hansen's disease ideologically undergirded the imposition of coercive biopolitical measures including the deportation and quarantining in an isolated internment camp of the indigenous patients. The 1865 'Act to Prevent the Spread of Leprosy'[10] authorized the arrest, forced removal and strict segregation of anyone alleged to have contracted the disease: a confused and counterproductive "law that was supposed | to get rid of the sickness by getting rid of the sick" (FC 143). Actual implementation of the Act from the early 1870s onward "fell most harshly on native Hawaiians, who soon discovered that the new regulation required them to send friends and relatives away" (Moran 2008: 318) against their will. One point that Merwin's text very strongly emphasizes is how this policy of singling out and expelling the afflicted from the community severely violates the most fundamental tenets of Hawai'ian ethics and is hence rightly perceived as an assault on cultural self-determination. In this vein, "the expulsion and banishment of the lepers is – at bottom – a colonialist ruse to squelch the whole native population, not just the stricken souls" (Lieberman 2012: 44). As the speaker of Merwin's verse novel notes, "It was the foreigners | whom the sickness almost never attacked who feared it most | and what the Hawaiians dreaded most was being taken | away from their families" (FC 126). It is for this reason that the "Hawaiians called the disease […] *mai hookawale*, the separating sickness, because of the strict segregation of the patients" (Frazier 2001: ix): it is not the sickness itself but the politics imposed around it that severs communal ties. To elude deportation, numerous of the diseased, often together with their families, went into hiding. On the island of Kauai, the setting of Merwin's historical novel in verse, it is the nearly inaccessible wilds of the valley of Kalalau that serves as a refuge for fugitive patients. For a couple of months, a sanctuary of self-determined, self-organized communal subsistence flourished in the valley: a convivial counter-colony to the governmental quarantine internment camp on the outlying islet of Molokai, dreaded by the Hawai'ians as "the grave where one is buried alive" (Frazier 2001: 10).

History, genealogy, socioecology

Merwin bases his narrative on the testimony of Pi'ilai, a returnee from the Kalalau valley, as told to and written down in Hawai'ian by the journalist Kahikina Kelekona, whose English name was John Sheldon. Kelekona/ Sheldon's Hawai'ian text was first published in 1906, and much later

---

[10] I will where possible avoid the historically loaded term 'leprosy', which can be easily replaced by 'Hansen's disease'; moreover I will, instead of the derogatory term 'leper', use neutral alternatives like 'sufferers', 'patients' or 'afflicted'; however, in citations (including from *The Folding Cliffs*) I will retain both 'leprosy' and 'leper' where necessary but will quote as sparingly as possible from passages containing these words.

translated into English by the Hawai'ian historian Frances Frazier with the title *The True Story of Kaluaikoolau: As Told by His Wife, Piilani* (first published in 1987 in *The Hawaiian Journal of History*, and in an extended and annotated version as a monograph in 2001). Pi'ilani was the wife of Ko'olau, a cowboy and expert marksman, who along with his young son Kaleimanu contracted Hansen's disease in 1892 and decided to join the refugees in the Kalalau Valley. As government agents finally started to forcibly round up the fugitives for deportation to Molokai, fighting ensued between the incoming forces and some of the inhabitants. In a series of encounters, Ko'olau first shot and killed Deputy Sheriff Louis Stolz, and later two provisional government soldiers who had been sent to arrest him. He vowed never to be taken alive and together with Pi'ilani and their son retreated further into the canyon, successfully evading discovery and capture for "three years and five or more months" (Frazier 2001: 32) until first Kaleimanu's and later Ko'olau's death of Hansen's disease in 1896. Pi'ilani who never contracted the disease buried both her son and her husband in secret places in the valley, and after a few more months of solitary existence in the wilderness finally returned from hiding to her family and, years later, related her story to Sheldon. Obviously, the fraught configuration of Vela and Alapati, of the transformation of the spoken word into literature, is further complicated here as the actual testimony triggers a veritable chain of Chinese whispers: Pi'ilani's oral account is first written down by Sheldon, then translated by Frazier and finally set to verse by Merwin, who in a prefatory note locates his own text in the interstices of history, fiction and legend:

> The central events of the story all happened and the principal characters existed but the evidence for both is fragmentary and most of it second or third hand, refracted and remote. This is a fiction but it was not my purpose to belie such facts as have come down to us. Some of them have been moving towards legend since they occurred. (FC n.p.)

More than that, earlier readers of *The Folding Cliffs* have detected how Merwin collates Pi'ilani/Sheldon/Frazier with a range of further textual material. Thus, Francoise Palleau-Papin (2016: 29) suggests that Merwin must have used Jack London's short story, 'Kolau the Leper', as "a foil against which to write a counternarrative"; Laurence Lieberman (2012: 48) makes out "a disguised take on Dante's hierarchical topography" in Merwin's representation of the Kalalau Valley as an inverse *Paradiso* (whereby Merwin neatly closes ranks with Walcott, Carson and Wendt, who, as we have seen, also refer to Dante in whatever different ways). Far more pertinent to the following discussion, however, is Merwin's recourse to a non-Western hypotext. Both John Burt and Jeff Westover point out that *The Folding Cliffs* "echoes the language of the Hawaiian creation epic, the *Kumulipo*, as translated by Martha Beckwith" (Burt 2015: 16),[11] or "adapts phrases from the *Kumulipo* [...], the Hawaiian chant of creation" (Westover 2019: 59). The politics of Merwin's recourse to the *Kumulipo*, I argue, is bent on two main effects: first, the democratization of a deeply inegalitarian tradition by endowing the plebeian protagonists of *The Folding Cliffs* with pedigrees that are modelled on the supreme genealogy that the *Kumulipo* reserves for Hawai'ian royalty alone; and second, the instantiation of a specific version of what Jason Moore, borrowing from Marx, has discussed as "historical nature" (Moore 2015: 116), and that in Merwin's scenario is tied in with precisely that telluric force that the *Kumulipo* appears to place as the site of origin of the world as such – *volcanism*.

As a "cosmogonic genealogy" (Johnson 2000: 34), the *Kumulipo* serves "two independent functions: (1) a chant about the earth's creation; and (2) a prayer that sanctifies the chief" (Fox and McDermott 2019: 2). The aristocratic Kamehamea family that rose to power in the early eighteenth century commissioned a 'songmaker' to compose a chant that would put forth the family's claim to divine origin. Like Wendt's Vela and indeed all composers in Polynesia before European contact, the unknown author of the *Kumulipo* was a spoken-word artist, and the first recorded written version of the chant is the 1889 publication by King Kalakaua in Hawai'ian, to be followed by his sister's, Queen Lili'oukalani's, first English translation (1897). Kalakaua and Lili'oukalani, who dates the original composition of the chant to 1700, were the last two Hawai'ian monarchs and members of the very family that the *Kumupilo* linked "not only to primary gods belonging to the whole people and worshipped in common with allied Polynesian groups, not only to deified chiefs [...] within the family line, but to the stars in the heavens" (Beckwith 1972: 7). Kalakaua's investment in the chant is therefore clearly political, inasmuch as the propagation of the *Kumulipo* was "to his interest and later to that of his sister as queen to uphold in every way the family claim to blood descent from the fountain source of the royal line" (ibid.: 29). Lili'oukalani accordingly frames her 1897 English translation of the *Kumulipo* as "being nothing less than the genealogy in remote times of the late King Kalakaua, who had it printed in the original Hawaiian language, and myself" (Lili'oukalani 1997: 10). It should be obvious that matters cannot have been much different even at the time of the text's first composition: it always was intended to serve as a eulogy to a ruling family striving to consolidate political supremacy by claiming for themselves divine origin.

---

[11]It should be noted that Merwin appears to have mostly relied on the 1981 translation by Rubellite Kawena Johnson, as a recent post from *The Merwin Conservancy* indicates; cf. https://www.instagram.com/tv/CFfGsfmD4wP/?utm_source=ig_embed (28 January 2023).

In the (narrow) sense of a delineation of ancestry, then, *mo'oku'auhau* – roughly translated as genealogy – "was in large part a political art and a chiefly practice [...] to establish the truth that one was descended from an illustrious ancestor of great mana and high rank, had inherited some of this mana, and were entitled to some of the rank that went with it" (Chang 2019: 100). Yet to restrict the ideological function of genealogy to the competition among rival families from the same chief class would certainly fall short of the more general societal impact that this kind of orature must have had in the re-enactment and reproduction of a massively stratified distribution of the sensible in a rigid caste society, "where inherited blood counted above all things in establishing the perquisites of rank" (Beckwith 1972: 30): "Retaining genealogical lineage has been particularly important to Hawaiian ali'i (chiefs) who recited their mo'oku'auhau to assert their political power" (Wilson-Hokowhitu 2012: 138–9). In this wider perspective, along with a range of other cultural practices and rituals (most notably the insidious *kapu* system), the cosmogonic genealogy serves primarily to buttress by deification the absolute rule of chiefs and priests over the vast majority of commoners and slaves.

If Nafanua's Samoa is a society founded on rank and hence completely devoid of the "promise of equality" (V 259), then the same holds true for the world according to the *Kumulipo*. And yet, of course, there is more to it. Wendt, certainly not a nostalgic, takes recourse to the epistemology and ontology of the Va as a primarily *spatial* paradigm of convivial relationality that allows to think alternatives to the devastations that anthropocentric hostility inflicts on nature. Similarly, the primarily *temporal* episteme of *mo'oku'auhau* cannot be restricted to the delineation of implicitly hierarchical kinship genealogies alone but, like the Va, enables the conceptualization of an essentially relational world, a "socioecology" (Nu'uhiwa 2019: 44): a term that serves "to highlight that Hawaiians did not just notice the interactions among other species around them, but also included their interactions among themselves, with other species, and also with their environment" (ibid.). This relational ecology manifests in the *Kumulipo* through the formulaic "dichotomy of land-ocean pairing" (Kanahele 1997: 3) that links apparently far apart species in custodial bonds across vast distances. Some lines from Beckwith's translation (cited subsequently as K + verse number) exemplify this poetics of composed relations: "The stingray living in the sea [is] | Guarded by the stormy-petrel living on land" (K330–1), "the jellyfish living in the sea | Guarded by the bamboo living on land" (K 456–7), "the Palaoa [walrus?] living in the sea | Guarded by the sandalwood living on land" (K 251–2).

In this wider understanding, genealogy may be familial as well as cosmogonic, and in this double dimensionality it emerges as the crucial epistemological paradigm in Hawai'ian traditions. As such it cannot be restricted to kinship as perceived by anthropology, but instead extends to an "interlinking, expansive web of connections" (hoʻomanawanui 2019: 64): "Knowing one's moʻokuʻauhau (genealogy) connects one to kupuna (ancestors) and ancestral homelands. Knowing mele koʻihonua (cosmogonic genealogies) enables understanding a Kanaka worldview through creation stories" (Rohrer 2016: 175). Numerous readers of the *Kumulipo* persuasively interpret the chant in this vein as expressive of a pluriversal mode of worlding that "articulates earth as a living whole emerging out of the manifold of interconnected biophysical, human and spiritual relations coexisting in time and space" (Fox and McDermott 2019: 10): a processual planet. Here of course everything depends upon what understanding of *moʻokuʻauhau* is at work: either the delineation of ancestry as an indigenous "tool for establishing and defending claims to power" (Chang 2019: 99) or the enactment of "connectedness with the ancestors, land and the surrounding environment" (Wilson-Hokowhitu 2012: 140). In the first, narrower understanding, where *moʻokuʻauhau* zooms in on humans (alone), genealogically grounded divisions of the sensible will appear as exclusionist and casteist, and the *Kumulipo* will be read as a Polynesian equivalent of, say, the infamous *Laws of Manu* that codify the hierarchical caste system in South Asian societies. As soon as one deploys the wider angle of a non-anthropocentric lens, however, *moʻokuʻauhau* shades off into *mele koʻihonua* and becomes an inclusivist paradigm that embeds humanity in the ramified assemblage of the web of life; in the words of Marie Alohalani Brown, "to perceive the world genealogically" means to acknowledge that "everything is relational [...]; as a theoretical and philosophical construct, it stands for relationality" (in Fox and McDermott 2019: 3). What is missing in most accounts is the negotiation of the gap that opens up between these two notions of genealogy.

Therefore, the appealing paradigm of pervasive and all-encompassing relationality, which articulates an ecumene of human and non-human life and beyond that, of biota and abiota, is all too often bought at the price of an incapacity to address inequality among humans as a problem – a problem that remains mostly unacknowledged but, in some instances, gets explicitly denied in a dismissal of "the supposedly egalitarian republic" (Chang 2019: 97). Can ecological justice come only at the cost of social justice, and vice versa? Wendt is aware of this cost and weaves its critique into *The Adventures of Vela*; but he posits the friction between social and ecological justice as dilemma, that is, as an irresolvable problem that explodes the society of Nei and leads to wholesale deforestation and ecocidal monoculturalism in present-day Samoa. Merwin by comparison goes further in that he delinks the socioecological potentials of cosmogonic genealogy from its cathexis to feudalist social systems and ideologies that, in the case of indigenous Hawaiʻi, buttress the stratification of the socius into the three castes of "the chiefs or *aliʻi*, the commoners or *makaainana*, and the outcastes or *kauwa*" (Levin 1968: 406). Where Wendt somewhat capriciously flirts with the ruling castes (for both Nafanua and Vela are clear representatives of the quasi-divine elite) in order to occasionally debunk as baroque excess the extreme social hierarchies prevalent in traditional Samoa, Merwin figures a deeply relational cosmos but places at its centre precisely those to whom neither the poet of the *Kumulipo* nor Vela, Alapati or even Wendt will attend: the commoners (or, with Lukács, the popular). While Wendt's verse novel is daring in its bawdy disrespect for the sentiments of cultural nationalists, in its iconoclastic violation of nativist pieties and in its fusion of traditional orature with pop-cultural repertoires, *The Folding Cliffs* moves the exact other way and takes an alternate but equally minor cosmopolitan path: instead of denigrating the elevated, it elevates the denigrated. Merwin's poetry leaves the superior tone of Hawai'ian hieratic and aristocratic tradition not only intact but enhances it even further by merging it with the hypercanonical authority of the European literary lineage enshrined in the odes and elegies of classical antiquity: Pindar, Ovid and, perhaps, Stesichoros. This, of course, is only the first step that Merwin takes; the second is the full democratization of this doubly enforced superior tone by repartitioning the sensible in a fervently anti-Aristotelian way: the cosmic chant and the solemn ode are being transformed into a radically egalitarian narrative whose protagonists are plebeian and heroic at the same time. More than that, as true commoners, the cowherd Ko'olau and his peasant wife Pi'ilani appear and act not primarily as individuals but as 'popular characters' expressing the productivity of the commoners. They are members of a communal body whose integrity is threatened not by the literal disintegration of those bodies that are afflicted with Hansen's disease, but to the contrary by the coerced exclusion of the patients from the communities of which they are an integral part. It is through this inclusivist move that Merwin attempts what Wendt does not venture, namely the reconciliation of social and ecological justice.

This minor cosmopolitan move is to some extent anticipated by Sheldon's translator, Frances Frazier, who makes out in Pi'ilani's testimony "a steadfastness and devotion that rivals any classical legend of faithful love" (Frazier 2001: x), endowing the narrator with a heroism that belongs to the sphere of legend rather than real life; and already Sheldon, Pi'ilani's first transcriber, appears to have embellished his text with a number of features that idealize the plebeian, as in the following passage describing the young Pi'ilani:

> There also was growing in this same land of Kekaha, a beautiful lehua blossom of the highest, a beautiful, nectar-sipping, yellow-plumaged Oo bird. [...] on a certain night when the mountains lay serene under the lady moon and her million twinkling stars, when the wings of the dew spread the deep fragrance of the blossoms over the winds which moistened the faces of the *pali* [cliffs] and the mountain ridges, in the season of Makalapua of the year of our Lord 1864, there budded forth a soft and beautiful blossom, without blemish: "Back as straight as a *pali*,

face like the moon, no bumps or crookednesses," and her mother called her precious child Piilani. (Sheldon in Frazier 2001: 7)

Where Sheldon heaps up excessive (and probably conventional) imagery reminiscent of fairy-tale formulae to drive home the point of Pi'ilani's exceptional beauty, Merwin re-activates the genealogical chant itself in order to produce a family tree for his protagonists that articulates the common in the diction of royal lineage. The first chapter of section 3, 'Born', provides a genealogy for both Ko'olau and Pi'ilani that opens with a selection of reassembled citations straight from the *Kumulipo* as the following synopsis will demonstrate:

Born in the dark wave the fragrance of seaweed	Born the tough seagrass living in the sea
born on the land the shore grass hissing while the night slips	Guarded by the tough landgrass living on land
through a narrow place a man is born for the narrows	Man for the narrow stream, Woman for the broad
a woman is born for where the waters open	stream (K 41–4)
the passage is for a god it is not for a human (FC 89)	The God enters, man cannot enter (K 106)

The opening lines from the third section of *The Folding Cliffs* (left column) thus recite freely from the first chant of the *Kumulipo* that relates the beginning of life on earth in the deep night of creation, the 'primal darkness' *kumu lipo* from which the title of the chant is derived. In the original chant it takes another 600 lines to enumerate the birth of manifold mineral, vegetal and animal life forms and species from corals and seaweeds, fish and birds to pigs and rats, to reach the moment where humans actually enter the world as "the first chief of the dim past" (K 619) is born. If the *Kumulipo* thus celebrates the advent of an aristocratic ur-chief organically embedded in the web of life, then Merwin emphasizes how hierarchy and subjection are always already woven into the very fabric of the pluriverse right from the beginning:

in the sea the child of the hilu fish is born in the night under the tides	The seven waters just float Born is the child of the *hilu* fish and swims
the child floats through the seven currents it is already someone to bow to in awe (FC 89)	The *hilu* fish rests with spreading tail fins A child of renown (K 131–4)

The *hilu*, a fish that is "among the most brilliant in colouring found in Hawaiian waters" (Beckwith 1972: 61), is prominently mentioned in the second chant of the *Kumulipo* as 'a child of renown' that excels over the latter-born fish of lesser status. Possibly a typological anticipation of the human chief-to-come, the *hilu*'s appearance ensures that rank is inscribed into the natural world order, and Merwin's addition – 'already someone to bow to in awe' –simply emphasizes for the present-day reader this apparently ineluctable hierarchy. But what if the preferred and privileged *hilu* were read not as an exceptional wonder child but as a commoner? Merwin's text in fact encourages precisely such a reading by leaping almost immediately from the creation of the awe-demanding *hilu* not to the advent of some ur-chief but to the birth of Kanemahuka, the fisherman and grandfather of Koʻolau. The aristocratic fish thus serves as an almost direct ancestor not to a chiefly dynasty but a plebeian family, whose actual genealogy Merwin lifts from another source text, namely, Frazier's translation of Sheldon. According to that account, the modest family trees of Koʻolau and Piʻilani are devoid of all cosmogonic deep-time dimensions but instead date back merely three generations that are reported in the unembellished minimalism of the basic *moʻokuʻauhau* template:

> Kanemahuka, the man, dwelt with Keawe, the woman, born was Kaleimanu, a male
>
> Nakaula, the man, dwelt with Kawaluna, the woman, born was Kukui, a female
>
> Kaleimanu, the man, dwelt with Kukui, the woman, born was Kaluaikoolau. (Frazier 2001: 5)

Merwin's text fuses these two hypotexts – the *Kulumipo* and the Sheldon/Frazier version of Piʻilani's testimony – to arrive at a genealogical account that merges myth and history, phylogenetic and biographical memory, the creation of the world and the reproduction of an ordinary family whose members are 'born to remember', hence to bridge the past and future. Their memories are of multiple experiences of violence ('killing'), loss ('burials', 'mourning') and, at best, hard labour ('oxen and crushed sugar cane'), so that the ancestors of Koʻolau and Piʻilani emerge as sufferers rather than actors, recipients rather than makers of history:

> The child
>   of the hilu fish is born in the night under the tides
> the child floats through the seven currents it is already
>   someone to bow to in awe born is the sandalwood tree
> on land the guardian of the whale in the ocean
>   born Kanemahuka to remember the sound
> of the stream at Pokiʻi and voices by the low fire

>   talking about a killing born is Keawe in the valley
>   of Waiaka whom he would hold in his arms Keawe
>   to remember crying above the rushing water
>   the burials along the valley the mourning from doorways
>   born to them both Kaleimanu to remember
>   the smell of oxen and crushed sugar cane in the mud
>   [...]
>   born is Koʻolau
>   to Kaleimanu and Kukui in a new year
>   a month of long waves born is Piʻilani. (FC 89)

Genealogy spills over from the cosmogonic to the ordinary, from the sanctification of the chief to the extrapolation of the dignity of the commoners, the undistinguished, whose very indistinction is beautifully ennobled in a rehearsal of that kind of "syntactical fluidity" that Christopher Ricks makes out in the verses of Hopkins, Rilke and most of all Milton, who, for Ricks, "achieves some of his finest effects precisely by leaving it possible for a word or a clause to look backward or forward" (Ricks 1963: 137). As a stout social formalist I am not so much out for taste judgments of 'finest effects' but more interested in the politics of such liquid texture as manifest in the last three lines of the citation given earlier: 'Born is Koʻolau | to Kaleimanu and Kukui in a new year | a month of long waves born is Piʻilani'. In the absence of punctuation it is not clear whether the temporal marker – 'in a new year | a month of long waves' – qualifies Koʻolau's or Piʻilani's birth. If there were a full stop after the name of Koʻolau's mother, Kukui, then it would be Piʻilani who was born 'in a new year' and 'a month of long waves'. If the full stop came only after 'waves', however, all these seasonal markers would belong to Koʻolau. This ambiguity of a markedly fluid syntax is of course deliberate and its effect is not only aporetic (and hence, epistemological) but more than that a flexibilization of ontological fixities. For in this liquid texture the newly born Koʻolau and Piʻilani shade off into each other as the boundaries of their respective temporal domains become porous. Instead of rigidly circumscribed individual identities, then, Merwin's verse evokes fuzzy and flexible subjectivities that are not grounded in bounded selfhood but communion, not in the accrual of properties but in what is shared commonly between them. Syntactic and metrical spill-over effects – 'gap negotiations', as McHale would have it – thus correlate to the positing of a constitutive openness of unbounded selves that exist and thrive in the indigenous continuum of a deeply interconnective socioecology. In this continuum, what counts is not what belongs to any one individual but what is shared; and what is shared between Koʻolau and Piʻilani – what 'looks backward and forward' between them and therefore belongs to none of them unequivocally, but instead to them both – is time, more precisely, the time of the seasons: 'a new year, a month of long waves'.

Moʻokuʻauhau identities are thus intimately entangled with *moʻokuʻauhau* temporalities, and Merwin's text gives a most indicative illustration of this in the character of Koʻolau and Piʻilani's son who shares his name, Kaleimanu, with his paternal grandfather and to some extent engenders a further confusion of the linear aspect of genealogy. As Koʻolau asserts, the young Kaleimanu 'repeats' his grandfather with a difference: "You are like Kaleimanu your grandfather | but not all the same" (FC 249). The close relation of the boy and his grandfather is most ostensible in the name they share, and more specifically, in the taboo meaning of that name: "The Wreath of Birds" (FC 20). It is a prophetic name that had been revealed in a dream to the 'first' Kaleimanu's mother who

> gave him that name because of something she knew
>   in the dream but her son he had to ask her
> for years before she would tell him any of the dream
>   and when our son asked his grandfather it was the same
> for a long time he would say only that it was a dream
>   of birds. (FC 20)

The secret of the dream is never lifted in Merwin's text but the precocious young Kaleimanu, "who for all his spookiness and wisdom never quite seems like a real child" (Burt 2015: 10), early on intuits the hidden dimensions of the enigmatic name he carries. The 'wreath of birds' indeed links the boy to the spiral temporality that we have already seen at work in *The Adventures of Vela*, and along with this unhinging of the linearity and irreversibility of chronological homogeneous empty time, it renders porous the boundaries between fact and fiction, life and story, action and trans-action. As Kaleimanu somewhat ominously asserts, garlands or wreaths (Hawaiʻian: *lei*) made of bird feathers partake of multiple temporalities, through which they are set apart from the more ubiquitous flower garlands. According to Kaleimanu at the age of five the

>   flowers and leaves in the leis
> had all been picked and ended but that in bird leis
>   the birds were flying only they were birds from before
> and from afterward so that nobody could see them. –   (FC 20)

In this reading of his own name, Kaleimanu identifies with and indeed *as* temporal heterogeneity embodied in the feather wreath in which past and future – 'birds from before and from afterward' – invisibly conjoin. Therefore, the near-identity ('but not all the same') with his grandfather in the spiralling loops of genealogical time is as natural to the boy as the co-presence of the legendary and the mundane: "He wanted to hear bird stories | from back before about people from then who were birds", and after having virtually incorporated all tales and legends available "he would ask about them as though the stories I were still there" (FC 21). The communion of story and reality, 'then' and 'now', leads to yet another boundary evaporating: the line between fact and fiction that gradually gives way as Kaleimanu makes up "stories of his own which he told as though they had happened I and he had seen them" (FC 262). The boy's constant concern with "something now in the story" (FC 21) indicates how the fictional spills over into the actual, reminiscent of the persistence of 'Nafanua's world' in the 'real world'. By investing Kaleimanu (both grandfather and grandson) with the traditional trope of the *lei* (the garland or wreath), Merwin virtually personifies a traditional Hawai'ian meta-metaphor of narrativity as such: a narrativity that proliferates gutter texts. For the narrative *lei* is not only interlaced but also, as ho'omanawanui (2014: 50) points out, resistant of closure and hence incomplete:

> While it is tempting to 'close' or complete the lei by bringing all the open strands together, I suggest that the lei is still being formed [...]. 'Closing' the lei also might incorrectly suggest that all variants are merging into a single master narrative.

This inherent incompleteness of the *lei* ensures, then, the coexistence and negotiability of plural narrative strands and versions, and thereby a centrifugal democratization. As a loop, moreover, the *lei* ideally emblematizes the spiral temporalities that connect Merwin and Wendt's diegetic worlds but that, in *The Folding Cliffs*, destabilize the aristocratic linearity of generational genealogies that Wendt, however playfully, ultimately confirms in his new testament. Meanwhile, as an embodiment of the *lei*, Kaleimanu the boy most effectively operates as a democratizing force in the medium of spiral heterotemporalities.

This becomes explicit in the child's identification with Lahi the 'Bird Man' whose story Merwin has probably adopted from folklorist William Hyde Rice's collection of *Hawaiian Legends* (Rice 1923: 47–8). 'The Bird Man' relates the adventures of Lahi and his uncle, Slow Man, who subsist as poachers in a remote mountain valley where they feed primarily on the *uwaua* birds that belong to the local chief. When the latter learns of the ongoing theft of his property on the fringes of his territory, he rallies an army of 400 to capture and kill the bird-catchers. Lahi and his uncle however retreat to a nook in the rocks that can only be reached through an extremely narrow passage that allows for only one man to pass at a time. One soldier after the other gets killed when entering the nook until it is the turn of the very last man, the chief himself, who recognizes Lahi as his own son and makes him his successor. Arguably the tale articulates a plebeian desire to turn aristocratic genealogy upside down as Lahi, the poacher, ends up as prince. Unlike conciliatory folk tales, however, this one does not arrive at the happy ending by way of the Proppian function according to which "the hero gets married [to the princess] and ascends the throne" (Propp 2009: 63) – a plot resolution that allows the underdog to join the exclusive ranks of the elite; instead it plays out the agonistic fairy-tale plot element of the victory over, and punishment of, the villain as a veritable revenge fantasy in the single-handed elimination of the king's army. Merwin's text therewith retrieves (or outright constructs) a subaltern tradition of counternarratives to the hierarchical master plot of dynastic genealogy. The boy Kaleimanu functions in *The Folding Cliffs* as the embodiment of that alternate tradition that, in line with the paradigm of spiral temporalities, repeats itself with a difference in the diegetic present.

The legend of Lahi is not mentioned in Piʻilani's testimony but introduced early on in Merwin's text as one of Kaleimanu's favourite stories that he demands to be told time and again. The decision to evade deportation by retreating into the Kalalau Valley is for the boy to a large extent made agreeable by the fact that the valley is the setting of the story so that the escape from government prosecution leads "to the place on the mountain where Lahi lived" (FC 21), and hence into the story itself. In fact, the Kalalau Valley, suffused with "the air of another time" (FC 177), appears as a landscape that spatializes a heterotemporal coexistence of the here-now and "the remote past" (FC 177) in the transcendental dimension of a "suspended time" (FC 204) beyond measure: "Piʻilani would look back on those first days in the valley | first days first weeks she could not tell how long it lasted | that time that season that age in itself" (FC 204). This suspension of chronology, however, is not a simple given enshrined in the land as such but rather the outcome of a complex interaction between the land and its inhabitants: "During those years in the valley sometimes she saw faces | and houses and moments from long before" (FC 283). This phenomenology of heterogeneous space-time comes most clearly to the fore, ironically, with regards to what appears as the very embodiment of linearity itself: the trail. Far from being a mere trajectory, it triggers in Koʻolau an epiphany of braided palimpsestic time:

> There were turns on the trail where Koʻolau
>   could see all the times he had passed there every step that he
>   had ridden among those trees along those rocks through
>   that light
>   they floated in front of him and then in a moment
>   they had moved on and it was a day like any other. (FC 183)

Iteration is always also reiteration, moving forward also always moving backward to 'all the times he had passed there'. The same transformation of linear movement into a spiralling loop shuttling between past and present occurs whenever Piʻilani revisits the valley after her return to her family. Each time she descends into Kalalau, "the way came and went in the braid of | later times when she had travelled down that trail" (FC 199). In such a setting, where then and now commingle in a 'syntactical fluidity' (to return to Ricks one last time), temporal irreversibility gets suspended along with the distinction between 'story' and 'history'.

Therefore, when Koʻolau manages to fight back his persecutors, Lahi's defeat of the chief's army is re-enacted. The fugitive family take shelter on a well-nigh inaccessible promontory above a waterfall, "veiled on the right and left by growing things, leaves and creepers, and could not be seen" (Frazier 2001: 24). As in the 'Bird Man' story, the fugitives cannot "be | approached except by one man at a time" (FC 250), and, as in the tale, the soldiers are being fought back single-handedly. In defence of himself and his family, Koʻolau shoots and kills three provisional government soldiers before the fugitives manage to secretly evacuate their beleaguered hiding place and escape even further into the wild interior. The defeat of the soldiers on the promontory is consistently interpreted by the boy Kaleimanu as an actualization of 'the story', a spill-over of legend into reality: "Kaleimanu whispered to him – Is it the story now – | What story Koʻolau asked him – Where the soldiers | come up the cliff one at a time and he throws them down" (FC 248–9). What is crucially different from the spiralling time in Wendt's verse novel is that, in *The Folding Cliffs*, the porosity of past and present, legend and fact, clears a space not only for an unsettling of homogeneous empty time but more specifically for a subaltern narrative and epistemic repertoire that runs counter to both settler–colonial and indigenous hegemonies.

Volcanic syllables, volcanic silences

Merwin's text does not abandon *moʻokuʻauhau*. To the contrary, it embraces the genealogical paradigm precisely by critically democratizing it. More accurately put, democratization is the very condition for the paradigm to hold. This is true not only for the politics of displacing the enumeration of ancestry from aristocratic dynasticism to plebeian family lines, but also for the genealogical envisaging of the web of life in toto, which brings us finally back to the cosmogonic and ecological dimensions of *moʻokuʻauhau*, and to the processes of world-becoming that Merwin, like Wendt, Carson and Walcott, identifies with the volcanic.

In this, his text again loops back on the *Kumulipo* in a loose intertextual entanglement, strongly foregrounding the volcanism at work at the moment of the earth's birth. In Queen Liliʻoukalani's translation of the *Kumulipo*, that first moment of creation occurs when, "at the time that turned the heat of the earth | [...] | Then began the slime which established the earth'; Beckwith renders these lines as 'at the time when the earth became hot | [...] | the slime, this was the source of the earth" (Beckwith 1972: 58). The Hawaiian scholar and commentator Poepoe, on whom Beckwith draws in her own interpretation of the chant, reads from this enigmatic description the idea that the world originates in volcanic eruptions, in "the coming of fire from the inside of the earth and leaving in confusion (inside out)" (in Beckwith 1972: 46). The original slime is, then, (similar to the 'uncreated tartar' in Milton's *Paradise Lost*) simultaneously the 'source of the earth' and the matter she ejects so that, in a magnificent temporal spiral, the question of chronological priority gets confounded beyond repair right at the outset.

As in Walcott and especially Carson, the notion of an externalization of the interior links the volcanic immediately to the psychic as the Hawaiian term for the primal matter, *walewale*, is in some versions of the *Kumulipo* rendered as *welawela*, "meaning 'intense heat' or 'strong emotion' " (Beckwith 1972: 45), thereby sliding effortlessly from temperature to temperament.

If the *Kumulipo* economically condenses the volcanic origin of the planet into a few hints at the earth's heat and ejaculated unformed matter, then Merwin's own rewriting of the creation chant not only elaborately fleshes out the creativity of volcanism but immediately cathexes it with language, more specifically, the spoken word:

The mountain rises by itself out of the turning night
    out of the floor of the sea and is the whole of an island
alone in the one horizon alone in the entire day
    as a word is alone in the moment it is spoken
    [...]
its fire came late among the fires in the dark of space
    its burning plume rose late through the plated shells of the globe. (FC 47)

The somewhat idiosyncratic combination of the telluric and the linguistic is here not so much grounded in the notion, so prominent in *Autobiography of Red*, that both volcanoes and words bring the inside to the outside; it is rather motivated by the tension between singularity and reiteration that illustrates how the spiral of time, the heterotemporality that Koʻolau, Piʻilani and Kaleimanu inhabit and foster, is woven not only into the folding cliffs of the Kalalau Valley but into the fabric of the world at large right from its very beginning. The mountain, having risen 'through the plated shells of the globe', shares with the spoken word the eventual singularity of the *parole*: hence the ineluctable solitude of both the volcano and the word 'in the moment it is spoken'. And yet are both, despite their concrete haecceity, also repetitions of forerunners and by that same token, precursors of followers who will repeat them like the boy Kaleimanu repeats his grandfather, and Koʻolau the birdman Lahi. As soon as Merwin moves from the biographical to the systemic, it becomes apparent that what is at stake here is a tension of event and form, singularity and reiteration, resulting in the paradox of "the pure reproducibility of a pure event" (Derrida 1992: 20). It is true that the word can be, and has to be, conceived as a singular event, "meaning what it means only then and meaning it only I once" (FC 47);

but at the same time, its apparently unique meaning can solely emerge through the compliance to *formal* constraints of repeatable patterns. To be intelligible, the word must be articulated

> with the same syllables that have arisen
> and have formed and been uttered before again and again
>   somewhere in the past to mean something of the same nature
> but different something continuing and transmitted
>   but with refractions something recognized in its changes
> something remembered from what is no longer there
>   and behind it something forgotten as the beginning
> is forgotten and as the dream vanishes the present
>   mountain is moving at its own pace at the end
> of its radius it is sailing in its own time
>   with the earth turning away under it as the day
> turns under a word and it came late as a word comes late
>   with a whole language behind it by the time it is spoken. (ibid.)

In the itineraries of the spoken word, then, the utterance-events relate to each other like Kaleimanu and his grandfather: 'like but not all the same', 'something of the same nature but different', 'something continuing but with refractions'. And obviously, the geological matter of which the planet is made partakes of the very same oxymoronic repetitive singularity. Why else should the opening lines of the lengthy quotation mentioned earlier describe the process of linguistic articulation as the combination of syllables that have 'arisen' and 'formed' exactly like the mountain itself that stands at the very beginning of creation? Indeed, the volcanic peak, once coagulated and ossified, is subjected to the forces of erosion, in that respect "following its elders the earlier usages | already invisible" (ibid.) except as "a submerged convoy [that] was continuing | the voyage consonants of an archaic language" (FC 48) under the sea. Linguistic obsolescence – 'earlier usages', 'archaic language' – and geological erosion coincide as the planet itself consists of 'plated shells' as well as 'ancient syllables' (FC 53) that assemble and disassemble to form a deeply perforated archipelagic gutter text made of "the line of faded atolls" (FC 53).

Going back to the volcanic origins of the Hawai'ian Islands in "the time before time" (FC 48), Merwin's text continues to condense and reassemble the genesis account of the *Kumulipo*, moving through the different stages of life's progress along the spiral of time and consistently suffusing "geological time" (Burt 2015: 16) with linguistic enunciation: a cosmogony in which matter and word, physis and logos, are inseparably entangled. Moreover, the birth of Hawai'i and the arrival of life and, finally, people on the islands are in multiple ways connected with the planet and the globe alike. Thus the advent of Pele, "the goddess of fire" (FC 53), coincides in Merwin's account with vastly discrepant progresses made

> by Arthur sailing for Iceland and by Merlin
> versed in the turnings of Western islands and by Brendan
> and the animals with him in the small ark of his summer
> and then by Charlemagne's veterans in the dark of Europe
> still furred in its forest that harked back to the ice. (FC 55)

Clearly this chronicle is deliberately oblivious of chronology and, more than that, of the difference between myth and history, inserting Arthur and Merlin into the same timeline as Charlemagne. Such a blurring of the demarcations of apparently distinct domains repeats (or prepares for) the porosity that Kaleimanu perceives between the real and the fictional. In this medium of blurry temporality Hawai'i is rendered part of the larger world so that Pele coincides with mythical and historical figures from other worlds. Later on, the insertion of the islands into a/the world system is consolidated through the trans-oceanic traffic, by English traders, of sandalwood from Hawai'i to China. In this trade triangle, Hawai'i serves as supplier of a rare and highly prized raw material whose extraction is systematically enforced by the profiteering local elite who enjoy a period of heightened conspicuous consumption:

> The years from 1811 to 1828 saw the sandalwood boom in Hawaii when the Hawaiian aristocracy lived high for a while on the profits of sandalwood cut by the common people: fourteen foreign sailing-ships and the best silks, liquors, tableware and clothing of Europe were among the purchases of the Hawaiian chiefs paid for in sandalwood. (Shineberg 1967: 9)

Merwin's rendition highlights how this quasi-feudalistic splendour comes at the expense of the ecosystem as well as the majority of Hawai'ians who are reduced to serfdom:

> The chiefs bought on credit to be paid in sandalwood |
> and the chiefs' collectors dug the commoners out of their
> family gardens and sent them farther all the time
> into the steep forests with axes to fill the quotas
> of sandalwood [...]
> [...] and their farms went to ruin while they were gone.
> (FC 78)

And while the local aristocracy "enjoyed the profits thus taken from the islands under them | [...] the ruin went before them and climbed the mountains" (FC 77). The ruthless exploitation of both labour and natural resources leads to mass starvation and large-scale deforestation that after the collapse of the trade around 1830 becomes the stuff of 'legend' among the commoners who recall how "the cutters | pulled up every sandalwood seedling they could find" (FC 78). These 'legends' of devastation wreaked upon the mountain forests and its inhabitants are not primarily focused on the effects of foreign invasion or settler colonialism but of the indigenous *kapu* system of hereditary privilege, religious prohibition and draconian punishment: a "merciless web of caste and ceremony | of ritual and dread and sacrifice" (FC 79).

The commoners' legends are not insurrectionary rallying cries but rather registrations of defeats, losses and destruction. In this sense they can be read as narrative reversals of the creation myth that Merwin lifts from the *Kulumipo*: instead of the proliferation of ever more, ever new life forms at the dawn of time, the sandalwood trade engenders the disappearance of entire species, and along with them a whole 'historical nature', a cultural mode of human interaction with, and embeddedness within, the *oikeios* (Moore 2015: 29) that in traditional Hawaiian philosophy is centred on the concept of land as *a'ina*, 'that which nourishes'. In that tradition, the ideal subject position, both individually and communally, is that of the *hoa'ina*: "A friend, caretaker, partner who is tied to and bound to a'ina" (Aikau 2019: 84). In the process of coercive labour extraction and deforestation, the praxis of *hoa'ina* comes under siege as the elaborate autochthonous technique of taro farming gets almost completely lost because "those | who still had strength for growing taro and mending terraces | and sluices and cleaning the channels were compelled to travel | far into the mountains for the receding sandalwood" (FC 84). As we have seen, *The Folding Cliffs* rehearses the creation myth of the *Kumulipo* with special emphasis on the importance that volcanic forces have in the genesis of the world. All the more it is significant that the survey of Hawaiian history up to the late nineteenth century artfully returns to the volcanic; but what might appear as a coming full circle is rather a vicious cycle: for the volcanic comes back as destructive artifice, as instrument of ecocidal extractivism and agrarian monoculture after the end of the sandalwood trade: "There were plantations of coffee | wide marshes of rice and the irresistible poison | and imperial promises of sugar with the volcanic | sounds and smells of its mills" (FC 85). The volcanic syllables of the early stages of world-creation are thus travestied in the hissing of life-devouring dark satanic mills.

Meanwhile, the 'language' of the material world that resounded all through the ages of 'the time before time' resiliently hibernates in the remote recesses where the fugitive patients of Hansen's disease hide from governmental policing and retain or regain, for the duration of their precarious idyll, a self-styled praxis of *hoa'ina*. Consistent with Merwin's emphasis on the indispensable nexus between social and ecological equity, this convivial praxis encompasses the human and the non-human alike. New arrivals to the commune are treated with an amount of hospitality that makes one newcomer feel as if he had entered a traditional tale:

> but what surprised me
> almost as much is the way those who were here before us
> in the lower valley have behaved toward us and how

good they have been to us we have heard in the stories
    that people once treated each other this way but I thought
that was long ago and probably was made up. (FC 205)

Joining the commune, then, amounts to joining a cultural revival that entails a stepping into both the past ('long ago') and the legendary ('in the stories'). Paradoxically it is the disease that enables such a recuperative re-enactment of a tradition that harks back to periods before not only European and North American settler colonial intervention but also the imposition of the rigid *kapu* system. The idealized conviviality of the fugitive community in the Kalalau Valley is therefore a utopian secession from manifold forms of oppression and an experiment in self-government. It is more specifically a retrieval not of paradise but of paradigms lost as exemplified by the reappropriation of traditional agricultural techniques: "Puheliko has restored a small taro pond | that had been abandoned down there a long time ago | and they all went and planted the first taro with him | and then ate and drank and danced" (FC 206). The revival of the concept and praxis of *hoaʻina*, then, comes through the solidarity of outcastes and the communal sustainable interaction with(in) the *oikeios*, understood as "the creative, generative, and multi-layered relation of species and environment [...] through which humans act – and are acted upon by the whole of nature – in our environment-making" (Moore 2015: 15). In the Kalalau community, this praxis of 'environment-making' is premised on and simultaneously generative of the *hoaʻina* paradigm, implying a perceptive openness to the submerged creative language of the land itself. It is Piʻilani in particular who acts as a paragon of this kind of perceptiveness, listening to the valley's "syllables [that] floated past out there like butterflies and she | tried to catch the sounds" (FC 279), or to a mountain stream's "colorless syllables" as they "hurried past her" (FC 39). What is most resonant, however, is the silence, the "sleep of the mountain" (FC 43), that Piʻilani lucidly hears and that subtly connects her to the creation myth and the origins of the Hawaiian world: "She heard the darkness of the mountain under her | all the way to the underside of the sea floor" (FC 37). In Frazier's translation of Sheldon's rendition of Piʻilani's testimony, both Koʻolau and Piʻilani are geologically framed: the former only bears the name of a volcano, but the latter actually embodies topography with her "back as straight as a cliff". It is these associations that link Merwin's protagonists not only to the planet but more than that to the cosmogonic dimensions of the *Kumulipo*. Carson's playful postulation of some 'link between character and geology' is here fully grounded in a mode of world and subject making that is alternate both to the dominant script of major cosmopolitan modernity and to the rigidities of the appalling autochthonous. The planet becomes here not only a verb (as in the other volcanic verse novels discussed earlier) but collective praxis.

3

In/verse Britain: The poetics of the post-nation

The contemporary verse novel coexists, collaborates and to some extent, no doubt, competes with the prose novel in its maximalist, often interlaced 'plot-of-globalization' format. With their planetary deep-time scope, the texts discussed in the previous section arguably have some affinities with those maximalist "world texts" (Ercolino 2014: 14) that have received much attention in (world-)literary studies as indicators of a transnational turn in literary praxis leading to the emergence of the allegedly new genre of the "world novel" (Irr 2014: 175). Verse novels, however, are also capable and prone to write the nation with a difference. They thus live along also with those more conventional and 'provincial' novels that keep "pinning the story at the centre of the nation-state" (Moretti 1996: 56). Even if the latter has never, not even in the period of the 'rise of the novel', been figured as a self-enclosed unit but a porous integral part of a much larger world, the centrality of the nation as imagined community keeps defining and delimiting the thematic scope of a significant portion of novels even in the age of globalization. The resurgence of ideological nationalism, frequently posing counterfactually as 'deglobalization', has newly re-enlivened the nation-and-novel nexus as, for example, in the British context the return of the condition-of-England novel in the wake of Brexit indicates. In works like Jonathan Coe's *Middle England*, Patrick Neate's *Jerusalem* or Sam Byers' *Perfidious Albion*, nationalism is exposed as a national malaise that those writers, paradoxically, address within a formal tradition that is itself national. In the following pages I would like to attend to a number of verse novels and novellas – Kae Tempest's *Let Them Eat Chaos*, Bernardine Evaristo's *The Emperor's Babe*, Patience Agbabi's *Telling Tales* and Malene NourbeSe Philip's *Zong!* – that perform the ostensibly novelistic function of 'writing the nation' with a difference: namely by inverting it in verse.

That all these texts have been written by women (or in the case of Tempest, a non-binary author), three of whom are Black or person of colour, will be discussed in the conclusion to this section.

3.1 A million epiphanies now: Kae Tempest's *Let Them Eat Chaos*

Kae[1] Tempest's *Let Them Eat Chaos* (2016) is a long narrative spoken-word poem that "was written to be read aloud" (C n.p.). Simultaneously issued as a book and as a record with a minimalist score of electronic beats as a backdrop to Tempest's energetic rap performance, *Let Them Eat Chaos* appears as a dense verse novella that in spite of its relative brevity (the performance takes short under an hour) all the same 'does the job' that is conventionally ascribed to a wholly different and much more bulky genre, namely the 'state-of-the-nation novel'. To call Tempest's text a verse *novella* rather than a verse *novel* is owed not so much to its scanty length but to its narrative specifics. Centred on a highly significant single and singular incident on which the denouement of the story hinges, *Let Them Eat Chaos* conspicuously fits the canonical Goethean definition of the form of the novella as the presentation of an "unheard-of occurrence" (*unerhörte Begebenheit*) (Weinig 1998: 54) and thus offers the "concentrated portrayal of one event" (ibid.) instead of the sprawling spread of multiple plots and constellated settings that the apparatus of the novel affords. Nonetheless it could be argued that, despite its novella-specific concentration, Tempest's text contains in its folds the multitudes of a novel without fully fleshing them out. For *Let Them Eat Chaos* fulfils the functions that some of the most influential social formalist approaches in the twentieth century have assigned to the novel: the evocation of an imagined community whose actually unconnected members are articulated by nothing but the basic fact of their "steady, anonymous, simultaneous activity" in homogeneous empty time (Anderson 1991: 26); or the configuration of the plurality of socially coexistent linguistic, stylistic and ideological registers in the text's realist rendition of the heteroglossia and inconclusive dialogicity of modern life (Bakhtin); or the shaping of an as yet amorphous but virulent common imaginary of a latent planetary connectedness (Ngai).

---

[1]In 2019, the writer formerly known as Kate Tempest asserted their gender as being non-binary and assumed the name Kae Tempest.

The state of the nation in verse

As if to rub in its claim to be an alternative to the novel form, Tempest's text bears striking narrative similarities with one of the epitomic specimens of the new social realism in twenty-first-century British writing, John Lanchester's *Capital* (2012). In that polyphonic novel a cast of rather unconnected characters take turns as focalizers and protagonists of their respective 'individual' sub-plots; they are held together by the mere circumstance that they all happen to live, largely unbeknownst to one another, in the same street in a traditionally modest, now rapidly gentrifying London neighbourhood. Of course, for the reader there are more connections than that since all those disparate lives are in one way or other affected, and in many cases transformed, by the one historical event in whose wake they unfold: the 2008 financial crash. That crisis provides the connecting tissue which assembles all these individual voices into the "panoramic view of a selected collective" (Yesilbas 2020: 130). By that token, "the metonymic structure proliferates and ramifies into a choral story involving the entwined lives of the characters cohabiting in that one street" (Bernard 2015). And this, exactly, could also serve for a precis of *Let Them Eat Chaos*. Like Lanchester's narrator, Tempest's speaker zooms in on a cast of characters who apparently have no other connection but their accidental residence in the same street. But again, there is more: all of them are suffering from insomnia so that the intrusive speaker of the poem, effortlessly sneaking in and out of the privacy of bedrooms and kitchens in the small hours, catches them half or fully awake each at the same exact moment in homogeneous empty time: 4:18 a.m. However, unlike *Capital*, Tempest's verse novella will not culminate in a 'panoramic view' but rather in a fractal geometry that does not stop short at the articulation of the seven individual segments into a socius but rather evokes an assemblage of interrelations that enfold entire galaxies as well as the tiniest "miniscule molecules" (C 70) in a space that is void but connective: a gutter text that is constituted through the tension of the molecular and the molar. Instead of reproducing or updating the nation as imagined community (as Lanchester does along with a whole range of twenty-first-century condition-of-Britain novelists), Tempest places their characters into a much vaster context, one that not only dissolves the circumscribed identities of detached individuals but also de-insularizes the bounded national community by inserting it into a fully planetary horizon in which cosmic dimensions (as we have seen them in the volcanic verses of especially Wendt, Merwin and Ngugi) are blended with a transnational historical depth and scope that recalls the panoramic vistas of Walcott and Carson. After reading Merwin, it is difficult not to feel reminded of the *Kumulipo* (and, by extension, the genre of the creation myth in general) when *Let Them Eat Chaos* opens as a full cosmogony, albeit one with a twist, with the undisturbed darkness of a universal void before the creation of the world:

> Picture a vacuum.
>
>   An endless and unmoving blackness
>
> Peace
>
> Or the absence, at least
>   of terror
>
> Now,
>   in amongst all this space,
> see that speck of light in the furthest corner,
>   gold as a pharaoh's deathbox
>
> Follow that light with your tired eyes.
>   It's been a long day, I know, but look –
>
>   watch as it flickers. (C 1)

From this initial little speck of light, precariously flickering 'in the furthest corner' of the vast darkness, first the sun and then the planets gradually come into view until "our Earth" (ibid.) emerges in all its precarity and beauty: "Its blueness soothes the sharp burn in your eyes | its contours remind you of | love. || That soft roundness. | The comfort of ocean and landmass. | Picture the world" (C 2). Arguably, this is an ekphrastic rendition of the 'Blue Marble' that, unlike its visual equivalents from the NASA corpus, does not feign seamless continuity but instead through excessive line breaks foregrounds its segmentive make-up and thereby engages the reader as co-producer of the text. Accordingly, 'picture' is a verb, not a noun, in Tempest's verses: 'Picture the world'. With an economy akin to the account in Genesis rather than the Hawai'ian chant, the initial 'vacuum' has been transformed into 'the world' within the space of some sparse twenty-odd verses. Who has made it? Here, no creator god is at work but the imaginative capacity of the speaker's addressee who is impelled to do the 'picturing' that will produce the world. Right from the start, reading (or in the case of performance: listening) is thus framed as an act of both envisioning and world-making. Inasmuch as they frame reception as productive, Tempest's opening verses position the act of reading within the paradigms of the gutter text as co-constructive gap negotiation. This assumes a particularly active reader since "the gutter – the gaps between panels – requires work on the part of the reader of a different nature than other narrative forms" (Gardner 2006: 800). In Tempest's lines, this active and productive mode of reading is rendered as fully fledged world-making, and it therefore has to entail a high amount of responsibility for the world that it makes. Against the tendency to shy away from responsibility, to complacently assert that *"it's not up to us to make this place a better land"* (C 71; emphasis in the original), the text rallies its whole energy in a culminating call, a secularized version of the Great Commission (but in a less solemn register, of the old Ian Dury song, too), to "wake up | and love more" (C 72).

Read in biblical terms, Tempest's text thus opens with Genesis but does not close on Apocalypse but the Great Commission given by Jesus on his ascension: a call to conversion. This ties in with the nature of the novella's climactic 'unheard-of event' in the evanescent moment of an urban "baptism" (C 66) that connects into a temporary community the "seven perfect strangers" (C 64) whom the speaker had earlier visited in the intimacy of their insomnia. All through the main part of the text, these seven unrelated neighbours figure as distinct and disparate individuals each caught up in their respective "lonely homes" (C 63). To some extent, then, Tempest seems to comply with the protocols of the condition-of-Britain novel when they assembles in their text a cast of apparently representative figures that may be read as stand-ins for entire social trends or groups – from the gentrification victim who has to give up her suddenly unaffordable flat to the successful PR manager; from the exhausted care-worker to the successful but stressed-out professional single mother. As the speaker's zoom closes in from the planetary to the local dimension, the focalized street somewhere in London with its diverse and stratified spectrum of houses and inhabitants initially seems to function as a synecdoche of the socius at large:

Smart flats. Rough flats.
Can't-get-enough-cat flats.
You know, seventeen cat flaps.
Rich flats, broke flats.
New flats.
Old flats.
Luxury bespoke flats.
And this-has-got-to-be-a-joke flats.

Pensioners, toddlers.
Immigrants and Englishmen.
Family with six kids.
Single businesswoman. (C 7)

As if to re-enact Anderson's model in which the imagined community of the nation gets articulated in the medium of the novel's "spectacular possibilities for the representation of simultaneous action in homogeneous empty time" (Anderson 1991: 194), Tempest ensures right at the start (and will repeatedly re-emphasize) that the isolated insomniacs are all held together by one common moment precisely located in clocked time: "It's 4:18 a.m. | At this very moment, on this very street, | seven different people in seven different flats | are wide awake" (ibid.). But it should be clear that *Let Them Eat Chaos* is neither a realist novel nor a revived village sketch in verse. This does not mean that its social acuity is not serious and committed; however, it is pervaded (invaded?) by a sense of detachment that almost naturally derives from its cosmic opening that puts everything that follows 'into perspective' and endows everyday existence with a sense of the provisional. In this respect it is important to note how the transition from the cosmic to the quotidian is structured as an immersion of a reader that is addressed as one who comes from elsewhere and is not (yet) fully at home in the world even without knowing it:

> Where have you landed?
>
>   Uncurl yourself.
> [...]
>
> This is a city.
> Let's call her
>
>   *London.*
> And these
> are the only
> times
>
>   you have known. (C 4–5)

What ensues is a categorical incongruity between accidental social existence and essential being – an incongruity that provides the substratum of a situational transcendence (as discussed by Karl Mannheim) reminiscent of the "transcendental homelessness" for which, according to the young Lukács, "the novel form is, like no other, an expression" (Lukács 1988: 41). Importantly, however, the social reality to whose representation the main textual body of *Chaos* is devoted remains visibly embedded into the much larger reality of the planet in space. Thus, whatever happens (or doesn't happen) in the privacy of the various bedrooms and in the lives lived (or not lived) in them, is always already nested in that ultimately ulterior reality of which the social actors, immersed as they are in their individual daily lives, remain largely unaware. The text thus establishes a cosmos (that is, an ordered, patterned world) consisting of a set of forms understood with Kornbluh as 'composed relationalities', at whose outer circumference "the planets are dangled around it [the sun] | and held in their intricate dance" (C 1), while "in the breeze" at street level "the beer cans and crisp packets dance with the dead leaves" (C 7).

Clima(c)tic truth events

Tempest's establishing shot ensures that chaos, despite its prominence in the book's title and in the experiential life worlds of the characters, is only an illusion as the structure of the 'dance' appears pervasive at all scales in infinite extension and infinite regress. Behind the surface of anomy and entropy, the composed relationalities of an ordered cosmos persist like a Va in waiting. Therefore, what appears to endow Tempest's text with a theological dimension that would encourage a virtually Christian self-positioning 'in the world but not of it' can in a planetary reading be interpreted as a secular reappropriation of eschatology as such: the apparently transcendent is in fact part of the immanent, even if an unseen, unexperienced and to some extent unrealized part. No clear demarcation exists between the seemingly disparate quotidian and the ordered cosmic planes: in outer space the planets 'dance' around the sun, just as in the empty street at night the litter 'dances' with the fallen leaves. This is not metaphysics but rather a fractal geometry as proposed by Wai Chee Dimock, for whom the repetition or reoccurrence of patterns and formal idiosyncrasies at multiple scales establish the relationality of a multilayered "'nested' formation" where the local – is this case, the London street – "is not purely indigenous but a 'cradling' of the global within one particular site: a sequence of diffusion, osmosis and readaptation" (Dimock 2007: 277). 'Diffusion' and 'osmosis' suggest a permeability and porosity between the various levels or scales; in this vein in *Chaos*, the larger order, invisible at the level of immersion, can and will recurrently break into the everyday: "At any given moment in the middle of a city | there's a million epiphanies occurring" (C 5). Even though Tempest, all through the verse novella, draws heavily on both the theological and the poetologic traditions, they uses the term 'epiphany' neither in the established religious sense of a sudden self-disclosure of the divine, nor as the flash-like revelation of the meaningfulness of the profane so typical of modernist aesthetics from Joyce and Woolf to Walter Benjamin and John Berger. The epiphanies in *Chaos* are strictly immanent as they consist of nothing but the irruption of the actually extant but unseen *form* ('composed relationality') of the world into the characters' experiential horizons that are devoid of any kind of relationality and hence, strictly speaking, unformed. Like all epiphanies, the ones in *Chaos* transform *chronos* into *kairos*, and moreover, a space that separates into a space that connects. Accordingly, they are not primarily contemplative but to the contrary intersubjective performatives of communion whose participants transform, for the duration of the evanescent event, their separateness into the experience of a gutter, that is, a gulf that connects: "The distance | that we share" (C 71). It is the enactment and full consummation of this communion in the narrative world through which *Chaos* departs from the protocols of novels like *Capital* that principally comply with the model that Anderson has suggested for nineteenth-century writing. In the diegetic world of these texts the nation is not manifestly performed; instead, it is the reader who is impelled to hold together the disparate subplots configured in homogeneous empty time, and to imagine a (national) community that for the intradiegetic characters remains by and large latent. The same latency is of course experienced by the readers themselves in their own social lives: The "secular, historically clocked imagined community" is "performed in silent privacy, in the lair of the skull" (Anderson 1991: 35). Not so in *Chaos*, where the hitherto isolated seven insomniacs are subjected to a collective truth-event that disrupts the regularity of clock time and "animates the frozen moment" (C 63) of 4:18 a.m. by exposing the "seven perfect strangers" (C 64) to "a shared thing, theirs as much as anyone's" that will make them "see each other" and join into a "chorus" (C 65).

What is this truth-event? According to Alain Badiou, from whose diction I have borrowed the term as a useful alternative to 'epiphany', truth-events are "*immanent breaks* with the situation" (Badiou 2001: 42; emphasis in the original), that is, with the given historical and sociocultural environment one is forced to inhabit. Into this normalized and routinized being, something may irrupt that exceeds and explodes the situation: an encounter with a newness that occurs as an event that is "beyond what is", "interrupts repetition" (Badiou 2003: 46) and makes "something appear in a world which had not existed in it previously" (Badiou 2006: 285). A truth is therefore "something extra, something that happens in situations as something that they and the usual ways of behaving in them cannot account for" (Badiou 2001: 41). Situational transcendence is thus not, as in Karl Mannheim, a disposition that is condemned to constantly register a lack in the given, but instead a full (if evanescent) experience of the unforeseen. For Badiou, the privileged sites of truth-events are "the arts, the matheme, love, and political invention" (Badiou 1999: 86) as instances with a potential to a maximal intensity "that changes your being as you are dragged away and come to depend upon an absolute elsewhere" (Badiou 2007: 126). While this is no doubt exactly what happens to Tempest's characters, the actual occasion for this kind of exposure to 'an absolute elsewhere' sits very awkwardly with Badiou's catalogue of possible areas where truth-events may occur. In *Chaos* it is neither love nor politics, science or the arts that 'drags the characters away' but – the weather. It is a rainstorm, a "force 10 gale" (C 71), that drives the non-sleepers from their isolated flats into the lightning-illuminated rain-drenched street where "they see their city || new" (C 64), and gradually expose themselves to the event:

        Shielding their eyes at first
            but then
                    tipping their necks back, unhunching their shoulders,
            opening their bodies up to
                        the storm. (C 65)

Of course, this can be read as an instance of the sublime and hence an aesthetic experience. More than anything, however, it is an occasion for communion, the banding of a community that need not be imagined as it is enacted and performed: 'They walk towards each other | dragging themselves like the wounded | and band close, close | shocked and laughing' (C 65). Unlike in the realist novel, the community is not happening behind the backs of those who form it. What they are not clearly aware of, however, is that they have been summoned by the storm – an actor in its own right that speaks of itself in the plural: a multiple that, following Sianne Ngai, by the very token of its pronoun embodies connexionism, and in fact declares explicitly that it is their mission to alert people to the perils of self-imposed insularity, and the fact of their implication in the larger world:

We're not the dread storm that will end things.
We're just your playful
            gale-force friend
                in the end times
Come to remind you
        that you're not an island
Life is much broader
        than borders. (C 43)

There is, then, a lesson in what the thunder said, and that admonition addresses the individual in their debilitating self-isolation as much as the insular nation in its strained self-sufficiency within "the walls of this fortress" (C 43). The seven neighbours are interpellated into the realization and consummation of their being-in-the-world by the storm's invitation to "come dance in the deluge" (C 41) and thereby to connect with the cosmos at all its scales; after all, we have already seen that the 'dance' serves for a pattern that is threaded throughout the world, from the planets circling the sun to the litter in the street. To 'dance' is therefore a connexionist act of communion in which the demarcations of bounded selves dissolve and individuals "spill like the flood" (C 41). At the scale of the polity, the same pattern operates as the chimera of national autarky gets blown away by the storm and gives way to the insight, voiced earlier in the text by one of the insomniacs, that not only 'no man', as John Donne has it, but also "no isle is an island" (C 18). Against the nationalist "tunnel vision" (C 71), then, the insight that "life is much broader than borders"; against the "myth of the individual" (C 72), the collective exposure to the 'shared thing' that no one need nor can possess – the stormy truth-event.

Such events, for Badiou, cannot be deliberately produced but like visitations require "an ontological passivity, [...] an uprooting abandonment" (Badiou 2007: 126) to the singular encounter. All the same they demand an active and sustained engagement after the ephemeral event has passed. What Badiou calls 'fidelity' is the actual *ethical* core of his whole edifice: the one to whom a truth-event happens has to decide whether or not he or she is willing to enter into the laborious "truth-process" that is based on "the decision to relate henceforth to the situation *from the perspective of its evental supplement*" (Badiou 2001: 41; emphasis in the original). Fidelity means not only to remain truthful and faithful to the event but also to treat that event as a turning point with consequences for one's future conduct in the social world. The process of fidelity can only begin when the event has been appropriately "nominated": It "must be named to occur for a being-faithful, thus for a truth" (Badiou 2003: 75). In this light, the last section of *Chaos* offers a sustained act of 'nomination' in which the text, as it were, testifies to the truth at its centre, a truth that attains a quasi-anagogic dimension as it confirms, against the 'myth of the individual' and 'the distance that we share', the intricate interconnectedness of the world in its entirety and at its multiple scales and layers:

> All things are, in their way, communicating.
> We're just sparks
> tiny parts
> of a bigger constellation. (C 70)

Apophenia revisited

By suggesting that the movement of the 'dance' is not limited to just one scale but much more deeply transitive, the text has subtly prepared for this pervasive yet largely unnoticed interconnectedness of everything with everything else: a world-wide connexionism that assumes one vast composed relationality that forms a total, all-encompassing 'constellation' into which every thing is inserted, and to which every thing contributes. Importantly, the gap – the gutter – remains not only visible but indeed constitutive of the text in its very structure: the wide empty spaces on the pages of *Let Them Eat Chaos* make for a sprinkling effect, where the distance between the verses and even individual words is as much foregrounded as their connectedness. Wendt, we have seen, retrieves a similar vision of a deep-structural planetary gutter relationality from the vital tradition of the Va. By contrast, Tempest has to articulate their own version of connexionism without such a reference point. They hence has to produce an interconnected world through their own acts of pattern recognition, and claim their validity through their own apophenic assertions. When sceptically defined as the "seeing of patterns where there is actually only noise" (Bratton 2013: 3), apophenia is a delusion: it imposes counterfactual order and form onto factual chaos and formlessness, and postulates relationalities where there may be none. However, for a discussion of Tempest's writing, the problem of apophenia is not so much one of epistemology or truth claims but of ideology. In this respect, apophenia offers a response, in fact a remedy, to a perceived entropy and its attendant phobia; it is therefore the exact opposite of the paranoia – the claustrophobic fear with stifling overdetermination – that served as the hallmark of the postmodernity of the Cold War period (cf. Jameson 1995: 63–79). In writers like Thomas Pynchon, William Gibson or Don DeLillo the slogan "everything is connected" (Pynchon 2000: 820) epitomizes the dread of a stifling hidden order behind the visible, and the threat of a sinister molar takeover. In contrast, the same slogan in the writings of Kae Tempest appears to soothingly confirm that not everything is just random. Paranoia assumes that "the discovery of connections is identical to the discovery of plots" (Bersani 1989: 102), whereas apophenia hopes for the discovery of precisely these connections. It is plotting – the construction of narrative syntagms – that remains the last resort of apophenic desire for what, with Jürgen Habermas, could be called "experiential contingency containment" [*erfahrungsnahe Kontingenzeindämmung*] (Habermas 1988: 93). In this respect, the author turns out as the ultimate plotter whose "careful construction of narratives would seem to suggest that any contingency within them is intentional" (Kneale 2011: 181).

The apophenic craving for a "spontaneous perception of connections and meaningfulness in unrelated things" (Gibson 2003: 115) is according to Hito Steyerl symptomatic of a cultural formation marked by corporate information overkill: "If paranoia was a standard Cold War narrative, apophenia happens when narrative breaks down and causality has to be recognized – or invented – across a cacophony of spam, spin, fake, and gadget chatter" (Steyerl 2018: 5). However, the patterns made out in the white noise of galaxies of data are not entirely phantasmagoric; in fact, there is a spillover from the patterns that governmental, police and corporate statisticians recognize in the data universe to the embodied life worlds of actual people: "In practice you become coextensive with the data-constellation you project. Social scores of all different kinds [...] as well as commercial and military pattern-of-life observations impact the real lives of real people" (Steyerl 2017: 60). In this logic, paranoia gets in again through the backdoor as apophenia becomes an instrument of the police (in Rancière's sense of that term). Against this development, Tempest attempts to reclaim apophenia for the political proper by profiling the insight into the pattern – the pervasiveness of the dance that gives form to the world at all scalar levels – as a truth-event that cannot be contained within the boundaries of self or nation but impels whomever it 'drags away' to 'spill like the flood' by joining the 'dance'. This in not just a simple celebration of communion but rather a recognition of an ineluctable implication in the pain of others: not just a dance but a 'dance in the deluge'. Thus the "atomized" (C 67) monadic and molecular self steps out of its isolation to acknowledge that connexionism implies, indeed depends on, responsibility in and for the world:

> The tragedy and pain
> of a person that you've never met
> is present in your nightmares,
> in your pull toward
> despair. (C 70)

Likewise, the nation can only reassert itself on the condition that it thoroughly locates itself within a worldly frame. This requires the acknowledgement that its shrinking island is "just one little clod off the mainland, sinking" (C 18), but that simultaneously the 'bigger constellation' is nothing but the composed relationalities of a multitude of "miniscule molecules" (C 70). As no isle is an island, the nation has to face its insertion and implication in the world, and most crucially, the past and present violence that it has inflicted and keeps inflicting on others:

> It was our boats that sailed,
> killed, stole and made frail
> it was our boots that stamped
> it was our courts that jailed
> and it was our fucking banks that got   bailed. (C 71)

Such a perspective implies precisely the existential incongruity, the ineluctable distance from one's accidental socio-historical location with which the poem opens as it beams the reader from the peace of the dark void of the cosmos to nocturnal London. The estrangement effects of this crashlanding are vicariously voiced by the speaker for the implied reader: "*Is this what it's come to?* | You think. || *What am I to make | of all this?*" (C 5; emphasis in the original). After immersing itself in so much privacy and intimacy, Tempest's text at the end returns to the initial distance and estrangement from socially established normalcy, but with a difference: what appears as merely vague situational incongruity without content or shape at the beginning of the verse novella, is at the end a formed and politicized relation of not-belonging to the situation: a veritable lesson learned in disidentification with what (one) is. So profound a rearrangement of desire can surely stand the criteria test for what Badiou calls a fidelity process as a specific way of *relating* to the situation 'from the perspective of its eventual supplement': "wake up | and love more".

It is important that *Let Them Eat Chaos* is a spoken-word performance that as such emphasizes its own eventual status. This strengthening of the performative and oratory aspect of poetry is part of a much larger trend, all over the Anglosphere, setting in with the emergence of poetry slams (cf. Somers-Willett 2005) and spoken-word poetry shows (D'abdon and Molebatsi 2011: 57) from the 1980s onwards. Tempest's performance, with its drum and bass score and energetic rap rhythms thus appears as a white variant of that kind of urban orature that Wendt's Vela celebrates as his own 'brand new beat'. In its own context of Brexit Britain it figures as an embellished version of the 'one-person poetry show': a format which, in the UK, has been deployed especially by Black women poets like Kat Francois or SuAndi, who use the format "to negotiate diasporic history and cultural memory in a public arena" and to "strategically challenge hegemonic notions of national identity" (Novak 2020: 325). That this challenging of hegemonic narratives of the nation through performance poetry is not restricted to Black spoken-word artists should be obvious. This is exemplified by Tempest's connexionist in-verse jeremiad that interrogates the myth of self-sufficient fortified Little Britain linking the fate of the nation with that of the imperilled planet by traversing the manifold separating yet connecting gutters that pertain between the manifold scales of the world.

3.2 'But I dreamt of creating mosaics': Bernardine Evaristo's *The Emperor's Babe*

If *Let Them Eat Chaos* is a poem that does the job of a condition-of-England novel, then Bernardine Evaristo's *The Emperor's Babe* (2001) is an in-verse postcolonial/diasporic novel that inverts that national narrative. Set in Roman-occupied Britain around the early years of the third century CE, Evaristo's text centres on Zuleika, the daughter of poor Nubian immigrants to Londinium, who at the age of eleven is spotted by a wealthy Roman aristocrat "thrice my age and thrice my girth" who marries (or rather, buys) "the nice ‖ simplex, quiet, fidelis girl" (EB 4) as a convenience. A social upstart against her own will, Zuleika first gets a crash course in upper-class conduct where she learns "how to get my amo, amas, amat right, and ditch | my second-generation plebby creole" (EB 4). She then gets installed in her husband's villa as part of the property. During the frequent and extensive absences of her husband (who prefers metropolitan Rome over peripheral Londinium), Zuleika spends much time with her streetwise childhood friends Alba and Venus until she catches the attention of Septimus Severus, the Roman emperor, who, during his military campaign against the Caledonians, makes Londinium his basecamp. Zuleika's ensuant affair with Septimus gives occasion to "some sensual poetry [...] dedicated to their loving encounters" (Rosenberg 2010: 387) but is abruptly terminated by the emperor's unexpected death on his way to the warzone, leaving the protagonist unprotected from her returning husband who retaliates for her infidelity by having her slowly poisoned.

Chick lit as imperial romance

As the (failed) bildungsroman of a Black second-generation Londoner, *The Emperor's Babe* overtly participates in one of the major traditions of diasporic and/or Black British writing (cf. Stein 2004). In this vein, numerous critics have observed that Evaristo's verse novel contributes to the figuration of "alternative visions of a hyphenated, hybrid country" that much postcolonial British writing has powerfully pitted "against the grain of the predominant narratives of the British nation" (Muñoz-Valdivieso 2010: 161). With the pleasure it obviously takes in the narrator's 'second-generation creole', *The Emperor's Babe* reinvigorates the hybridizing impetus that the heteroglot poetics of the postcolonial British novel from Sam Selvon, Buchi Emecheta, Salman Rushdie and Hanif Kureishi to Caryl Philips and Zadie Smith has foregrounded. Indeed, as Evaristo has stated herself, "the language that Zuleika uses is very now, very hip. The novel is peppered with Latin, Italian, Cockney-rhyming slang, patois, American slang, pidgin Scots-Latin, and in the case of Severus, broken English" (in McConnell 2016: 109). However, unlike Selvon's Moses, Galahad and Tolroy, or Kureishi's Karim Amir, or Smith's Samad Iqbal and Clara Bowden, Evaristo's characters don't live in London but Londinium, and in their diegetic world they don't speak creolized English but (some kind of) Latin. While it is true that this circumstance is easily forgotten in the reading process of a text that is, after all, written in English not Latin, the other main difference between Evaristo's and (most) other postcolonial texts remains obvious all through: its being written in verse. If there is an aspect of *The Emperor's Babe* that has been extensively and insightfully discussed, it is arguably the deliberate anachronisms with which Evaristo superimposes ancient Roman Londinium and turn-of-the-millennium London onto each other by parallelizing the multiculturalist mishmash of both these chronotopes. Antiquity, in those readings, does not simply serve as an estrangement device through which contemporary hybridities can be profiled by defamiliarization; it is also, and perhaps even more so, a reference field in its own right for Evaristo's "project to inscribe the historical black presence in London" (Cuder-Domínguez 2004: 179) by tracing that presence much, much further back than the usual landmark of post-Windrush postcolonial immigration. Zuleika, as already indicated, *is* a second-generation diasporic whose parents have moved to Britain from northern Africa. This migration of a Black family to Britain is, however, far removed from a Saidian 'voyage in'; it rather resembles a trajectory from the empire's southern periphery to its ultimate north-western outpost located on the very border of 'civilization' with a view of the heart of darkness lurking across the Thames in "the jungle that was Britannia | teeming with spirits and untamed humans" (EB 12).

The Conradian resonances are obvious here but strikingly it is the Black speaker that shudders at the thought of venturing forth into the thick of the land of the white natives: "To leave || the city wall was to risk unknown horrors" (EB 242) that surpass – like Conrad's never specified "abomination" (Conrad 2006: 6) – any atrocity that the empire may inflict upon its slaves and outcastes. No doubt, therefore, Evaristo's text playfully inverts the racist dichotomy of civilization and wilderness that underpins imperial romance from Haggard to Conrad, Doyle and beyond, but at the same time it would be equally correct to state that it simply fleshes out an inversion that is already articulated in *Heart of Darkness* itself. After all, in Conrad's text, imperial London is not only the "biggest, and greatest, town on earth" (ibid.: 3), the centre of the world, but at the same time "the monstrous town" that spreads its "brooding gloom in sunshine" (ibid.: 5). If that passes for a rough description of the Empire's capital city in the late nineteenth century, then Marlow's imaginary sketch of Roman Britannia appears to give a genealogical explanation for that essential substratum of 'darkness' that appears to cling indelibly to the metropolis which was, and somehow has remained, "one of the dark places of the earth" (ibid.: 5). In an oft-quoted passage, Marlow continues to envisage the British wilds, the jungles and swamps along the Thames, through the lens of a 'civilized man', perhaps a Roman officer or an Ovid-like exile:

> Sand-banks, marshes, forests, savages, – precious little to eat fit for a civilized man, nothing but Thames water to drink. [...] Here and there a military camp lost in a wilderness, like a needle in a bundle of hay – cold, fog, tempests, disease, exile, and death, – death skulking in the air, in the water, in the bush. [...] Land in a swamp, march through the woods, and in some inland post feel the savagery, the utter savagery, had closed round him, – all that mysterious life of the wilderness that stirs in the forest, in the jungles, in the hearts of wild men. (ibid.: 6)

Such a projection of antique Britain as a zone of underdevelopment is by no means original to Conrad, who in fact builds his imagery of swamps and 'savages' on a much older tradition of English historiography from Bede to Milton, where Roman occupation regularly features as a civilizing mission *avant la lettre*, and the imperial colonizers "as severe but efficient teachers" (Wiemann 2007: 53), of whom, as Milton puts it, "we have cause not to say much worse, than that they beate us into some civilitie" (Milton 1991: 60). In this scenario, the position of Zuleika – not in spite but because of her migrant family background – on the privileged Roman side of the colonial divide introduces a further inversion of contemporary British conditions: in the virtual settler colony of Britannia, being autochthonous implies no prestige or entitlement but to the contrary equates aboriginal inferiority, as Zuleika's response to a surprise gift from her absentee husband, Felix, drastically illustrates:

> Two ginger girls arrived, captured
> up north, the freckled sort (typical
>
> of Caledonians). Felix ordered them
> before he left for Rome.
>
> When approached, they clawed the air
> with filthy talons, mucus ran in clotted rivers
>
> from pinched little noses,
> their eyes were splattered mosquitoes,
>
> courtesy of Tranio, to shut them up.
> Fascinating, so vile, yet something
>
> just for me, id and ego. Pets. (EB 55)

In Conrad's fantasy, the ultimate horror consists in the unacknowledged correlation, the repressed "remote kinship" (Conrad 2006: 36), between the primeval outside and the atavistic forces and drives that lurk beneath the sheen of civilization. The two 'fascinating' and 'vile' Caledonians for a brief moment confront shallow Zuleika, "the self-regarding 'babe' or 'it girl' whose world is reflected in the pages of the 'Daily Looking Glass'" (Scafe 2015: 220), with her potential psychic depths. Yet the 'id girl' soon gives way again to the 'it girl' as, on the very next day, Zuleika has her new 'girls' thoroughly bathed, oiled, perfumed and with the help of "hairdresser, dressmaker, manicurist" transformed into "little ladies" who, in the course of time, "I hope will become – I my devotees" (EB 56). The civilizing mission here boils down to grooming the Black woman's burden to the fickle aspiration for popularity as a substitute for fame (of which more later). Marlow and Kurtz heroically fail to ward off the lure of the primeval, and this failure forms the tragic fulcrum of imperial romance that, in all its equivocality, is unmistakably outspoken about one thing: the sublime magnitude and abysmal depth of both the jungle and the self. By contrast, Zuleika's "world [is] *so* small, inside and outside" (EB 220; emphasis in the original), and it is only her own personal summer of love with the Roman emperor that opens up her universe a little more. Apart from this affair, Zuleika's small world, incarcerated in the golden cage of marriage, consists of shopping sprees, conspicuous consumption, ganging up with her two childhood friends Alma and Venus and a rather vague aspiration to somehow achieve fame, "to leave a whisper of myself in the world" (EB 159). Zuleika in this light resembles less the heroine of some inverted imperial romance but much more a chick lit protagonist "seeking personal fulfilment in a romance-consumer-comedic vein" (Knowles 2004: 2). Or perhaps it would be more accurate and productive to think of Evaristo's verse novel as a form-ideological hybrid that pits imperial romance against chick lit without any of the two definitely winning the day.

By the time of the publication of *The Emperor's Babe*, chick lit had come fully into its own especially in the UK in the wake of the immense success of Helen Fielding's *Bridget Jones's Diary* (1996). Chick lit, a specific subspecies of "commercial women's fiction" (McNulty 2019: 440), has often, and often for good reason, been put down as a deeply conservative, hackneyed, shallow and "most trivialized literary genre" (ibid.). More specifically, it has been accused of an anti-feminist ideology that reduces femininity to a "preoccupation with Cosmopolitan culture and consumerism [...] primarily embodied in women's obsession with appearance issues" (Montoro 2012: 94), dieting and dating. Hostile critics observe that, instead of *écriture feminine*, chick lit unabashedly offers texts by, about and for "silly little women with silly little concerns" (Mazza 2006: 26). In this vein, the chick in chick lit is seen to embody "an oddly conservative approach [that] may bear out arguments made about backlash against feminism, ideology fatigue among the 'postfeminist' age group, and the persistence of anxieties about women's ambition" (Wells 2006: 57). If the chick lit text ideally follows the pattern of the bildungsroman told in the confessional mode of first-person narration, then it does so by seriously downgrading the genre to a form where "the frequency of the I pronoun facilitates the heroine's development, or, as critics have claimed, produces a juvenile solipsism" (Harzewski 2006: 38).

The right to be stupid

How does that contemporary genre tie in with the imperial romances of such writers as Rider Haggard, Conan Doyle, Edgar Wallace, Frank Savile, whose potboilers invariably combine puerile misogyny with aggressively racist (and more often than not, classist) fantasies of white male supremacy and mastery? In many respects these two genres appear as far apart as possible on the spectrum of formulaic literature and yet there is one perhaps somewhat inconspicuous commonality that might prove useful and fruitful for my discussion of *The Emperor's Babe*, and of Evaristo's politics as a Black feminist writer working towards an in/verse Britain: both the imperial romance and the typical chick lit novel gravitate around stupidity. This may immediately be persuasive for chick lit. The stupidity charge is in fact duplicated in *The Emperor's Babe* when Zuleika's aristocratic sister-in-law dismissively summarizes her verdict on the new family member: "Cute, yes. Young, even better. | Stupid, no doubt" (EB 52). Cute, young, stupid: no wonder that authors and readers of chick lit novels full of charmingly clueless heroines frequently encourage each other not to "take offense at reviewers and critics who call Chick Lit 'fluffy,' 'frothy,' or 'dumb' " (Yardley in Montoro 2012: 165), and remind an allegedly hostile environment that "young women aren't stupid. We do actually know the difference between literature and popular fiction" (Colgan in Misler 2017:22).

In contrast, it will at first appear counterintuitive to locate stupidity as a crucial feature for the genre of imperial romance that very obviously fantasises mastery and control. This mastery, however, is routinely delegated in the texts onto the figure of the weird eccentric mastermind who, like Doyle's Professor Challenger or James de Mille's Dr Congreve, requires to be idealized through the lens of an admiring, often mystified and decisively mediocre gentleman narrator whose job it appears to be to anticipate the questions of an implied reader posited as not only puerile but (perhaps) even stupider than the narrator himself. Through his constant self-reduction to muscular virility, this type of narrator (who may, as in Rider Haggard's Allan Quatermain novels, at times coincide with the masterful hero) ensures that "the space given to any intellectual activity is minimal" in a sociocultural climate that expected that "chivalrous gentlemen were not only not very bright, but proud of it" (Girouard 1981: 166, 269). Doyle's self-described "sun-burnt, young and vigorous" Malone is a typical representative of that distrust of intellectuality paired to a puffed-up masculine physicality: "I'm fifteen stone, hard as nails, and play centre three-quarter every Saturday for the London Irish" (Doyle 2008: 21, 78). Their pronounced ignorance notwithstanding, these sporting gentleman narrators all the same claim and get their share of male bonding and general approval that appears to be their natural due. They benefit, obviously, from "the high valuation of stupidity in nineteenth-century gentlemen" (Sedgwick 1985: 223, FN4) that makes lack of intelligence a positive distinction marker. The less-than-average narrator's address, then, interpellates readers of imperial romance as beneficiaries of a set of "social webs that tie male unknowing to new forms of power" (Halberstam 2011: 58). In contemporary popular culture around the time of the publication of Evaristo's book, it was especially feminist critics who, in the wake of such blockbusters as *Forrest Gump* (1994), *Dumb and Dumber* (1994), *As Good As It Gets* (1997) or *Dude, Where's My Car?* (2000), started to register an increasing and celebratory "portrayal of regressively stupid white males [...] as a kind of Hollywood pandering to the anti-intellectual machismo of its buyer" (Boose and Burt 1997: 18). What is celebrated here is not so much stupidity as such but, as in Victorian and Edwardian imperial romance, the privilege that 'empowers' its bearers to get away with their "wilful [...] often intractable ignorance" (Jenemann 2013: 37). I have lifted this last phrase from a discussion of the cultural politics of stupidity that, proceeding from Adorno and Horkheimer, defines stupidity as "a symptom of domination, not of disability" (ibid.: 35). In the Frankfurt School tradition, stupidity is thus intimately tied in with the ideological perpetuation of dominance by way of manufacturing consent and inducing "the subject to arrest thought in platitudes, clichés, and positivist truisms" (ibid.: 40). While it is therefore apt to see stupidity as a 'symptom of domination', it is at the same time with the same plausibility a symptom of dominance, an important factor in the unequal distribution of the sensible. As Jack Halberstam has extensively discussed in view of turn-of-the-millennium popular culture, the unapologetic and often celebratory re/presentation of white male stupidity indexes certainly no individual or communal 'disability' but much rather the extent to which white male supremacy is naturalized as lived hegemony. As such it grants white men the extreme privilege of stupidity understood as "a relaxed relation to knowing" (Halberstam 2011: 63) that, in a more popular/populist format has been exposed in Michael Moore's devastating portrayal of George W. Bush in *Stupid White Men* (2001). If the early 2000s witnessed the "refashioning of the self-undermining power of 'Bushisms' themselves into a conservative way of accepting and tolerating pure stupidity" (Zupancic 2008: 34), the rise of right-wing populism in the second decade of the millennium has transformed this 'tolerance' into unabashed admiration of the kakistocracy of stupid white men, as the ascendancy of a model of hyper-entitled and hyper-offensively stupid white masculinity performed by figures like Donald Trump, Joao Bolsonaro or Matteo Salvini indicates.

Given this reading of stupidity as masculinist privilege, can chick lit, in spite of all its obvious consumerist and heteronormative ideological limitations, perhaps be seen as a complicated feminist response that stakes a claim *for women* to the 'right to stupidity' from which they have so far been exempt? What makes this move so complicated is the obvious fact that women *have* invariably been rendered as inherently 'stupid', but in a very different way and to very different exclusionary effects. Whereas male stupidity betokens jovial serenity and embodied privilege, hegemonic patriarchal scripts and the concomitant gendered knowledge formations naturalize and punish female stupidity: "Unknowing in a woman indicates a lack and a justification of a social order that anyway privileges men" (ibid.: 55). To claim stupidity as a 'right' rather than a debilitating ascription therefore interferes with the social distribution of agency options and advantages and is hence a profoundly political move. In the following reading of *The Emperor's Babe* I will suggest that Evaristo reclaims stupidity as a *universal* privilege by reactivating and refracting the male domain of imperial romance through the generic protocols of chick lit. As I will argue further down, the gutter textuality of the verse novel offers the congenial formal features for such a redistributive venture.

As we have already seen, the 'taming' of the Caledonians occurs and succeeds by way of grooming, that is, a mere surface operation. The transformation of the two 'savages' into 'little ladies' involves no pedagogy – not even in the degraded form of mechanistic behaviourist drill (as in Shaw's adaptation of the Ovidian Pygmalion story) – but only the enforced application of personal hygiene. 'Civilization' here is instant but merely cosmetic and its superficiality a far cry from the Victorian ideal of colonization as unselfish educational toil: the notorious notion of the white man's burden that the heroes of imperial romance so bravely shoulder in their mission to "humour | (Ah, slowly!) toward the light" the "new-caught sullen peoples | half devils and half child" out there in the colonial wilderness (Kipling 1922: 231). Zuleika is not interested in that kind of colonial enlightenment. There is no superior ideal that she claims to be capable of transmitting apart from the standards of fashionable looks – a 'taming' all the same as the formerly unkempt Caledonians' post-coiffeur hairdo indicates: "Their red curls piled high | are charmed serpents" (EB 56). What thus ensues is an unapologetic banalization, hence an offensive debunking, of the masculinist narrative of colonial pedagogy that here, through rigorous feminization, gets deflated to an unabashed superficiality.

Evaristo does not only debunk the paradigms of colonial pedagogy and the civilizing mission but also the perhaps most central trope of the imperial romance, namely the dramatization of the 'discovery' and exploration of the uncharted territories 'out there'. When Zuleika actually ventures forth from her '*so* small' world into the vast wilderness that encircles Londinium, her sorties occur in the form of pompous outings with the emperor and his entourage escorted by an armed guard of 300 soldiers. Crossing "the wild sloping grassland of Mayfair" and "the humid jungle at Bayswater", the picnic party sets up tent in "an overgrown clearing | where the jungle swept down at Portobello" (EB 218). Of course, the contrast between the allegedly wild jungle and the anachronistic familiar placenames creates an incongruity that undermines all claims to adventurism and overcodes the wilderness exploration as a city tour. There is nothing left here to be discovered as all these places have obviously already been named. All the same, Zuleika imagines herself, if only briefly, as a heroine of imperial romance – "I went exploring, wolves, bears | savages were unwelcome visitors | in my mind" (EB 219) – only to remind herself and the reader immediately that "I knew I was safe, here with you [the emperor] | and three hundred soldiers" (ibid.). There is arguably something ironic about this outing under high security, and it goes without saying that the presence of a private army may ward off all potential hazards but definitely all promise of adventure, too. This, according to James McClure, is the paradox built into imperial romance as a narrative pattern that purports to glorify the bringing of order into the uncharted wilderness but that more fundamentally bemoans the disappearance of precisely those unordered spaces to whose domestication its protagonists all the same actively contribute:

The ultimate enemies of romance, then, are not the foreign foes confronted on the field of battle in the text itself, but the foes held at bay by these essential antagonists: the banal, quotidian world of calculation and compromise from which the heroes of romance are constantly in flight, and the globally routinized world that only became imaginable about one hundred years ago, a world utterly devoid of romantic regions. (McClure 1994: 3)

The quotidian is however not only the mere mercantile or capitalist 'world of calculation and compromise', it is also the feminine domestic sphere: Zuelika's '*so* small world'. If the later Victorian male authors nostalgically complained how "the world is disenchanted" as "oversoon shall Europe send her spies through all the lands" (Lang 1888: 84), this disenchantment is to a large extent underpinned by a deep-seated misogynist contempt for the feminized world of the regularized everyday domestic 'from which the heroes of romance are constantly in flight'. Coexisting with these masculinist fantasies of a vanishing world of adventure out there, much of women's popular romance moved exactly the other way: (re)enchanting the drab and debased domestic scene. That George Eliot summarily dismissed this popular/populist literature as "silly novels by lady novelists" (Eliot in Harzewski 2006: 29) is nothing but yet another indicator that we are here in the sphere of the stupid. Notably, in late Victorian Britain, it was almost exclusively as writers of domestic romance that women could openly appear as authors at all. If the author persona of the 'silly lady novelist' ineluctably implied low symbolic capital, then this disadvantage was outweighed, for many writers, by an "ever-increasing potential for high financial capital – that is, large popular sales and the very real possibility of the author's economic independence" (Hipsky 2011: 26). The charm of domestic bliss that these novels invariably propagate may be as hackneyed and conventional as the consumerist superficiality of contemporary chick lit (which is the legitimate heir to the Victorians' 'silly ladies' novel'); but it is in any case a viable antidote to the inconsolable nostalgia of the masculine adventure romance caught in the double-bind of imperial desire for order and disorder, control and danger at the same time. Women's romances envision precisely that as enchanted, which their male counterparts decry as hopelessly mundane: the *so* small world of the domestic. There is no real need, therefore, to venture out to the fringes of empire or the swamps and jungles that encircle Londinium: miracle and wonder are waiting to be discovered and enjoyed much closer at hand in the privacy of the home (for the Victorian 'silly lady novelist') and, for the contemporary chick lit writer, more explicitly in the bedroom. The Victorian domestic romance impelled its audience "to read stories about heroes who are both gentle and tender and to imagine the details (rather than read a thorough accounting) of the couple's sexual encounters" (Click 2015: 18); the postmodern chick lit text, as a contrast, is as explicit as the cultural situation to which it speaks and caters to a readership who utilize these texts' "recurrent themes of fantasy, romance, and sex to make sense of the sexualized cultural environment in which they are immersed" (ibid.: 17). Evaristo's Londinium is clearly such an environment, teeming as it is with "off-duty soldiers" prowling the markets and "watching for lumps | on our chests, to see if your hips grew away | from our waist" (ibid.), and with

drunken machistos who loitered

outside bars and wolf-whistled at cute
young chicks, whilst grabbing their dicks,

pursing their lips and gyrating their hips. (EB 165)

Fame fatale

More than anything, sex (which in chick lit is almost invariably heterosexual and consensual) offers repetitious occasions to constantly reconsolidate intimate homosocial bonds among women. The experience of sex and the city is thrilling only to the extent that it becomes a conversation topic, joyously analysed and dissected in extensive postmortems in which "female friends frequently gather to discuss [...] and share the details of their sex lives" (Smith 2008: 95). "The Babe Three" (EB 187) – Zuleika, the highly promiscuous Alma and transvestite Venus the "Glitzy Glamour Queen" (EB 139) – form an intimate circle of friends strongly similar to the one around Carrie, Samantha, Miranda and Charlotte in *Sex and the City*, but it would be inaccurate to reduce this posse to the mere consumerist orthodoxy and 'stupidity' that hostile critics assign to average chick lit protagonists. For Zuleika is not primarily after heterosexual pleasure (even though she is that, too) but more than anything after fame. In this light the intimate postmortems with the two close friends form a feminized version (discredited as 'gossip') of the highly prized public praise of men's valorous deeds. In the privatized and secluded forum of Zuleika's *peristylium*, narratives of sexual exploits are exchanged and evaluated in analogy to the orator's eulogies of men's political or military achievements. If it is the praise and not the deed that ensures that the hero "will become a god when he dies" (EB 140), then the poet or rhetor is the true source of power. As in Vela's chronicles of Nafanua, so in Zuleika's Londinium: the epitaph immortalizes. Everything depends upon whether it will be inscribed "on lengthy stone plaques for posterity" (EB 171) or, as Zuleika anticipates in her siesta drowsing, ephemerally scribbled on the wall to evaporate as "a puff of steam" – "my lengthy epitaphium, | listing my great achievements: || *Zuleika Woz' Ere*" (EB 72–3). As Zuleika's friend

Venus succinctly points out, women cannot expect more than this unless they "immortalize" themselves: "Ain't no one never gonna write ‖ about your life but you. Once you're dead | you never existed, baby, so get to it" (EB 45).

With this metatextual zoom on the powers of literature *The Emperor's Babe* clearly departs from the conventions of chick lit and imperial romance and instead reflects its own status as a loosely knit gutter text. It is then not just a romance or even a bildungsroman but more specifically a *Künstlerroman*, and it is this reflexivity that chick lit routinely evades by consistently

> avoiding the subject of the development of women's literary talents, an evasion that is particularly remarkable in light of the overwhelming popularity in the genre of first-person narration and the prevalence of heroines' careers that involve some kind of writing. Every heroine who tells her own story to the reader is, in a sense, writing her own novel, yet in no case does she acknowledge this. (Wells 2006: 56)

As a contrast, all through her narrative, Zuleika emphasizes her ambitions to become a poet, even if that ambition is initially not so much motivated by some aesthetic impulse but by the craving for celebrity status: "I'm going to become a great poet. ‖ I'd love to be famous for something" (EB 45). If this is still the 'cute, young, stupid' stance of a virtual chick lit protagonist, then it is precisely this 'babe' positionality by way of which Zuleika manages to carve out an alternate authorial persona not foreseen in the masculinist literary system. For, as just discussed, the immortality that abiding fame provides is in Roman Londinium clearly a man's privilege, so that any reclamation of the same for women amounts to a first-order gender-political intervention. This becomes even more pertinent when considering the gender bias inherent to the literary system itself. Immediately after her wedding, Zuleika begins to take poetry lessons in which she is first taught that naturally "all the notable poets were men", then force-fed the canon of heroic epics from Homer to Vergil and finally informed that "anyway | I'd never write good poetry because what did ‖ I know about war, death, the gods | and the founding of countries?" (EB 85). Serenely unperturbed, Zuleika reveals herself as "a thoroughly modern miss" (EB 85), not an imitative epigone but an innovative poet-to-be, not interested in epic monumentalism but in the here-and-now of the multicultural mashup she comes from – a mashup that, as so often in *The Emperor's Babe*, is both of Londinium and of London:

> What I really want to read
> and hear is stuff about us, about now,
>
> about Nubians in Londinium, about men
> who dress up as women, about extramarital

peccadilloes, about girls getting married
to older men [...]. (ibid.)

This is the stuff of neither Homeric epic nor imperial romance nor chick lit. This is postcolonial, queer and feminist stuff: a kind of writing for which Zuleika gets no models from her poetry tutor so that she has to attempt to generate it out of her own resources. Notably, however, this is not yet another portrait of the artist as a young whatever but instead the story of a failure to become an artist. But even more importantly, this failure is not primarily due to some lack in Zuleika but to the literally irresponsible setting in which she tries to find her voice. Whenever Zuleika attempts to get herself heard, she finds that she is being ignored. Her father, for one, replies to her offer to recite one or two of her "ditties" ("I know they're not brilliant yet") with the inconsequential question, "In a throaty sleepy voice", when she will finally get "bambino" (EB 86). Similarly, both her patrician husband and her imperial lover turn a deaf ear on her literary ambitions by demanding that "silence is a woman's best adornment" (EB 143): an adage that Zuleika internalizes to such an extent that she dare not speak up even if only to "fill his pause" (EB 142). Most devastatingly, when she and her two friends curate a "recitatio-cum-orgy" (EB 192), a classical forerunner of contemporary poetry slams, Zuleika's own performance goes completely unnoticed with her personal house slave, Tranio, "the only person listening" (EB 201) and everybody else busy fornicating or just drunk to a stupor. It is not a question whether or not Zuleika's poetry is 'good' by whatever standards but that all through the novel it passes completely unnoticed. Of course, there is a performative contradiction here inasmuch as the whole text *is* Zuleika's poetry: a decisively readerly, un-virtuoso, apparently 'stupid' – that is, relaxed – kind of poetry almost exclusively composed in non-metred unrhyming couplets that read, over vast stretches, as if they were simply prose typographically dispersed and thus perforated by gaps that appear as regular as the gutters of a conventional comic strip. This guttering of the text, I argue, introduces a virtually ekphrastic dimension in which poetry and the visual are intimately correlated. Thus Zuleika's self-interrogation of her own poetic talent raises the question of her pictorial competence: "Poems were meant to fulfil me instead | but I failed to create pictures || with my words – or did I?" (EB 143). The equation of visual and verbal arts (as in the poetological formula of *ut pictura poesis*) is looming large here, and in Zuleika's self-questioning it imposes a normative horizon of expectation that no poet can answer to due to the fundamental difference between word and image: the image "does not describe at all but merely presents; or better, it depicts, in the original etymological sense of that word: renders in pictorial form", whereas the verbal text, incapable of that kind of depiction, has the prerogative to "assert" (Chatman 1980: 128).

Zuleika's contradictory inhibitions about her poetic vocation is in that sense in league with her silenced gendered positionality. Poetic vocation, literally speaking, is a matter of voice and address that requires an auditorium. If, as a contrast, "images do not speak, they do not tell a story, they do not have listeners" (Locher 2011: 454), then it is only consequential that the muted Zuleika should be drawn to the visual arts. Already in her prologue, she informs the reader that she "dreamt of creating mosaics | of remaking my town with bright stones and glass" (EB 3). That dream seems to evaporate over the course of the narrative and is explicitly reiterated only on her deathbed, when she confides in her best friend Alba that she "wanted to be a great poet or mosaicist | or something" (EB 249). In a more indirect way, however, the mosaicist ambition resurfaces in the first 'post-coital colloquium' with the emperor. Notably Zuleika feels the urge to communicate to her new lover her artistic aspirations not as a budding poet but in a precise repetition of her idea of mosaics: "*I wanted to remake my town | with bright stones and glass!* || Oh, to fill his pause with my truth" (EB 142; emphasis in the original). The impulse to speak is, as already discussed, immediately contained by the patriarchal demand of women's silence so that the pause in the 'colloquium', the gap in the conversation, will not be filled by the evocation in words of an imagined visual work of art that would 'remake my town'. That imagined mosaic is, like all mosaics, a gutter text whose segments of 'bright stones and glass' remain distinctly visible even as they connect to form the coherent picture of 'my town'.

The resonance to Joyce, who famously claimed that it was his aim "to give a picture of Dublin so complete that if the city one day suddenly disappeared from the earth it could be reconstructed out of my book stone by stone" (in Tymocko 1994: 158), subtly dissolves again the boundary between the visual and the verbal, *pictura* and *poesis*. The model for the mosaic that Zuleika dreams to create would be a novel, and ironically one that is itself a reworking and reappropriation of the very Homeric epics that Zuleika so vehemently rejects. In critical discussions of *Ulysses*, "the image of Joyce as a mosaicist recurs with notable frequency" (Baron 2020: 21) – from Frank Budgen's comparison, in the mid-thirties, of Joyce's meticulous technique with that of "the mosaic artists of Rome and Ravenna" to R. B. Kershner's suggestion of "a postmodernist portrait of Joyce [as a] mosaic-worker" who recombines borrowed materials (in Baron 2020: 24–5). Of course, in a postmodern understanding of writing, any text will then be a mosaic: a reworking of available segments rearticulated into a new but ineluctably intertextual syntax. In this sense, "any text is constructed as a mosaic of quotations; any text is the absorption and transformation of another" (Kristeva 1980: 80), or more accurately, numerous others. What is specific about gutter texts, is that they leave the segments they are made of only loosely articulated and hence the gaps between them visible, and are hence particularly transparent about their mosaic status. This, for sure, is the case when it comes to Zuleika's poetry: like any well-wrought mosaic, *The Emperor's Babe* is neatly framed (with prologue and epilogue) so as to ensure the integrity of a bounded text that, however, inside the frame retains a looseness and segmentivity that makes it dissolve into a set of deliberately weakly connected episodes. *It can but be contiguous in this world.* Moreover, what holds for the macrostructure of the whole book is repeated, fractally as it were, at the microlevel where the visual distribution of the inherently prosaic as poetry – more specifically, unrhymed couplets – further emphasizes the overall gappiness. What ensues is the coherent but discontinuous 'reworking of my town' in a decisively anti-epic mode whose effect is the figuration of an inverse Britain not only as colonial heart of darkness but also as an inconclusive mosaic waiting to be reassembled time and again.

3.3 Detoxing England: Patience Agbabi's *Telling Tales*

Where Tempest de-insularizes Britain, *Telling Tales* (2014) by Patience Agbabi, another prolific and prominent performance poet, rewrites the nation in verse explicitly *as an island* – a island that is however, as I will argue, as emphatically implicated in the larger world as Tempest's 'little clod off the mainland'. Agbabi's speaker introduces *Telling Tales* as a "remix" of "Chaucer Tales" (TT 6), thereby foregrounding its self-placement in the recycling practices of contemporary pop cultures but at the same time, with its status as a twenty-first-century adaptation of *The Canterbury Tales*, in the inner sanctum of the national as well as the world literary canon. For Chaucer's collection of narrative long poems – not a verse novel but rather an in-verse story cycle – has traditionally been codified as *the* founding text of English Literature and by that token, a privileged member of the central canon of world literature, understood as a limited corpus of 'timeless masterpieces'. By announcing itself in the diction of global sampling and piracy culture as a "remix", Agbabi's text claims for itself the status of world literature in a different understanding of that term as a constitutively transnational literature that can no longer be grasped through the lens of national philology or national tradition. In this vein, *Telling Tales* promises the subcultural reappropriation of a canonical piece for a multi-ethnic and always already transnational Britain.

The nation between incompleteness and wholeness

By describing her text as a "track by track remix", Abgabi playfully sends the reader, whom she posits as well versed in postmodern intertextuality, on a scavenger hunt: Does *Telling Tales* actually contain the complete *Canterbury*

Tales? Do all of Chaucer's narrators have their say? A brief comparison of the tables of contents is enough to establish that Agbabi indeed lives up to her 'track-by-track' claim of providing a complete rewriting. From the 'Prologue' to the 'Retractions', Agbabi's remix follows the original accurately, even if Chaucer's Prologue is now called 'Grime Mix' and the concluding Retractions are now called 'Back Tracks'. But the pretence of completeness is at the same time all too obviously questionable: in contrast to Chaucer's endless columns of iambic pentameter (my Penguin edition, which omits Chaucer's prose passages, runs to just under 500 pages), *Telling Tales* is a slim volume of just 120 sparsely printed pages. And while the first of the tales, 'The Knight's Tale', is 2,249 verses long in Chaucer's version, Agbabi reduces it to a mere 39 lines. However, there are also opposite tendencies: 'The Cook's Tale', in Chaucer a narrative fragment broken off after only fifty-eight lines, is stretched in Agbabi to more than twice its length and – unlike in the original – rounded off into a halfway coherent narrative. At its macrolevel, *Telling Tales* is thus an apparently unabridged rewriting of the original none of whose segments are missing from Agbabi's 'faithful' reiteration. To drive this home, each of the chapters in *Telling Tales* comes with a many-layered paratextual framework consisting of not only the chapter's title and the name of its ostensible author (whose bionote is included in the appended "Author Biographies") but also of a capitalized headline whose function it is to identify each remix chapter with its respective Chaucerian pretext. All the more, of course, does the substantial discrepancy between Chaucer's voluminous collection and Agbabi's compact rendition come to the fore. If *Telling Tales* is therefore an incomplete remix, then this does not diminish its fidelity to the original: rather to the contrary. For why should one expect completeness in a copy when its original is itself incomplete? After all, "Chaucer Tales were an unfinished business" (TT 2), as Harry 'Bells' Baily, Agbabi's host-turned-MC, points out right at the outset. Unfinished indeed: while Chaucer's 'Prologue' announces 120 tales, only 24 are realized or preserved in *The Canterbury Tales*; and some of these – notably the aforementioned 'Cook's Tale' – break off in open stretch or, like 'The Monk's Tale' and 'Chaucer's Tale of Sir Topaz', are interrupted by other pilgrims or the host. If one follows Timothy Stinson's neo-materialist philology, incompleteness is in a sense constitutive of the *Canterbury Tales*:

> The best-known example of an unfinished literary work is The *Canterbury Tales*. It is difficult for a partial work to become canonical, especially one missing as much as *The Canterbury Tales* evidently is, and yet it is also difficult to find an author or work more unarguably canonical than Chaucer and his *Tales*. (Stinson 2017: 120)

Despite its incompleteness, since the nineteenth century at the latest, Chaucer's text has had the aura of having represented the totality of the nascent nation for the first time and at the same time in perfect form and, as Nevill Coghill (1970: 17) postulates, of having sketched a "concise portrait of the entire nation" – a nation that did not even exist as such in Chaucer's time. Literature is thus an anticipatory constituent of reality: a national imagination is articulated *avant la lettre* as a socioculturally representative cast of characters from all walks of life and "from every shire's end | in England" (Chaucer 1970: 19) joins in composed relationality to *form* a productive community.

Of course, this is an imagined community, to use the familiar term that Benedict Anderson proposes for the modern secular nation. According to Anderson's social formalist account, the constant reproduction of the nation is partly achieved by a particular literary genre: the (realistic) novel. Its essential affordance as a form is to configure simultaneous parallel action in an uninterrupted temporal continuum and thereby symbolically articulate the form of the nation: "The idea of a sociological organism moving calendrically through homogenous empty time is a precise analogue of the idea of the nation, which also is conceived as a solid community moving steadily down (or up) history" (Anderson 1991: 26). Similar to Anderson, Arjun Appadurai identifies the "historically situated imagination of persons and groups spread around the globe" (Appadurai 1996: 33) as a socially productive force that plays a central role in shaping a transnational, globalized present and the ways in which subjects relate to that present. Given the multiple transnational cultural flows that constantly reassemble in the ongoing processes of globalization, Appadurai expands the term of the imagined community to the concept of "imagined worlds" that "many persons on the globe live in" (ibid.). This notion of a multiplicity of imagined worlds implies a principal plurality, but not necessarily the peaceful co-existence of these worlds; there is always also the potential for polemical contestation, in other words, the political. Unlike Anderson, however, Appadurai says nothing about literary forms that would be particularly suited to generating, articulating or representing such imaginative worlds.

Yet given their protean provisional character, imagined worlds are, unlike national imagined communities, not based on the suggestion of guaranteed continuity in the medium of empty homogeneous time, but rather presuppose an always incomplete and inconclusive sense of provisional belonging. In this respect they arguably bear more affinity to a non-novelistic, gappy textuality as the one presented in Abgabi's cycle of poems and stories that draw on the pre-novel tradition of a Chaucerian text type – a text type for which incompleteness is constitutive. In this reading, *Telling Tales* goes back to the always already incomplete *Canterbury Tales* in the spirit of brotherly/sisterly dissimilitude: not as a polemical appropriation in the sense of a postcolonial writing back, but rather a gesture of fraternization/sororisation through which Agbabi's text frees Chaucer's original from its nationalistic immurement and refers back to precisely what, on closer inspection, was always already clearly laid out in the *Canterbury Tales*: namely, that 'England' is not a self-contained self-sufficient entity, but already appears as porous and deeply incomplete the moment it first finds a cultural expression in Chaucer's text. Not only that the settings of the majority of the narratives are all over the world – Syria, Flanders, Egypt, India – and that already the first embedded narrator, the Knight, is introduced as a world traveller who has visited Prussia and Russia, Alexandria and Armenia, Morocco and Arabia. More than that, not only the personnel but also the narrative resources are decidedly transnational in Chaucer's work. The father of English poetry was at heart mostly and 'merely' a translator of found European, Arabic and Persian materials:

> Although Chaucer's career lies well before the full establishment of the kind of nationhood Anderson describes, his is the figure that later generations associate with the beginnings of a specifically English sensibility. This association is all the more arresting when we consider how many of Chaucer's productions were in fact translations from Latin, Italian, and French 'originals'. (Knapp 2004: 131–2)

Agbabi's reverence for this father figure hinges precisely on the fact that with Chaucer 'English poetry' has its founding moment as an always already mongrelized and transcultural formation: "*The Canterbury Tales* was always a European text, a cross-cultural celebration" (Agbabi 2018: 1). This, however, is a highly selective construction that deliberately omits the 'darker sides' of Chaucer. For neither Chaucer's work nor the vision of Englishness that speaks through it lend themselves too easily to the tolerationist affirmation of hybridity that Agbabi's appreciation suggests. It can indeed be argued that Chaucer "speaks for a comparatively narrow and exclusive English national community" (Nakley 2010: 370) despite the international resources and influences on which he draws, and that the England that *The Canterbury Tales* evoke can be read as a pre-emergent national community in the process of constituting itself as a homogeneous body whose "communal wholeness" requires the maintenance of "a closed society" vigilantly safeguarding itself against potentially threatening "pollutants" (Despres 1994: 426). To some extent the very genre of *The Canterbury Tales* as a many-faceted and polyvocal story collection works against such a purist thrust. Yet it is this very pluralism that allows Chaucer to accommodate, next to prankish rowdy tales like the Miller's or the Shipman's, chivalric romances like the Knight's, or the Wife of Bath's pleasurable innuendoes, stories that make *The Canterbury Tales* a serious embarrassment for a present-day reception like Agbabi's that is bent on reading the text as a celebration of hybridity.

Toxic ingredients

There are tales in Chaucer's collection that "cannot be ignored but the modern reader feels uncomfortable with and apologetic about them" (Bloomfield 1972: 384). This embarrassment is triggered for sure by 'The Man of Law's Tale' or 'The Squire's Tale', both reinscribing a "widely disseminated late medieval 'Orientalism'" (Lynch 1999: 411) that requires a heavy dose of sophistry to be 'redeemed' as "something one might well call a 'strategic Orientalism'" (Johnston 2015: 6) that Chaucer ironically makes turn in on itself. Far more appalling, however, is that, with 'The Prioress's Tale', at least one piece of toxic anti-Judaist persecution literature has found a prominent place in the collection. Over that discomfiting little piece Chaucer studies have been divided for more than a century into the opposing camps of 'hard' and 'soft' readers: the former exonerating Chaucer by putting the blame for the tale's vapid antisemitism on the embedded narrator, the Prioress; the latter ready to concede that, "even though we might wish it otherwise, Chaucer, as a man of his time, was not perturbed by antisemitism" and hence not specifically hesitant to reproduce it (Besserman 2004: 322). While 'hard' readers interpret the tale as "a satire on the Prioress's antisemitism", 'soft' readers "understand it to be an example of a kind of medieval devotional literature that unfortunately depended on anti-Judaism for its effects" (Blurton and Johnson 2017: 24). In this light it is important to note that anti-Judaism, even if not rampant in *The Canterbury Tales*, is by no means confined to 'The Prioress's Tale'. Both 'The Pardoner's Tale' and 'The Parson's Tale' charge 'the Jews' with the gratuitous "dismembering" of "our blissed lords body" (Chaucer 1970: 558, 695) – an assault on Christ/ianity that the Prioress's story displaces into the diegetic present by re-literalizing the alleged Jewish ritual of host desecration as child murder.

The genre deployed for this is the conventional 'Miracle of the Virgin' narrative (Besserman 2004: 322) that Chaucer latches on to the equally generic late medieval tradition of "Eucharist miracle stories in which the Host appears as a child" (Despres 1994: 416). In such stories, child abuse or murder and the desecration of the sacramental wafer symbolizing the body of Jesus spill over into one another. This is exactly what 'The Prioress's Tale' is about: a Christian choirboy gets killed by Jews who hire a murderer to stop the child from singing in their district the hymn "O Alma redemptoris" to the Virgin Mary. The body is cast into an open sewer but miraculously the dead boy continues to sing and does so until his mother and a group of Christians find him. Without court hearing, trial or formal judgment, a provost condemns an unspecified number of Jews to be tortured and executed, whereas the dead boy explains how the Virgin enabled him to continue singing after his throat was slit. Eventually the Prioress's story culminates in the boy's soul's ascension to heaven, so that a transubstantiation from flesh to spirit provides a narrative closure that reiterates the structure of the Eucharist: "The final, solemn, ritual action of the tale – the resting of the slain child 'biforn the chief auter, whil masse laste' – [serves] as a eucharistic sacrifice familiar to its audience through the bleeding-child-as-Host motif" (Despres 1994: 423). Surely a plot like this stands on the shoulders of and reproduces a thick tradition of European anti-Judaism that then forms yet another transnational cultural and narrative resource that the cosmopolitan Chaucer integrates into his constitutively transnational text: a toxic ingredient whose presence in the concoction that is *The Canterbury Tales* makes detoxing crucially imperative for the remix. For it cannot go unmentioned how important the vapid ideology of anti-Judaism obviously is for the community-building effects within the diegetic worlds of both 'The Prioresses Tale', where the Eucharist miracle performatively consolidates the Christian congregation, and the frame narrative of *The Canterbury Tales* where after listening to "this miracle every man | As sober was it was a miracle to see" (Chaucer 1970: 502). This "notable moment of unity among the pilgrims" that "immediately after the Prioress finishes her story confirms the unifying potency of her tale" (Wilsbacher 2005: 11) surely resonates with the community-forging dynamics of othering, whether coded in religious or secular terms, in the social world at large: as a demonized figure "'the Jew' was central not only to medieval English Christian devotion but to the construction of Englishness itself" (Tomasch 2000: 244). In this context it should not be forgotten that the 1290 Expulsion had put a violent end to the presence of Jewish communities in England so that the prioress and her audience as well as Chaucer and his readership inhabited a country without Jews whose symbolic presence they nonetheless have to continuously reinvoke as pollutants to be expelled: "Between 1290 and 1656 the English came to see their country defined in part by the fact that Jews had been banished from it"; and if the pre-emergent nation to some extent required "the English to define themselves as different from, indeed free of, that which was Jewish" (Shapiro 1996: 42), then this negative other had to be kept present in (spite of) its absence; hence the "ongoing [...] allosemitic production of the virtual Jew" (Tomasch 2000: 255) to which Chaucer (or only his Prioress?) contributed.

I expand on these issues not with the aspiration to contribute anything new to the substantial body of scholarly work that has gone into the discussion of 'The Prioress's Tale' but with the sole intention to point out how deeply problematic the reference point is that Agbabi draws on in her project of rewriting the nation by remixing Chaucer. The England that emerges from the assembly of Chaucer's pilgrims is all too clearly posited on the ideologeme of othering, most obviously in religious, sexual and racial dichotomies. At a closer look, then, Chaucer's 'portrait of the entire nation' is disturbing. Whether this is due to the flaws of the sitter or the painter or both is a moot point for a historicizing approach that tries to understand "how the poems connect not just to the self-aware intentions of the poet and the explicit expectations of his audience, but to larger patterns of social practice and ideology" (Patterson in Blurton and Johnson 2017: 39). This holds true even more strongly for a discussion of Agbabi's project "to showcase this island's | love of retelling tales in its fierce pun", that is, to rewrite neither the author nor his historical subject matter, but the text that serves for her pretext: "The *Tales*' grand story of England" (Nakley 2010: 372). That cherished canonical founding text, as we have seen, contains poisonous substances. To remix it in a spirit of a minor cosmopolitanism means to detox it. Focusing in the following, especially though not exclusively, on her 'remix' of 'The Prioress's Tale', I would like to explore whether and (if yes) how Agbabi manages to enact such a detoxification.

For this enquiry it might be useful to recall earlier 'remixes' of *The Canterbury Tales* such as Lumiansky's 1948 rendition in modern prose which Gregory Wilsbacher (2005) has analyzed with admirable sensitivity. First published three years after the defeat of Nazi Germany and the revelation of the horrors of the Shoah, Lumiansky's edition all but omits the Prioress and offers instead of a prose version of her 'tale' a brief summary from which all references to Jews are edited out and no mention is made of the antisemitism of the story. It is only in the paratextual apparatus that Lumiansky points to the troubling qualities of the tale and the reasons he had for omitting it:

> The Prioress's story of the little choirboy who is murdered by the Jews possesses an unpleasantness which overshadows its other qualities. For most of us, 'The Prioress's Tale' is ruined by the similarity between this sort of story and some of the anti-Semitic propaganda which was current in Nazi Germany, and which is still in operation, not only in numerous foreign countries but also here at home. (Lumiansky 1948: xxiii in Wilsbacher 2005: 4)

In this perspective, the dangerous tale has to be censored in order to contain it. This resort to policing is legitimized by the immediate threat that Lumiansky identifies in the tale, a threat that for numerous readers lurks not so much in its antisemitic content but its formal appeal, its economic dispatch in the artfully crafted rime royal format of which "Chaucer was one of the first users, if not the inventor" (Dean 1991: 251): a stanza of seven decasyllabic (in Chaucer, usually iambic) verses rhymed ababbcc. For a reading that focuses on these formal aspects, Chaucer's *Prioress* delivers her hate speech as a well-nigh irresistibly seductive siren song whose effect on the reader is craftily woven into the frame narrative where her tale leaves the company of pilgrims awestruck and for the first time *united* as a community articulated into the silent admiration of the beauty of the words. This does not necessarily imply a consent to the Prioress's anti-Judaist propaganda but an appreciation of the elegance of its rendition: "The sober silence of the pilgrims [...] does not result from the open assent to the bigoted message but from the silent closure of assent brought on by the aesthetics of the tale itself" (Wilsbacher 2005: 16). What, however, if that silence does *not* signal 'assent' but rather embarrassment? What if the pilgrims do not reverently reenact the silence of the martyred boy after his soul's ascension but the silence that the story organizes around the 'justice' meted out at the Jewish community – a 'justice' that may plausibly be read as camouflage of a pogrom. The collective murder is thus neither completely hushed up nor actually represented, rendering the tale a transitional document between (typically medieval) 'naïve' and 'distorted' persecution texts. While "account[s] of persecution told from the perspective of naive persecutors [...] hide none of the objective traces of their persecution" precisely because "they are convinced that their violence is justified" (Girard 1986: 6, 26), distorted representations displace the target of the collective violence from historically identifiable stigmatized groups onto textual stand-ins who, in the course of mythologization, tend to appear as sacred agents of societal purification by way of self-sacrifice based on a "free and voluntary decision" (ibid.: 59). The Prioress's tale is neither fully here nor there. It parades a sacrificial victim in the figure of the Christian boy transformed into a martyr but the actual "scapegoat *of* the text" (ibid.: 118) – the unacknowledged agent who bears the burden of community stabilization by way of embodying that which the community violently expels from itself – is clearly the Jewish community. In this light the Prioress's tale may well be read as an only half distorted persecution account of the largely 'forgotten' atrocities that must have accompanied the 1290 Expulsion of the Jews. Such a reading sheds a very different light on the reaction of the pilgrims to the Prioress's story:

> The atrocious silence of a Jewish community wiped off the map with almost genocidal fervor thus also haunts the pilgrims' own stunned silence. Chaucer-the-pilgrim appears unable to bring himself even to look at his fellows because of it: 'What man artow,' probes Harry Bailly when no one breaks the increasingly uncomfortable lull, "Thou lookest as thou woldest fynde an hare, I For evere upon the ground I se thee stare" (VII 696–7). Indeed, in order to break the silence that the *Prioress's Tale* stuns its auditors into, Chaucer himself must tell the next tale. (Albin 2013: 112)

Read in this way, 'The Prioress's Tale' would effectively constitute a community of accomplices uncomfortably aware of their implication, if only by 'inheritance', in acts of collective violence the memory of which is as stunningly embarrassing as its distorted and displaced rendition in the pious tale. The story that the nation tells itself about itself involves collective memory as much as collective amnesia, as Benedict Anderson argues with recourse to Ernest Renan, for whom the stability and cohesion of the nation requires that its members remember certain events but also that they "already have to have forgotten" (Anderson 1991: 200) certain others – especially those where the community violently turns against itself. Renan's prime example for an event that "all Frenchmen must have forgotten" are the Bartholomew Massacres that he himself rendered as an aberrant fratricidal feud among fellow French citizens: clearly, a presentist projection that reenvisages a murderous sixteenth-century religious conflict through the nationalist lens of a nineteenth-century sensibility as if the participants in the 'Holy War' had seriously imagined the combatants not as enemies but "cozily together as 'Frenchmen'" (ibid.). What if we apply this hermeneutic to the tale of the Prioress? In this light its political and aesthetic impact, especially its nation-building thrust, would change in one crucial respect: as a story that reminds its auditors to a submerged fratricidal episode in the nation's chronology – to an event that they 'are obliged to have had forgotten' – the 'Prioress's Tale' would depend for its efficacy on an understanding in which Jews, now absent, are integral to the fullness of the pre-emergent English nation. The Expulsion would then figure not so much as a purge but an amputation with all its attendant phantom pains embodied in the virtual Jew whose "spectral presence [is] strongly felt and yet just as strongly derealized" (Kruger 2006: xvii). The omission of anti-Jewish collective violence from the narrative of the nation corresponds thus with the editing out of 'The Prioress's Tale' from Lumiansky's 1948 modernized prose version of Chaucer's collection.

Not by rap alone

Agbabi, by contrast, not only includes the tale of the murdered boy but thoroughly detoxes it. Its remixed version, I will argue, transforms the Prioress's/Chaucer's persecutor's tale into a narrative of reconciliation that interrupts the cycle of communal mimetic violence whose victim the dead boy became as the 'scapegoat *in* the story' and the Jewish minority as the 'scapegoat *of* the story'. Agbabi achieves this transformation by massively reformulating Chaucer's tale in terms of both 'message' and form. Of course, these two levels are intimately entangled with each other but for the sake of clarity I will discuss them separately, beginning with the most significant modifications to which Agbabi subjects the diegetic content of 'The Prioress's Tale' before I address the intricacies and implications of the formal features of her remixed version.

The title of Agbabi's version, 'Sharps an Flats', refers immediately to the dead choirboy's passion for music: in Western notation systems the key of a given piece is indicated by the number of flats or sharps, with sharps raising, and flats lowering, a musical note by half a step on the scale. At the same time, however, 'sharps' explicitly associates the "switchblade" (TT 81) with which the boy is killed in Agbabi's version: "They stabbed with a *sharp*"

(TT 82; emphasis added); while 'flats' underscores that the violence inflicted on the boy is to a significant degree embedded already in a whole fabric of structural violence of which an environment of brutalist architecture is one crucial element: the text is set in contemporary multiethnic London, more specifically in urban council estate territory, and the perpetrators – "2 boys from the back *flats*" (TT 82; emphasis added) – are themselves victims of this structural violence just as much as the young boy they kill. Not only does Agbabi transfer the tale to contemporary London; the most striking alteration is that in her version, the murder victim is the speaker: the poem as a whole is structured as a letter (or more likely, a podcast message) from the dead boy to his mother, to whom he speaks as "your son, J, chatting on a mix | Made in heaven" (TT 81). That posthumous narrator is (for most readers) easily identified as Black on account of his style and register that deploys "a distinctive form of 'nonstandard' English (in terms of spelling, sounds and vocabulary) to tell the story of a Black British schoolboy murdered on the streets of southeast London" (Hsy 2021: 132). The speaker evokes actual cases of racist murder in contemporary Britain, especially when he identifies as a "spar" of "Damilola", thereby referring to the killing of the Nigeria-born schoolboy Damilola Taylor who in November 2000 "on his way home from the library [...] was stabbed with shards of glass and bled to death" (ibid.). Through these references, the victim *in* the text is transformed from the Prioress's choirboy killed out of religious hatred into a Black youth mistaken for a "star scholar" and murdered for being perceived by the '2 boys from the back flats' as an upstart. Agbabi's achievement, however, lies not primarily in this displacement from white to Black but in the evacuation of the persecution logic that so blatantly mars the pretext. For in 'Sharps an Flats' there is no victim *of* the text: while it is true that the murderers get convicted and jailed ("boys got shut up"), this punishment is a far cry from the persiflage of justice that, in 'The Prioress's Tale', barely camouflages the communal violence inflicted on the Jewish minority. Nor does Agbabi's remix generate a communalist unity posited on the eviction (if not annihilation) of some stigmatized other. The dead boy does not call for retaliation but "peace". The only manifest intertext with Chaucer's original is precisely that element which the Prioress so openly displays and yet so blatantly betrays: the motto "*Amor vincit omnia*" embossed on her "broche of gold" (Chaucer 1970: 421). What the Prioress offensively forgets over the course of her annihilationist fantasy is exactly what Agbabi's speaker, J., reminds his mother of, ironically referring this gentle reminder back to the prioress who failed to uphold it: "Peace! Remember what the nuns say, | *Love conquers all*" (TT 82; emphasis in the original).

Agbabi frames her own work not only in terms of its poetics – as a 'remix' – but by the same token also in terms of its politics of form: as an inclusive democratization that materializes in the diversity of *forms* that the collection programmatically accommodates "from the grime to the clean-cut iambic | rime royale, rant or rap" (TT 1). The formal pluralism of *Telling Tales* thus merges or configures "distinctly black" (Wacker 2019: 256) formats like grime or rap with 'white' idioms like the 'Chaucer stanza' of rime royal. Among other forms, the collection includes the sonnet cycle of 'Joined-Up Writing' ('The Man of Law's Tale'), the 'old school' rap of 'Roving Mic' ('The Cook's Tale'), the elaborate mirrored macrostructure of 'Unfinished Business' (Chaucer's prose 'Tale of Melibeus') and the rime royal of 'Tit for Tat' ('The Reeve's Tale'). Given this display of virtuosity, the author's exasperation at being repeatedly mistaken for a rap-only spoken-word artist should not come as a surprise:

> I grappled with a huge range of poetic forms and registers throughout this project. [...] every single poem is written in a different style [...]. But some critics, working to impossibly tight deadlines, have made the mistake of thinking that *most of the poems* are written in rap form. Maybe it's because I is Black and have occasionally written raps. Maybe it's because the set-up is a poetry slam, making people mistakenly think that means rap. (Agbabi 2014)

As far as 'Sharps an Flats' is concerned, however, any critic is licensed to such a labelling as Agbabi herself declares her poem "a *rap* based on the Prioress's Tale" (Agbabi 2011). And indeed the formal structure of the text – the eight-line stanza reiterating rap's eight-bars street stanza and the extended end-rhyme riffs enhanced by dense internal rhymes, alliterations and assonances – bears very clearly the imprints of the poetics of rap with its "extended runs of the same rhyme sound over a series of lines, often with both end and internal rhymes" (Bradley 2009: 51). This densely knit sound structure has a hypnotic, "often incantatory" quality as "rhyme takes on a kind of rhythmic function here, underscoring specific patterns of sound to achieve its desired effect" (ibid.: 75). The heightened importance of rhyme as a structuring device correlates with the rhythmic flexibility of the bars that make for a wobbly irregularity of the verse. In performance, this flexibility contrasts with the metric regularity of the underlying drumbeats so that a "dual rhythmic relationship" (Wacker 2019: 257) ensues between "the regularity of the beat and the liberated irregularity of the rapper's flow" (Bradley 2009: 34): "The fixed meter of traditional prosody is externalized in the beat of the music. The rap itself is free of a fixed meter, yet grounded in prosody and form" (Collins 2017: 2). On this account, then, Agbabi remixes the Prioress's rime royal as rap, replacing a specifically sophisticated and uniquely Chaucerian format along with its distinct afterlife in white English elite literary practices with the equally but differently elaborate 'brand new beat' of Black street culture. The poem's diction and typography – "don't hit the fade switch b4 it's played" – underscore this reading, giving critics like Jonathan Hsy good reason to summarily dub 'Sharps an Flats' a "rap poem"

(Hsy 2021: 125). Through this 'becoming-Black' of 'The Prioress's Tale', the victim *in* the text becomes a target of anti-Black race hatred instead of the alleged murderous anti-Christian aggression that Chaucer and/or his prioress ascribes to the Jews.

But where does all this leave the victim *of* Chaucer's text? Does Agbabi's evacuation of the persecution logic also evacuate the Jews from her text? As long as this version of 'The Prioress's Tale' is unequivocally read as *only* a rap remix, everything seems to point to a displacement of the story into the world of contemporary urban Black life. If in the following I argue for a reading that restores a Jewish presence to Agbabi's text, then this is not at all meant to disclaim any of these obvious Black connotations. And why should it? After all 'Black' and 'Jewish' are not mutually exclusive, and it is indeed one of the tacit tropes of current antisemitism to project Jews as necessarily white. Rap has its own tradition of disclaiming this myth with acts like the Wu-Tang Clan celebrating the "Islamic Asiatic Black Hebrew". It is in this ecumenic spirit that I would wish to read 'Sharps an Flats' as a poem whose obviously Black speaker may simultaneously be Jewish, too, thereby giving voice to the silenced scapegoat that the prioress needs for her narrative of cleansing. Perhaps it is not by accident that Agbabi's dead boy, whose Chaucerian predecessor remains nameless all through, should identify himself as "J.": not by a name, then, but by an acronym that may be plausibly read as a typically street-credible self-stylization; yet it also arguably triggers a number of Jewish connotations, not least the stigmatizing scarlet letter J that the Nazi regime forced Jewish subjects in Germany and later occupied Europe to have stamped over their names in their passports. While this semantic association remains ultimately unverifiable and speculative, the text yet contains a structural clue that links the Black speaker to the theme of Jewishness, and more specifically, to the theme of diaspora and minoritarian speaking positions that are just as crucial for any project (such as Agbabi's) of inscribing a postcolonial, transcultural and post-white version of in/verse Englishness as they have always been for Jewish self-positionings in largely gentile societies.

By way of its specific stanzaic form and its tendential deployment of the alexandrine verse, "Sharps an Flats" draws on a little-known hybrid Christian Jewish textual tradition of which an erudite formalist like Agbabi is probably aware. Of course, "Sharps an Flats" *is* a rap but it is also, in its macrostructure, a recycling of a most eccentric stanzaic form that consists of two continuously rhymed quatrains (aaaabbbb) – a form that, to my knowledge, has hardly ever been deployed in English poetry (certainly not by Chaucer!) except for such rare examples as Sir Thomas Wyatt's 'A Renunciation of Hardly Escaped Love' (*c.* 1540). Yet the unusual pattern of four consecutive lines with the same end rhyme has a veritable tradition outside Britain in late-medieval Spanish poetry with the strictly regulated *cuaderna vía* form that prescribes the exclusive use of monorhymed alexandrine quatrains. The *cuaderna vía* was very visible (or more correctly, audible) as a medium of instructive, but also vilifying and indoctrinatory spoken-word performance poetry especially at Christian pilgrimage centres that competed with each other for donations from pilgrims along the St James Way. *Cuaderna vía* poetry served

> as a tool for drawing greater numbers of pilgrims to monasteries. As a component of their education, Castilian clerics learned how to cast a wide net by composing cuaderna vía poems in which the vilified figures (such as the Devil, Jews, lepers, Muslims, and sorcerers) were familiar to pilgrims arriving from throughout Europe. (Kaplan 2019: 3)

Given this widespread practice it is all the more remarkable that in the thirteenth and fourteenth centuries, *cuaderna vía* was increasingly adopted by Jewish authors who started to write not for an exclusively Jewish readership in the vernacular Castilian rather than Hebrew. The medievalist Paloma Díaz Mas (in Wacks 2015: 230) identifies a small corpus of poems that fuse Christian and Jewish positions in what she evocatively calls "*clerecía rabínica*" (priestly-rabbinic literature): hybrid texts in which the Jewish writer appropriates and 'detoxes' the very form in which, all around them, anti-Judaist propaganda articulates itself. As a consequence, a proper "Jewish *cuaderna vía* poetry" emerges so that the peculiar form, virtually dispossessed, no longer belongs to any one group as "Christians and Jews both grouped their alexandrine verses in quatrains with consonant rhyme" (Kaplan 2019: 41). In a spirit of resolute social formalism, various critics have emphasized the importance of this eccentric stanzaic pattern, not least the hiatus that bifurcates the alexandrine line into two halves and thus allows for the meditation on the bivalence of a given problem or example: a structural affinity with "the Christian didactic disposition of the authors of *clerecía*, who sought to explain their narratives in terms of worldly and heavenly significance" (Nepaulsingh in Wacks 2015: 106). Where the 'original' clerical tradition thus utilizes the doubleness of the alexandrine and at the same time, arguably, the quatrain's resonance with the four levels of patristic hermeneutic exegesis, the adoption of the form by Jewish authors engenders a "diasporic turn in the *cuaderna vía*" (Wacks 2015: 107). As a result, a minor literature emerges in which the Jewish writer deploys and deterritorializes the given majoritarian language and style of *cuaderna vía*: "The dominant verse form that [...] takes its structure from Christian theological cues (body/soul)" that the Jewish poet "adapts not to a related Jewish theological problem, but rather to addressing the political reality resulting from living in galut: the need to advocate, carefully, the position of the diasporic community" (ibid.). The type of minoritarian self-articulation that Jewish *cuaderna vía* poetry enacts is therefore not separatist but integrationist, not *demanding* but symbolically and performatively *instantiating* an inclusion that, in actual social life, was never granted. These texts, then, embody a counterfactual actuality that is grounded in literature's capacity to dissensus – the 'putting of one world into another' (Rancière) – and to "figure the impossible" (Spivak 1999: 54). Where the late-medieval Spanish Jewish writer "exploits the cuaderna vía poetic form in order to create a platform for guiding his [*sic*] public toward greater social harmony" (Kaplan 2019: 53), Agbabi unearths that submerged form as a medium that brings into the present and future "a *virtuality* inherent to the past and betrayed by its past actualization" (Žižek 2004: 12; emphasis in the original): an unredeemed past whose claim on the present "cannot be settled cheaply" (Benjamin 1968: 254). Exemplarily in 'Sharps an Flats', but generally all through the remixing of Chaucer's 'unfinished business', Agbabi demonstrates what this claim means for an in/verse re-vision of the nation:

> Our intent was to showcase this island's
> love of retelling tales in its fierce pun
> not to cut out the gem from its pierced tongue
> so we're keeping it real on the papyrus
> all that's written is written to inspire us .... (TT: 113)

Chaucer's claim in the appendix to *The Canterbury Tales*, the "Retractions", that "all that was written is there to instruct us" (Chaucer 1970: 507), gets here updated and adapted to the project of a transnational Britain. What Agbabi retains from Chaucer is the emphatic optimism that a 'we' be constructed and made to cohere by the power of the word, no longer assumed as Christian doctrine but as 'fierce pun'. Where Chaucer imagines a pre-national community assembled from "every shire's end" by the force of storytelling, Agbabi envisages an internally diverse and heteroglot postnational community united in its 'love of retelling tales' that are realized in writing and 'kept real on the papyrus' in/as *Telling Tales*.

3.4 Untelling tales: Anagrammatic Blackness in M. NourbeSe Philip's *Zong!*

Yet not 'all that's written' 'inspires us'. It may be possible to 'detox' individual texts – and we have seen in Agbabi's remix of Chaucer what effort even such a relatively limited project requires. But what if that updating of Chaucerian prenational optimism for a postnational present and future runs against the hard rock of the *actual* history of a nation that for centuries excelled in colonial domination of large tracts of the globe and the systematic dehumanizing of millions of non-Europeans? Inverse Britain may come into its own in Evaristo's playful inversions of coloniality or Agbabi's rewriting of the inaugural moment of English literature in her re-vision of Chaucer; but what is required before all these rearticulations is the disaggregation of the murderous matter that is stored in the nation's archive, where 'all that's written' turns out to be neither instruction nor inspiration but mere obfuscation. Through the lens of the exploited, colonized and enslaved – those who actually made and in modified ways continue to make modern Britain – the hegemonic hi/story of the nation must be a hopelessly incomplete gutter text even though it presents itself as a continuous narrative; and it is this obstinately long-lived continuous narrative that needs to be ripped apart time and again. What is consistently written out of that hi/story is the perspective of subalternity and specifically enslavement. Nowhere does this get more poignantly apparent than in the disturbingly complete and incomplete archive of the Atlantic slave trade and the Caribbean plantation economy that were indispensable in the making of modern Britain. Here the most sober and rational discourses of all – those of the law and of commerce – turn into sheer "irrationality and confusion", as M. NourbeSe Philip (2008: 195) observes, pointing to the ill-logic of "a system that could enable, encourage even, a man to drown 150 people as a way to maximize profit" (ibid). In her poetry cycle *Zong!* (2008), Philip, a Tobago-born Black poet and lawyer resident in Toronto, Canada, faces the impossibilities of negotiating the gaping gaps of that archive and offers, besides many other things, a most devastating *pharmakon* that puts Britain in/verse. Saying this, I am not suggesting that Philip is writing primarily *about* Britain; far from it: her poems speak of and to a racialized *world* rather than one specific location. But this does not rule out a scene of reading where *Zong!* as a whole takes on particular poignancy and relevance in a British perspective. For while it is true that the *Zong* massacre of 1781 can and should be interpreted as emblematic of the atrocities of the Atlantic slave trade in general, the fact remains that the perpetrators were British seamen under the command of a British captain of a British ship. More than that, it was British judges and attorneys applying British laws that performed in the subsequent trials and produced – British texts. In fact, it is one of these texts, the minutes of the *Gregson v. Gilbert* hearings, 1783, that provides the verbal material, the "word store", that Philip most extensively draws on for *Zong!* so that her text is most basically constituted from the materials of a British text. This, of course, does not make *Zong!* a British text but for sure one that intervenes into debates on Britishness past and present by rendering Britain in/verse. I will come back to this question further down but at this point would briefly like to add one remark on the question of genre. Like *Telling Tales*, but far more obviously so, *Zong!* is not a verse novel, at least not in the sense of a large-format narrative in verse. Where Agbabi remixes a pre-novelistic hypotext that assembles a whole panoply of stories and hence an excess of narrative, Philip extinguishes narrative entirely in a collection of radically spatialized poems that tend to sheer visuality. And yet, I argue, *Zong!* can be read as a series of verses that in concert 'do the job of a novel' – not by telling a story but by articulating a narrative address of the nation: only that, in this case, the narrative cannot be narrated as "there is no telling this story", but it "must be told" all the same. This paradox runs all through *Zong!* and complicates any reading, not least one that tries to grasp that text as *also* a project to in/verse Britain. Before addressing these questions in light of Philip's text itself, I would like to situate *Zong!* within current debates on enslavism and the *Zong* case in particular.

The archive of enslavism

The archive of the Atlantic slave trade is both alarmingly incomplete and shockingly complete as every historian worth their salt reiterates. What is almost entirely missing is the voices of the enslaved so that we do not only not have their testimony but not even the vaguest idea of "what happened to their memories" (Walvin 2011: 211). These are gaps that no visit to the scenes of crime can close and that defy but at the same time also painfully energize the constellating impulse that gutter texts trigger. Saidiya Hartman's sojourn to Ghana leaves her baffled with the void that she faces in the dungeon of Cape Coast Castle, the fortified British slave port from which alone up to 250,000 enslaved Africans were forced to embark on the Middle Passage:

> NO ONE IMPRISONED in the dungeon of Cape Coast Castle had ever described it. There was no record left behind by the captives who entered and exited the underground. Not a single account. All the journals, reports, letters, and trade documents belonged to merchants and company men. The rare instances of slave testimony described neighboring forts or slave holds elsewhere on the West African coast, but these recollections didn't amount to more than a few lines, none of which provided the merest hint of their experience in the holding cell. (Hartman 2007: 93)

What Hartman only wryly mentions in this context is the reverse side of this gaping lacuna, namely the uninhibited text production on the side of 'merchants and company men'. In fact there is no paucity of archival material to reconstruct the logics of the system at work, from its logistics to its legal framing, from its economic accountancy to its ethnographics. By no means was the slave trade taboo in British society; rather to the contrary, from the mid-eighteenth century to the abolition of the slave trade in 1807, "the friction between successful slave-based commerce and traditional English liberties" (Walvin 2011: 328) was constantly debated in public, where its beneficiaries and profiteers declared the slave trade and plantation economy inevitable as "the main spring of the machine, which sets every wheel in motion" (anon in ibid.: 70). Yet even if contemporary public discourse thus unabashedly avows that the rapid growth of Britain's wealth and accelerated modernization are dependent on and generated by the systematic exploits of slave labour, that very same discourse is simultaneously strained to organize a concerted silence around the concrete conditions under which these welcome benefits are reaped. The hidden abodes of production where modern Britain was made – the cargo hold of the slave ship and the sugarcane plantation – are rendered purely functionary sites in the abstracting logic of "computational colonialism" (Beller 2016). The actuarial "imagination of finance capital" demands and makes real the reduction of all particulars "to a general, abstract, typicalizing standard of (knowledge) value" (Baucom 2005, 162, 205) – as in the designation of the insurance value of each person stored on board the slave ship *Zong* at an average sum of thirty pounds. This computational logic – "the il/logics of colonization, [...] the il/logic of Black life in the wake" (Sharpe 2016: 89) – is visually manifest in the iconic sketch of the tiered decks of the *Brooks*. This diagrammatic abstraction of bodies in the hold has through its "ubiquitous dismemberment and endless recycling" long since become "a sort of visual shorthand used in popular treatments of slavery and the slave trade" (Wood 2010: 164). As Anouk Madörin persuasively suggests, the visual effect of the sketch is to render the Black bodies pressed into the ship's cargo hold standardized units whose arrangement appears to anticipate the barcode:

> Seen against the white background of the slave ship floor, the Black bodies captured in the *Brooks* sketch present an early version of digital measurement: the zeroes and ones from the binary code assigning a pattern of binary digits, or bits, to each character, instruction, or rule. These classificatory mathematics were one of the logics accompanying the Middle Passage as it stripped the enslaved off their individuality and singularity and reduced them to specimens within the transatlantic economy. (Madörin 2022: 22)

Black life is thus reduced to fungible typicality: "Typical risk, typical life expectancy, typical value of a given commodity" (Baucom 2005: 39). It is against this 'il/logics' of computational colonialism that white abolitionism mobilizes the "discourse of the spirit" (Thomas 2000: 36) in the attempt to restore the humanity of the dehumanized. The often graphic and lurid descriptions in white abolitionist writing of the Middle Passage or the plantation regime speak of this aspiration of recovering the individual suffering and therewith individuality as such. Saidiya Hartman demonstrates this strategy and its inbuilt shortcomings with reference to William Wilberforce's 1792 parliamentary move for the abolition of the slave trade. Wilberforce attempts to intensify the force of his argument by illustrating his plea with the account of the fatal torture of an unnamed young enslaved woman during the Middle Passage at the hands of a sadistic British captain. The appeal to empathy and compassion make it prerequisite that the victim should be individualized as

> too many dead slaves would have had the opposite effect and diminished the significance of the tragedy. From the *Zong* case he [Wilberforce] had learned that 132 live slaves dumped into the sea were just cargo. It was easier to feel fully the loss of one life [...] Too many deaths were unmanageable. (Hartman 2007: 108)

But, as has often been pointed out, even where this "melancholy realism" (Baucom 2005: 34) manages to articulate a counternarrative to the hegemonic actuarial logic of computational colonialism, it remains inadvertently complicit with the enslavement system it combats insofar as it, like that system, rules out Black agency. From the standpoint of the slaveholder, "the slave is indisputably outside the normative terms of individuality to such a degree that the very exercise of agency is seen as a contravention of another's unlimited rights to the object" (Hartman 1997: 62). Eerily similar is the standpoint of the white abolitionist mainstream, where the very idea that there could be such a thing as "African self-determination was soon abandoned when texts depicted silent victims who depended upon outside intervention" (Ferguson 1992: 257). In this convention, "the sentimental representation of victimised Africans was overdetermined by the slave's status as objectified property" (Rupprecht 2007: 338). By constantly reiterating this objectified status, white abolitionism's "bid for emancipation reproduced the abject position of the slave" (Hartman 2007: 167).

Yet I am not arguing here for a simple reversal of the enslaver/abolitionist construction of the Black figure as essentially passive recipient of either white terror or white benevolence; it would be too easy to generally postulate Black agency or even resistance as a given that was merely obscured by enslavist law or do-good paternalism. To assume that those who were exposed to the extreme violence of the slave ship or the plantation will 'necessarily' be resistant would be naïve at best for it would occlude exactly the de-subjectifying effects of that violence, not least its systematic denial of "legal personhood" (Weheliye 2014: 11). Given the structural disarticulation that enslavement entails, the expectation of resistance and agency needs to be "bracketed" since these concepts "assume full, self-present, and coherent subjects" (ibid.: 2) that the exposure to enslavism works to erase. Alexander Weheliye therefore emphasizes the no-body status of the Black subject that is not constituted by the fiat of habeas corpus but instead interpellated as mere "flesh": "If the body represents legal personhood qua self-possession, then the flesh designates those dimensions of human life cleaved by the working together of depravation and deprivation" (ibid.: 39).

It is precisely for this reason that Fred Moten opens his exploration of Black radical traditions with the assertion that Black resistance (which he, unlike Weheliye, does not bracket but put centre stage) is not to be misread as the deed of some agentive self-centred subjectivity or person as imagined by the European Enlightenment. To the contrary, "the history of blackness is testament to the fact that *objects* can and do resist" (Moten 2003: 1; emphasis added). Black radicalism, Black resistance thus emerges from the historical and persistent fact of dehumanization from which it wrests a moment where "objecthood becomes subjecthood" (ibid.: 240) in a reversal or displacement of categories. Christina Sharpe identifies this inversive process as "anagrammatical blackness that exists as an index of violability and potentiality". Anagrammaticality is not recuperative or redemptive; like Weheliye's notion of enfleshment rather than embodiment, or Moten's apparent oxymoron of the subjective object/objective subject, anagrammatic Blackness hovers between two poles: on the one hand, the violability of *imposed* unintelligibility as coerced structural exclusion from discursive agency and instead reduction to "the mere noise of suffering bodies" (Rancière 2010: 139); on the other hand, the potentiality that the undoing of the grammatical order, in the dual sense of that term, implies. This implies the disarticulatory practice of ripping apart the hegemonic given script but, beyond that, also the creative rearticulation of new, hidden, minor constellations and networks. As potential, the anagrammatic then undoes the master script and redoes it for its own purposes. There are, Sharpe (2016: 75) suggests,

> moments when blackness opens up into the anagrammatical in the literal sense as when 'a word, phrase, or name is formed by rearranging the letters of another' (Merriam-Webster Online). We can also apprehend this in the metaphorical sense in how, regarding blackness, grammatical gender falls away and new meanings proliferate; how 'the letters of a text are formed into a secret message by rearranging them' or a secret message is discovered through the rearranging of the letters of a text.

The *Zong* case

This brings us significantly closer but not yet quite to Marlene NourbeSe Philip's *Zong!*, a both literally and metaphorically anagrammatic verse collection designed to probe the violable as well as the potential in the impossible attempt to tell a story that "must be told by not telling" (Z 190). The story at hand is that of the *Zong* massacre in which the atrocities of the Middle Passage crystallize as much as the proliferation of discourse – both actuarial and 'melancholy' – around that unspeakable core. In the last weeks of November 1781, the crew of the British slave ship *Zong* threw more than 130 enslaved Africans overboard because water supplies were deemed to be running short: due to a series of navigational errors of the captain, the *Zong* had already taken some eighteen instead of the average nine weeks for the Middle Passage when the killings were done. Of the 442 people pressed into the cargo holds below deck, only 208 were still alive on arrival in Jamaica. The *Zong* massacre became a public issue in Britain only when the Liverpool-based ship owners, the Gregsons, tried to claim on the ship's insurance for the Africans killed at sea. After the insurance company had turned down that demand, the Gregson syndicate filed a case that would eventually transform "the story of the *Zong* [...] from a murderous secret among the small handful of sailors who carried out the killings, and their employers in Liverpool, into a highly visible political and legal issue" (Walvin 2011: 3). However, at stake in the courtroom hearings was not the fact of mass murder but the liability of the underwriters for 'loss of cargo': the court was "called upon to sit in judgment, not of the killers, but of whether mass murder was covered by an insurance policy. [...] African deaths were mere numerical and financial details in a commercial transaction" (ibid.: 173). This framing of the massacre entirely in terms of the actuarial rationale of computational colonialism speaks with chilling clarity from one of the very few official *Zong*-related document that have survived (the ship's logbook and manifest having disappeared already in 1782): the minutes of the court hearings in the *Gregson v. Gilbert* case, 22 May 1783, that Philip appends to (or includes in) *Zong!* During the court hearings, the conflict is whether the "throwing overboard of goods [...] to save the residue" was necessitated "by the perils of the sea" (in Z 211), as the owners assert, or whether "there was only an apprehended necessity, which was not sufficient" (Z 210), as the insurers claim. Both sides – and along with them the court itself – are united on one point: that this was not a criminal but an insurance case. There is unanimous agreement that any "argument drawn from the law respecting indictments for murder does not apply" since slaves, though "fellow-creatures", are by general consensus not humans but property, in Weheliye's analysis, not 'bodies' but 'flesh': "It has been decided, whether wisely or unwisely is not now the question, that a portion of our fellow-creatures may become the subject of property" (Z 211). Therefore, according to the steering subtext of the "contract plot" that dominated the trial (Baucom 2005: 201), whatever happened on board the *Zong* was not mass murder but the destruction of insured property.

However, that the court in its final statement should at all feel obliged to explicitly rule out the possibility of indictments for murder indicates that such a possibility must have been raised during the proceedings or in its context. And indeed it has, as historical research amply demonstrates. Abolitionist activists Olaudah Equiano and Granville Sharp not only observed and took minutes of the *Zong* trials but were actively involved behind the scenes at least in the May 1783 trial through their counsellor, one

Solicitor Haywood, who on their behalf placed the plea for a prosecution of the surviving *Zong* hands as murderers (cf. Dellarossa 2014: 137). None of the solicitor's argument appear in the official minutes (where he figures as 'Heywood'), but definitely in Sharp's transcripts of the May sessions that he forwarded, after the trial, to the Admiralty Department as that body to which "the cognizance and right of enquiry concerning all Murders committed on board British Ships belongs properly" (in Faubert 2019: 127). Sharp's transcript and missive are remarkable in their to-the-point conceptuality and their restraint from the sensationalism that characterizes most of the better-known writings from the white abolitionist canon. Where Clarkson or Wilberforce, in their attempts to trigger empathetic responses in their audience, frequently included detailed descriptions of the atrocities inflicted on suffering individuals, Sharp "made no attempt to publicize the horrors of slavery, to stir the emotions or touch sensibilities" (Brown 2006: 179). Instead, he argues a principal cause of Black "Right to Life itself" (in Faubert 2019: 151) and aims to performatively claim habeas corpus for the Black body. I wish to suggest, without there being any viable evidence, that this exceptional thrust and political acuity of Sharp's rhetoric is to a large extent owed to the fact that his text was not only his as it was composed in close collaboration with a co-author, Equiano, whose speaking position was fundamentally shaped by the fact of Blackness.

There may well be a certain amount of disillusionment in this rhetorical restraint. For Sharp and Equiano appear to be fully aware that they operate under conditions where everybody knows, hence nobody needs to be told about the slave trade that, indeed, "formed a mundane feature of the social and economic fabric of British life" (Walvin 2011: 174). Therefore the *Zong* case "involved no 'whistleblowers' tearing the lid off a secret, since there was no secret. It was commonplace for slaves to be killed on slave ships" (Faubert 2017: 181). Under these auspices, abolitionist strategy as pursued by Sharp and Equiano could not be premised on the naïve expectation that the horrors of the trade could be terminated simply by exposing them to the public, by dragging them into discourse. Rather, the *Zong* made hypervisible what had anyway been visible all along, hiding in the light for everyone to see. Abolitionism therefore was not primarily about conveying knowledge of the always-already-known but about making a scandal of what everybody knew. This scandalization, for Sharp and Equiano, appears to have been a matter of rational deliberation. The addressee of their discourse is the Enlightenment public whom they attempt to win over by pointing out the inconsistences, the ill-logic of the system. In this understanding, the abolitionist project was not so much an information campaign but a re-education programme: a national pedagogy with the aim to interpellate British subjects into proper rationality.

The other, more prominent and perhaps also more effective strategy to scandalize was, as mentioned earlier, the affective appeal of 'melancholy realism' with its lurid descriptions of atrocities that were presented to ultimately create an awareness of the brutalizing impact of the system on everyone. In the writings of Wilberforce this impulse is most explicit: "God has set two immense tasks before me: the suppression of the slave trade, and the reformation of manners" (Wilberforce in Rouse 2018: 15). Both these tasks are inseparably intertwined since for Wilberforce the slave trade is an immediate outcome of the corruption of manners and at the same time, as long as it is practiced, a constant source of further degradation and brutalization not only of the perpetrators but also of its indirect beneficiaries (i.e. almost all Britons). Substituting political principles and moral standards for short-term economic self-interest, the abolitionist educational programme promises its clientele primarily "the moral benefits that the abolition of the slave trade [would] deliver to the nation (rather than to the Africans)" (Rupprecht 2007: 339). In this figure of thought, beneficiaries incur losses, and perpetrators become victims, if only of their own deeds. The *Zong* "answered the need to represent the dehumanisation of slave trafficking" (ibid.: 341) and thus became a powerful collective symbol of a narrative through which a British audience could be taught to face their own brutalized condition.

At the same time, the *Zong* served as a shorthand for the sheer unrepresentability of the actual concrete horrors of the Middle Passage and enslavism as such. If the facts were generally known, then part of that knowledge was that the African experience was unknowable. In this sense, "the *Zong* served, in its above-decks visibility, as a stand-in for the below-decks invisibility of an experience of which there are almost no eyewitness accounts left by those who experienced it" (Armstrong 2007: 347). This concession that the system's actual atrocities are beyond representation is integral to the national pedagogy of abolitionism even when, as in Wilberforce's rhetoric, atrocities are sharply set into relief. It excludes the below-decks perspective from discourse by building a firewall around it, and it thereby serves in effect to annul and erase the Black experience of enslavement by rendering it only noise: unintelligible, anagrammatical, again.

A new narrative address

Zong!, I argue in the following, breaks through that firewall by deliberately embracing Blackness as anagrammaticality and wresting from it a poetry of the unspeakable and unrepresentable. As stated earlier, I am not arguing that *Zong!* is first and foremost about inversing Britain – certainly not in the same way that Tempest's, Evaristo's or Agbabi's texts are. What I wish to suggest though is that Philip takes up and appropriates the speaking position of the pedagogue in the second part of her book where, especially in the 'Notanda' section, the opacity of the poems of the first parts is 'ameliorated' by explanation and instruction. In other words, Philip's text bifurcates into a poetic, increasingly 'unreadable' first section and a second part which explains that inexplicable text. This constellation of a sprawling textual perplexity with a didactic instruction of how to read this chaos is structurally akin to the duality – that "tension between the pedagogical and the performative" – that Homi Bhabha has postulated as the hallmark of the "narrative address of the nation" (Bhabha 1990: 298). For Bhabha, this double-writing or dissemi-nation complicates and ultimately destabilizes the majoritarian project of implementing the nation as internally homogeneous and thereby clears "a place from which to speak both of, and as, the minority, the exilic, the marginal, and the emergent" (ibid.: 300). I would love to think that *Zong!* (among the many other things it does) reinvents this double scripting for a new kind of narrative address of Britain. To repeat: Philip's book is not a verse novel. In fact, it appears essentially anti-narrative while at its core there is a story that must be told but cannot be told. Here it is important that the full title of the book reads: *Zong! As told to the author by Setaey Adamu Boateng*. This paratextual inscription has at least two major consequences: First, it evokes a shared authorship in which an ancestor – probably a victim of the *Zong* massacre (and even the survivors were victims) – is named as the source whose message the author conveys; second, it indicates that that message was *told* and therefore must in some ways have been (a) narrative. *Zong!* is then the re-telling of that narrative in a necessarily non-narrative performance, since "that story can only be told by not telling" (Z 191). And yet the paratext keeps this un-actualized narrative visible under erasure and overcodes the whole book as one long ghostly story that will not manifest as one. Given this it will be permissible to argue that *Zong!*, though clearly not a verse novel proper but a cycle of experimental poems, is yet not entirely removed from the domain of narrative, and that in that respect it can still take on the function that has traditionally been associated with the novel: to deliver a 'narrative address of the nation', with the important caveat that this address will be radically non-narrative.

In its first part, 'Os' (Latin for 'bone'), *Zong!* comprises thirty-two poems of which the last six form a subsection of their own, titled 'Dicta'. The most immediately conspicuous feature of these poems is their extreme reductionism and the graphic quality they attain through the foregrounding of their massive gappiness as single words or small clusters of words are meticulously constellated and at times widely dispersed across the pages of 'Os'. The ensuant sense of disconnectedness gets intensified by the lack of grammaticality that right from the start discourages a narrative reading for the plot. *Zong!*'s spatial form appears to arrest linear (hence temporal) directionality and forces the reader to skim these pages for whatever morsels of meaning might be gleaned from their blank spaces.

"*Zong!* #4" (Z 7) is one of the more accessible poems in the book. It could be read as a meditation on the verb 'to be' which the text in its two vertical columns (Figure 3.1) conjugates through various modes and tenses. Yet even if the poem to some extent is exactly this – an exploration of 'to be' – its

Zong! #4

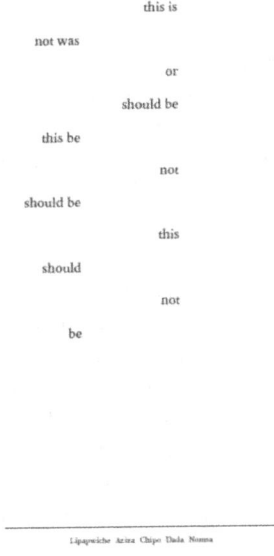

FIGURE 3.1 M. NourbeSe Philip, *Zong!*

Source: M. NourbeSe Philip, *Zong!*, p. 7. Reproduced with the permission of the author.

effect is in light of the topic at hand deeply disturbing. In spite of the vertical linearity of the spatial form, and in spite of the deceptive grammaticality and commensurability of the opening lines – "this is | not was | or | should be" – no coherent syntax can be construed in the middle part of the poem, until the concluding verses offer again a foothold: "This | should | not | be", only to add as a resounding non sequitur the isolated copula "is" whose typographic dis-placement to the far left of the rest of the text tips the visual balance of the two columns that make up the main body of the poem. One plausible way of making sense of '*Zong! #4*' is to assume that the pronoun 'this' in the poem refers to the massacre on board the *Zong*, an event whose presence in the present the first lines assert by rejecting the preterit: 'this is | not was'. To the extent that the grammatical verb form of the indicative present tense ('is') here trumps the past tense ('not was'), the text underscores that the event stands for a past that is not over and cannot be put to rest. In the reflexive 'pedagogical' 'Notanda' section (of which more further on), Philip ponders how the recollection of the trauma of the Middle Passage makes the atrocity repeat itself again and again so that it is happening always – repeating always, the repetition becoming a haunting. Do they, the sounds, the cries, the shouts of those thrown overboard from the *Zong* repeat themselves over and over until they rise from the ocean floor to resurface in *Zong!*? (Z 203)

What also returns, however, is the verb *to be* in its constative conjunction as 'is': at the final moment of the poem, its reoccurrence is a repetition with a difference as it now no longer overrides the notion of pastness but the normative notion according to which an event like the *Zong* massacre 'should not be'. The verb form 'is' now insists on its indicative force as opposed to the conjunctive mode of 'should'. What is remarkable is how Philip's poem works through and defaces the affirmative impact of the constative 'is'. For a poetic text to arrive at the confirmation of the actual existence and presence of something or someone is usually to be interpreted as an endorsement of being as such. The reading of '*Zong* #4', so far, renders this kind of endorsement *unheimlich* and ultimately impossible since it implies the embracing (or at least acceptance as fact) of enslavement and mass murder. What appears to be being as such is thus contaminated with the annihilation of Black being that it implies. For that which is confirmed as present by the concluding 'is' is precisely that: the killing of enslaved Africans declared to be cargo. Read in this way, the poem culminates in the suggestion that *being itself should not be*, and in this negativity, the Afropessimist thrust of Philip's poetry appears to come to the fore: being as it is hegemonically institutionalized rests on the "erasure and forgetting of the be-ing and humanity of the Africans on board the *Zong*" (Z 204) and everywhere. From this perspective, Blackness as non-ontology is the cornerstone of a politically constituted world order based on the colour line: an "entrenched visual schema predicated on the fungibility of the Black body" (Sexton and Copeland 2003: 54) that constantly reiterates and reproduces as categorical and essential the premise of white supremacy. This Manichean politics posits an essential "difference between a sentient being who is positioned as a *being in the world* and one who is positioned as a *thing of the world*" (Wilderson 2009: 123; emphasis in the original) – the former the non-racialized white subject, the latter the racialized Black non-subject/object/thing.

Zong! writes itself not only into this violent discursive formation but actually constitutes itself from the very material of that discourse. In its first section, Philip's text is literally *made* of nothing but enslavist speech, more precisely, from the minutes of the *Gregson v. Gilbert* hearings in May 1783, the one official document of the *Zong* case that has survived. For the thirty-two poems that make up 'Os', Philip decides to

> use the text of the legal decision as a word store; to lock [herself] into this particular and peculiar discursive landscape in the belief that the story of

these African men, women, and children thrown overboard in an attempt to collect insurance monies, the story that can only be told by not telling, is locked in this text. (Z 191)

The poems pilfer that 'word store', rip the internal relations of its words asunder and reassemble them anagrammatically in entirely new ways, apparently at random. In the 'Notanda' section, Philip discusses this procedure as intensely violent and eerily (and not least: deliberately!) "similar to the activity of the random picking of African slaves – selected randomly then thrown together, hoping that something would come of it" (Z 193). The Afropessimist text thus adopts its poetics from the technique of the enslavers and symbolically inflicts it on them by violently randomizing precisely that legal "language in which those events took place", a language that "promulgated the non-being of African peoples" (Z 197). The trial document, Philip notes, appears as "a certain kind of entity – a whole, a completeness" (Z 192), and it is this apparent coherence and consistency that the poems in *Zong!* so radically undo: "Philip's text unlocks her source text, the *Gregson* case, in order to release a story of the *Zong* massacre" (Shockley 2011: 815). But obviously that 'story' does not reveal itself from the fragments of that dismembered archival document. As long as the words and clusters of the poems in *Zong!* are in fact treated as *fragments* of a broken-up 'whole', they cannot serve as *segments* of a future assemblage (perhaps) to come. They can only serve as reminders to the lost 'completeness' of the *Gregson v. Gilbert* text and thereby constantly point to the abjectness built into that wholeness and perhaps wholeness as such, akin to the categorical negativity of the constative 'is' in '*Zong!* #4'. From an Afropessimist standpoint, this is not a tragedy. The tearing-apart of the archival text is not a *sparagmos* – a ritualistic dismemberment – that in Hegelian teleology "creates the conditions of the *denouement* and carries the action forward to a resolution" (White 1973: 126). Here there is no resolution but a constant mourning of that which remains absent even after the dismemberment of the master text:

> Philip's experimental poems do not tell a story so much as convey the ghostly presence of lives within a document that treats those lives as immaterial. They summon transported Africans caught between life and death, filled with humanity and also drowning in its negation. (Sharpe 2014: 473)

Yet even if the poems do "not tell the story that is missing from the archives so much as indicate the limits of its telling" (ibid.: 466), they still do not come to rest on the positive assertion of negativity and impossibility but instead form an irresolvable aporia that provides the leitmotif that runs all through *Zong!*: "There is no telling this story; it must be told" (Z 189). In this perspective it is the darkest of ironies that the last and concluding section of the book should consist of a verbatim reproduction of *Gregson v. Gilbert* as an intact document, as if to assert that all the ripping and mutilating, the reshuffling and reclustering of that 'mother document' had been futile and to no avail. This, indeed, would confirm the radical Afropessimist standpoint that enslavist anti-Blackness is so inextricably woven into the fabric of the world that only the end of the world can make it at all possible to put an end to the fundamental "impossibility of Black life" (Wilderson 2014: 12). Anything short of complete annihilation does not suffice; a mere ripping apart will only lead back to the reassembling, again and again, of the dehumanizing hegemon. In this light the gutter-text fragments in *Zong!* are also segments of that evil 'mother document' that at the end returns in full and forceful coherence after all these assaults on the integrity of its body, triumphantly declaring that it 'is'. And that its very being predicates and indeed eternalizes Black non-being.

But there may be another reading, too. For after all, the return to (and of) *Gregson v. Gilbert* at the end of *Zong!* occurs at a scene of reading whose terms have been constitutively shaped by Philip: both by the performance of the poems and the pedagogy of the notanda. The reader who finally arrives at the trial transcript will be a reader who has been exposed to a long instruction on how to read that language and its apparent orderliness and consistency as inversions and perversions of what it claims to promulgate. Philip's poems wear disorder and confusion on their sleeves but may all the more be read as logically consequential articulations of the disorder and confusion they are about; whereas the legal document comes in the guise of reason and deliberation but propagates an "order which hides disorder; its logic hiding the illogic and its rationality, which is simultaneously irrational" (Z 197). What Philip excavates from the text is its subtext, its "'underwater' ratio [...] that the law supercedes being, that being is not a constant in time, but can be changed by the law" (Z 200) in quasi-miraculous acts of pure nominalism that may, for example, transform people into cargo or things. The performative force of the law is by no means disclaimed when Philip exposes "its potent ability to decree that what is is not" (Z 196) as magical or religious thinking. Before we actually come into the presence of the law (as enshrined in the document that closes the book), the lens through which we read the law has thus been significantly recalibrated and, arguably, sharpened. To visit the law after reading Philip's poems and reflections, performance and pedagogy, amounts to entering the hidden abode of production of an anti-Black world but also the cell of a madman. If the main, anagrammatical part of *Zong!* seems "to be bringing chaos into the language", then this reading of the ostensibly grammatical and ordered language of the law "reveal[s] the chaos that is already there" (Z 205) and has always been there. Behind its sober façade, then, the legal document hides its delirium, which the *Zong!* poems vicariously perform. But they do more than that:

> The ratio at the heart of *Zong!* [...] is simply the story of be-ing which cannot, but must, be told. Through not-telling. And where the law attempts to extinguish be-ing, as happened for 400 years as part of the European project, *be-ing trumps the law every time*. (Z 200; emphasis added)

In this light, the poems are not only about the annihilation of Black subjecthood and indeed ontology, even though they are about all that very much; they are also about Blackness as resilient survivalism that makes an alternate reading of '*Zong!* #4' possible. What if this reassemblage of matter from the madness of the trial transcript is not about the mass murder but about Black 'be-ing'? On such a reading, the poem's speaker would voice the position of the law that has to concede that 'this' (Black ontology), though it by fiat 'should not be', yet *is*, not was. The concluding constative 'is', set precariously off-centre below the two columns as if to shift the ground on which they stand, is now an assertion of precisely that Black being that the law has set out to extinguish as that which 'should not be'. In this reading, it becomes important that the displaced 'is' may be the last line but not the actual ground zero of the poem. For underneath the first twenty-six poems there runs an ongoing frieze of names that are arranged underneath a long horizontal line that evokes the ocean's waterline under which the victims appear to be submerged. Their names are not recorded. This is not a memorial but a space of counterfactual and yet historically precise commemoration. It is on this basis of a virtual memory site that the poems in 'Os' precariously stand. How do the five names underneath '*Zong!#4*' communicate with the in-conclusive 'is' of that poem? The dead, who may or may not have borne the names that appear under the waterline: 'are' they or 'are' they 'not'? Can a work of poetry return to them the very being that they were so violently deprived of? *Zong!* says no. It is one of the most lasting shocks in the reading process when the space beneath the waterline remains empty in the six 'Dicta' poems. All that poetry can do is counterfactually name the losses and register the inhumane indifference of the ocean and the ship that moves on, away from the scene of crime, as in Turner's painting.

The following sections – 'Sal', 'Ventus', 'Ratio', 'Ferrum' and 'Ebora' – break open the confines of the *Gregson v. Gilbert* word store by configuring it with segments from numerous other verbal repertoires and various languages including Spanish, Portuguese, Italian, Yoruba, Shona, French, Hebrew, Greek and West African Patois. What ensues is a series of sprawling assemblages that appear paradoxically both amorphous and ordered, both anarchic and regular in their 'equal' treatment of all the loosely constellated verbal matter on the page (see Figure 3.2).

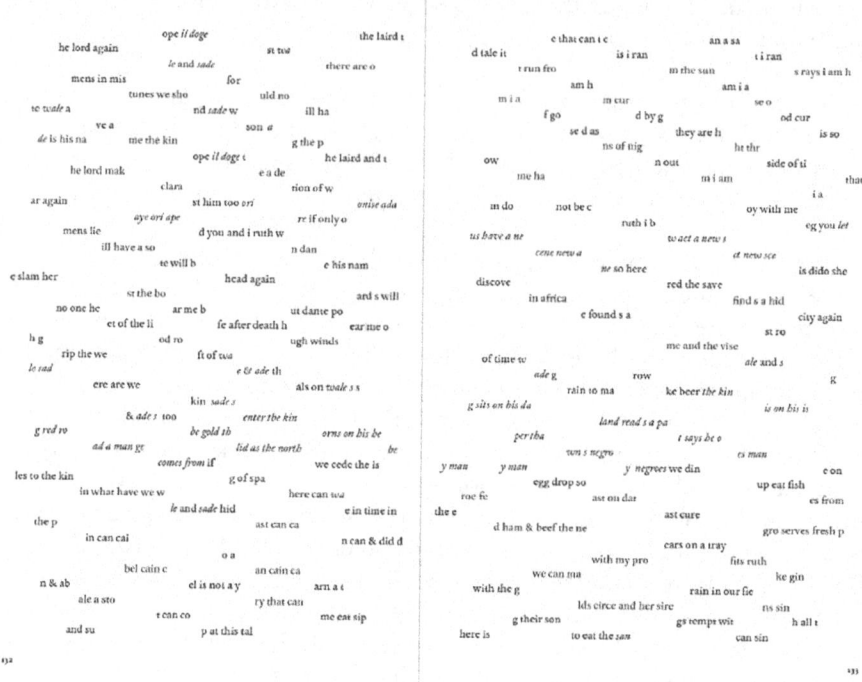

FIGURE 3.2 M. NourbeSe Philip, *Zong!*

Source: M. NourbeSe Philip, *Zong!*, pp. 132–3. Reproduced with the permission of the author.

This extremely guttered textuality visually emphasizes the well-nigh non-negotiable gaps between these clusters of verbal molecules. At closer inspection it turns out that this anagrammaticality pervades the text down to its microlevel where it is composed of decomposition, of the disarticulation and ripping apart of words that are spliced up, "separated by small and large spaces, and sometimes divided across a line" (Fehskens 2012: 420). One plausible reading would see in this procedure the text's striving to re-evoke the violence of separation and even bodily mangling and mutilation that the system of enslavism inflicted on millions of Africans; and more specifically the disorientation of the captives on board the *Zong*: "How did they – the Africans on board the *Zong* – make meaning of what was happening to them? What meaning did they make of it and how did they make it mean?" (Z 194). This confusion is passed on to the reader for whom "reading vertically or transversally becomes a challenge as words suffer splicing and mangling more and more frequently" (Fehskens 2012: 420) while all the same, splinters of minimal coherence (and even narrative!) emerge here and there like coagulated clods of meaning only to get submerged again in the white noise of the cacophonous zone of indeterminacy that the poem is. This strategy of disarticulation is paired to the establishment of a general equivalence as none of these dispersed clusters seems to possess a particular centrality or specific gravity of its own. Every particle appears roughly equivalent to all the others, and as none of these particles forms a self-enclosed entity but more often than not, massively incomplete component parts of larger units, the text's minimal molecules are, precisely due to their foregrounded incompleteness, readable as materialized embodiments of that "literary disincorporation" (Rancière 2004b: 40) that contemporary political theory perceives as literature's specific capacity to contribute to the overcoming of anthropocentric humanism. For Jacques Rancière, for example, literature enacts, by virtue of its democratic indifference, a redistribution of the sensible "that cancels the difference between two kinds of humanity, between beings destined for great deeds and refined passions and beings doomed to the practical and positive life" (Rancière 2011: 55). However, that logic, according to which writing instantiates "the equal value of every subject" (Rancière 2004a: 157), looks very different through the lens of a text that stretches 'democratic indifference' to its extreme limits while writing (but not telling) of the mass murder of some 150 people each prized at the 'equal value' of thirty pounds. This is not to polemicize against the political aesthetic theory of continental thinkers like Rancière but to specify where Philip departs, and must depart, from such agendas that from the perspective of Blackness do not apply: disincorporation and indifferentiation may appeal as liberatory and de-hierarchizing for subjects interpellated into the latest ideological revampings of possessive individualism but not for those interpellated as non-subjects. From a Black perspective, disincorporation can only entrench the withholding of habeas corpus; indifference can only confirm all over again 400 years of systematic desubjectification as exchangeable commodity in the medium of the universal equivalent: thirty pounds each. The poetics of the later sections in *Zong!* therefore does not celebrate the white noise it produces but rather mourns "the loss of language and meaning on board the *Zong* [which] levels everyone to a place where there is, at times, no distinction between languages – everyone, European and African alike, has reverted, it appears, to a state of pre-literacy" (Z 206).

It is from this reversion that the text derives its 'optimistic' dimensions. Already at the immediately graphic level, not only the amorphous dispersal of bits and bytes is conspicuous but also their networked arrangement across the pages that allows for a minimal structure to emerge. What is evoked thereby is nothing more (but also nothing less) than connectivity as a potentiality as clusters engage in putative relations with adjacent clusters in horizontal, vertical or diagonal, left to right, right to left, top-down or bottom-up directionalities. This poses a significant challenge to the reading process but simultaneously opens up multiple paths of exploration and tentative meaning making.

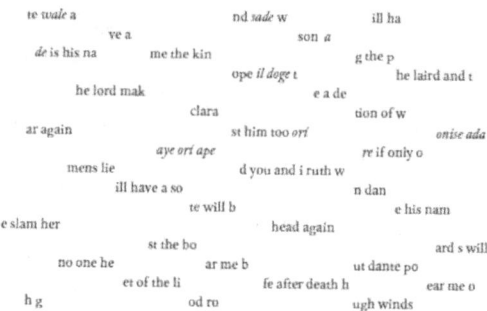

FIGURE 3.3 M. NourbeSe Philip, *Zong!*

Source: M. NourbeSe Philip, *Zong!*, p. 132. Reproduced with the permission of the author.

It is true that a strictly conventional left to right horizontal reading results in the retrieval of the intact text that is hidden, as it were, in this gutter constellation: only an extract of a much longer fugue-like series of variation on the theme of how enslavist politics shapes or unshapes personal lives. There are different foci and voices that are interlaced by the theme of generational reproduction in the destructive forcefield of enslavism. The first 'episode' – "*wale* and *sade* will have a son *ade* is his name" (Figure 3.3) – appears to introduce a minimal narrative of a family genealogy that gets immediately interrupted by the grotesque mobilization of the collective forces of an anti-Black world: "The king the pope *il doge* the laird and the lord make a declaration of war against him". Ade, yet unborn though named in the present tense, gets thus beleaguered by a universal alliance determined to annihilate him even before his birth. His father, Wale, has been introduced much earlier in the 'Sal' section as "a most uncommon negro he hopes to regain africa one day" (Z 88) and is later seen wooing Sade with a "rush ring" and building a "hut of rush and reeds" (Z 130) for the young family who are last seen when, probably, jettisoned from the ship. The story of Wale, Sade and Ade is thus a thin thread that is woven into the network from which it resurfaces recurrently only to disappear for good with the assertion that "wale sade & ade are prey" (Z 165).

There is, however, the story of another couple overtly interlaced with the Wale and Sade thread. An undisclosed intradiegetic speaker repeatedly sends his thoughts homewards to his partner, 'Ruth', reminiscing "the dray cart with hay where we two made one the cairn where i left a note for you ruth" (Z 130). 'Dray cart' and 'cairn' make this voice discernibly British (probably Scottish), and in fact the speaker, although he remains anonymous throughout, had already introduced himself properly in an earlier passage in

'Sal': "I come from the north the dales land of mist of hoar frost dear ruth" (Z 80). In the 'Notanda' section, Philip muses about her own astonishment with this uninvited yet strangely endearing presence:

> One of the strongest 'voices' in the *Zong!* text is that of someone who appears to be white, male, and European. Had I approached this 'story' in the manner of wanting to write the story about the *Zong* and the events surrounding its fateful journey, I would not have chosen a white, male, European voice as one of the primary voices in this work. My 'authorial intention' would have impelled me toward other voices. And for very good reason. (Z 204–5)

It is indeed striking to what degree the subplot of the 'Scotsman' doubles the Wale, Sade and Ade plot. Like Wale for Sade, the speaker has made a "rush ring" for Ruth (Z 130) with whom he imagines parenthood in a formulation that repeats the theme of the future son almost verbatim: whereas '*wale and sade* will have a son *ade* is his name', the 'Scotsman' imagines how "you and i ruth will have a son dante will be his name" (Z 132). Again, violence abruptly terminates the reverie, this time not as a 'declaration of war' by a universal anti-Black alliance of god, pope, doge and kings, but as an imperative to concrete physical abuse: "Slam her head against the boards". In the zone of indeterminacy of the *Zong* (and of *Zong!*), it cannot be clarified on whom this violence is inflicted by whom; nor can it be ascertained whether this is an imperative or a truncated constative from which the subject has been deleted: 'I'? Nothing, therefore, can exonerate the endearing but deeply implicated 'Scotsman' whose "story nests in the net" (Z 152) of the enslavist system from whose generic violence he hopes to reap his profits, as another reverie of a settled and saturated life with Ruth reveals: "We dine on egg drop soup eat fish roe feast on dates from the east cured ham & beef the negro serves fresh pears on a tray with my profits ruth we can make gin with the grain in our fields" (Z 133). Ruth-lessness and ruthlessness cannot be held apart. As for the violence against the woman or girl whose head is slammed against the boards, no further narrative specification is given in this passage so as to underscore that this text will not repeat Wilberforce's identificatory strategy of singling out individual cases but instead point to the routine seriality of that generic violation. The only one conspicuously standing out *as named* is the imagined son, Dante, whose rather improbable name is a few inches further down associated with the "poet of the life after death", whose smuggled-in presence 'nested in the net' of *Zong!* has much to say about the text's preoccupation with the afterlife of the trauma of the Middle Passage but also, in generic terms, about the epic dimensions of Philip's "recombinant antinarrative" (Z 204).

And yet the fact remains that the perpetrators and profiteers – the Scotsman and Ruth – are intimately and disturbingly parallelized with their dispossessed and dehumanized victims, Wale and Sade. Such parallelisms point to the deep connexionism that informs Philip's text in a most catastrophic way. For the integration of the 'Scotsman' and his voice indicates no reconciliation but is testimony to the fact that the system of enslavism is so total that all that are enmeshed in it are in whatever perverse and toxic ways connected, inescapably. Mbembe would call this relatedness 'convivial'; Said has made out something similar in the totality of imperialism and the "overlapping territories [and] intertwined histories" it creates or more accurately imposes (Said 1994: 61). Herein lies the motivation for "the organizing principle of relationship used in *Zong!*" (Z 205). But even if the "'governing principle' in *Zong!* is relationality" (Khan 2015: 18), then this surely does not entail the utopian expectation of some harmonious merger nor the attainment of some kind of wholeness. Here, the irreparable absence of all who were destroyed and dispossessed impels "a sentient recollection of connectedness experienced at the site of rupture, where the very consciousness of disconnectedness acts as mode of testimony and memory" (Hartman 1997: 73–4). Connectedness is here derived from the shared experience of disconnectedness in the same way as *Zong!* tells a story by not telling. Philip's 'governing principle' is thus a relationality that emphasizes the non-negotiability of the gap, the bottomlessness of a gutter that yet serves as a fragile bridge as "every word or word cluster is seeking a space directly above within which to fit itself and in so doing falls into relation with others either above, below, or laterally" (Z 203). Words thus become agents of connexionism that, however, can never repair the anagrammatical damage done to the order of syntax. The coherence of the text lies in its incoherence, in "the recognition of the amputated body in its amputatedness [...]. it is the ravished body that holds out the possibility of restitution, not the invocation of an illusory wholeness or the desired return to an originary plenitude" (Hartman 1997: 74). The strategy that Philip develops in her performance is to carry this impossible connectivity to its extremes where the voices, stories and word clusters in *Zong!* are "jammed together – 'crumped'" on the page to a point where precisely this squeezing together, reminiscent of the cargo hold, engenders a loosening as "the ordering of grammar, the ordering that is the impulse of empire, is subverted" (Z 205) and the text becomes a well-nigh unreadable cloud of blurred, scrambled and superimposed segments all struggling for space on the page (Figure 3.4).

But *Zong!* does not allow the reader to get away with the positive assertion of the text's unreadability. For sure, this is the outcome of Philip's 'performance', but her 'pedagogy' as laid down in the 'Notanda' section disclaims precisely that notion of unreadability by providing a set of reading instructions that make the radical opacity of *Zong!* transparent to some extent. To my knowledge, all critical engagements with *Zong!* (including this one) draw and rely heavily on Philip's own explanations in 'Notanda'.

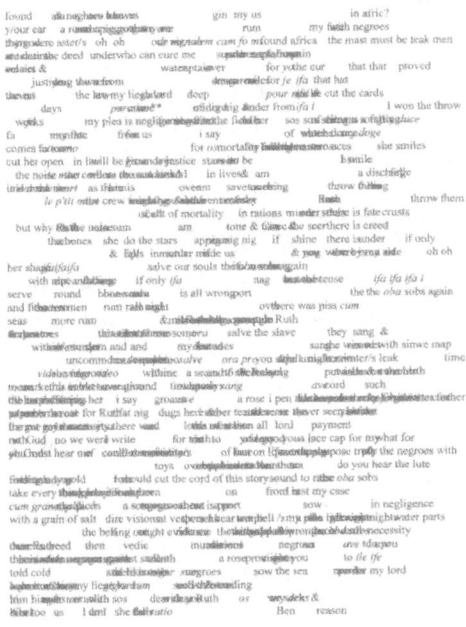

FIGURE 3.4 M. NourbeSe Philip, *Zong!*

Source: M. NourbeSe Philip, *Zong!*, p. 182. Reproduced with the permission of the author.

Strange enough, then, *Zong!* is a literally self-explanatory text. To the extent that its double structure of opaque perplex performance and explicatory and instructive pedagogy repeats the doubleness that Homi Bhabha discerns for the 'national address', it may be read *also* as an intervention into the ongoing interpellation into nationhood of that polity or socius that is responsible for the history and even the very matter from which *Zong!* is constituted: Britain. To repeat, I do not wish to argue that the project of *Zong!* is to write an in/verse Britain. Very clearly, Philip's text is operating within a far larger orbit than that of a shrinking island off the European mainland. Regardless of 'authorial intention', however, *Zong!* can and indeed should be read as a thorn in the side of a triumphalist self-description of Britain as the nation that transformed itself from "being the world's greediest and most successful traders of slaves in the eighteenth century [...] to being able to preen themselves on being the world's foremost opponents of slavery" (Colley 2002: 350–1).

Published one year after the series of commemorative events around the bicentenary of the abolition of the slave trade in Britain, Philip's book encountered a public sphere in Britain in which that history had once again been taken for an occasion of festive celebrations and national self-congratulations. "Most spectacular" among all these events and items was the "replica *Zong*" that for a few weeks "was moored alongside HMS Belfast in London and hosted a series of commemorations of the *Zong* killings and the slave trade" (Walvin 2011: 188). As spectacular sight and heritage site, the reconstructed ship contributes to the integration of the legacy of the slave trade into the palatable idiom of an abstracted national history that "purged of political tension [...] becomes a unifying spectacle, the settling of all disputes. Like the guided tour as it proceeds from site to sanctioned site, the national past occurs in a dimension of its own" (Wright 2009: 65). 'Purged of political tension' this sanitized and reified past can be presented (in the literal sense of making present) in objectified, dramatized or immersive forms of re-enactment that effectively overcode heritage with "avoiding the fragmentary process of history and with demonstrating the ongoing value of [...] completeness" (DeGroot 2016: 106). The replica *Zong* on display in its apparent wholeness and authenticity is of course a simulation, a hyperreal object: the ship moored in the Port of London in spring 2007 was in fact an old square rigger, the *Madagascar*, that was only temporarily renamed to act as stand-in for the absent *Zong*. It is this closing of the gaps that characterizes heritage history as obsessed with the 'invocation of an illusory wholeness', which sets it irrevocably apart from Hartman's Black politics of memory based on 'the recognition of the amputated body in its amputatedness'.

As the 2007 commemorative festivities of abolition demonstrated, Britons had no "desire to go beyond the original myths in which the emancipation moment of 1807 was enshrined" (Wood 2010: 187). However, pedagogy, pace Gayatri Spivak, is the "uncoercive rearrangement of desire" (2003: 101); an interminable task to be pursued in the hope "to relocate the desire to reassemble humanism so that it can appear in conjunction with a renewed analysis of the alienated modes of social interaction that still derive from the racialization of the world" (Gilroy 2016: 122). A reading of *Zong!* also (but emphatically not only!) as a project to in/verse Britain by way of a new national address would have to begin with this: with the uncoercive rearrangement of the entrenched desire to uphold the celebratory myth of British heroic self-transformation, from slaver to abolitionist, towards the very different desire for a no longer racialized world. This makes it imperative, in a first move, to disarticulate the as yet persistent script of enslavism as enshrined in *Gregson v. Gilbert*. This is, roughly, the burden of the poems in *Zong!* as they rip apart that abject script so as to clear a space for a putative anagrammatical rearrangement, and for a biting new national address that insists how the inverse Britain that emerges from the poetry of *Zong!* still has no referent outside Philip's pages.

4

Epilogue: ... looking at the stars

'We are all in the gutter but some of us are looking at the stars'. The preceding discussions of verse novels from numerous and diverse locations have explored the gutter and its doings. These close readings have hopefully demonstrated the variability with which the basic parameters of the gutter text – the countermeasure of sequence and segment paired to a foregrounded textual gappiness and incompleteness – are deployed and played out. Yet given all this attention to the gutter, what about the stars? In Wilde's aphorism, they are obviously a simple cipher for some lofty unsullied beauty that stands in pristine detachment and in sharp contrast with the debased condition on the ground. Now given that the gutter in this book is not the gutter that Lord Darlington invokes but a formal and generic category, the stars may as well take on a slightly different aspect and enable a move from the merely specular ('looking at the stars') to the speculative. After all, in aesthetic and literary theory, the stars have often served as shorthand for a nostalgically evoked premodernity imagined as naïve and organic wholeness, most emphatically perhaps in the exclamation with which the young Georg Lukács opens his *Theory of the Novel*: "Happy are those ages when the starry sky is the map of all possible paths – ages whose paths are illuminated by the light of the stars" (1988: 29). Picking up Schiller's distinction of classical 'organic' and modern 'artificial' civilizations, Lukács imagines the 'happy ages' of Greek antiquity as an epitome of "integrated" as distinct from "estranged" civilizations (ibid.: 29, 64); and following in the footsteps of Hegel's evolutionary systematization of literary forms, he defines those premodern ages when "the world is wide and yet like a home" as times of the epic, whereas the unhappy consciousness of modernity finds its adequate narrative matrix in the "novel form [which] is, like no other, an expression of this transcendental homelessness" (ibid.: 41) in a wholly prosaic world. Insofar as they interrupt the dominant flow of prose, gutter texts – and the verse novel in particular – may then be seen as the return of a mode of writing that is 'looking at the stars': certainly not in the sense of a return to the organic wholeness that hellenophile German idealists projected onto the sanitized and lactified screen of 'Greece', nor in any other nostalgic gaze through the rear-view mirror. If the residual form of the epic resurfaces in the contemporary verse novel – and the constant references to Homer, Vergil, Dante, South Pacific orature and East African creation myths seem to substantiate this idea – then the epic definitely does not return as a form that celebrates some re-enchantment of the administered world. And yet, it can and has been argued that the prosaic, disenchanted world of global modernity has of late undergone a process where disenchantment reverts back to magic, albeit a malign one which charges social reality once again with sheer unpredictability and elemental archaic danger. Joseph Vogl reads Eric Packer, the finance CEO and protagonist of Don DeLillo's *Cosmopolis* (2003), as a twenty-first-century version of the epic hero and DeLillo's text as a return of the epic proper "in the most modern form imaginable":

> If the notorious 'worldliness' of the modern and contemporary novel is bound up with the question of how events are ordered and by which rules, then DeLillo's novel registers a return to archaism in the most modern form imaginable; it leads us to suspect that the world of finance economics is battered by the storm winds of events signifying the gravest possible danger. Stock market transactions are coupled with the fatality of brute force [...]. Financial markets in a state of turmoil mirror zones of elemental danger. Together, they shape a narratological program that converts the dynamics of exchange rates into a pattern of epic fatefulness, making the advent of the unlikeliest outcome appear utterly inevitable. (Vogl 2015: 8)

Vogl's point is that the digitally enhanced and accelerated variant of finance capitalism has, like a malevolent wizard, bewitched social reality from the planning utopias of modernism (back) to a danger zone of hazardous quests and errands: a wider world for sure, but certainly not 'like a home'. The gutter text (and *Cosmopolis* is of course one, too) registers this transformation and gives a form to this 'return to archaism'. Similarly, Mark Fisher assigns "the forces that govern our lives and the world" of contemporary capitalism quasi magical potency when he asserts that

> it should be especially clear to those of us in a globally tele-connected capitalist world that those forces are not fully available to our sensory apprehension. A force like capital does not exist in any substantial sense, yet it is capable of producing practically any kind of effect. (Fisher 2017: 64)

The experience of being exposed to such a 'force', insubstantial yet omnific, verges on the sublime with the proviso that, unlike with Burke's avalanches, or Kant's starry night sky (!), we are now fully and defencelessly immersed into it instead of situated at a distance. Where Burke's spectator or Kant's stargazer ultimately have confirmed their supreme status as subjects in control of the external object world, the subject itself in Vogl or Fisher's accounts disintegrates into a gutter text in its own right as "gaps and inconsistencies are constitutive of what we are" (ibid.: 69). The subject disaggregates as it loses its mastery over a malignantly re-enchanted world informed by capitalist structures that no longer appear to operate on the principle of rationalization. For whereas "the battle against magic has always accompanied the *development* of capitalism" (Federici 2004: 173; emphasis added) – not least because magic "rested upon a qualitative conception of space and time that precluded a regularization of the labor process" (ibid.: 142) – the current avatar of capitalism appears to impose precisely an experience of the magical, one that is "premised on the belief that the world is animated, unpredictable, and that there is a force in all things" (ibid.: 173). To call this, with Vogl, a 'return to archaism' makes sense – but only from the perspective of the European masterful subject that feminist, postcolonial, Black, queer, environmentalist and much of Marxist criticism have debunked in concert as "the western configuration of the human" (Weheliye 2014: 135) that universalizes one particular form of subjectivity at the expense of all others: "The heteromasculine, white, propertied, and liberal subject that renders all those who do not conform to these characteristics as exploitable nonhumans" (ibid.). What however about all those who never were *in* control but always, as 'exploitable nonhumans', *under* control? There is, after all, a crucial difference between subjects that, like the ones envisaged by Vogl or Fisher, register their sudden lack of agency and command, and subjects that never were subjects in that strong agentive sense in the first place but instead envisioned "as object and dehumanized other" (Hartman 1997: 35). While the former may be conceived to be dragged into a 'temporally bound state of exception' by the newly hazardous and unpredictable 'storm winds of events' on the digital trading floor, the latter are members of those "different populations – often racialized – [that] are suspended in a *perpetual* state of emergency" (Weheliye 2014: 88; emphasis added): Benjamin's "oppressed" for whom "the 'state of emergency' in which we live is not the exception but the rule" (Benjamin 1968: 257). As we have seen, Achille Mbembe (2017: 4) has adopted this insight for the neoliberally globalized world, where the "tendency to universalize the Black condition" engenders a "becoming-Black of the world". From that perspective, the exposure to a threateningly unpredictable world is not a 'return' of (or to) something overcome or residual but rather a vitally integral part of a mode of existence that has always been 'epic' in the sense of Vogl's danger zone.

It is in keeping with this that Walcott saturates his postcolonial Caribbean village plot with "Homeric association" (O 25) and Dantean rhyme pattern.

Homer's arch-hero, Achille, here is "a black fisherman [who] scans the opening line I of our epic horizon" (O 13) where "the stars would renew their studded diagrams" (O 73). Yet these epic times are certainly not the 'happy ages' imagined by Lukács. Those times, for sure, were never as happy as modern nostalgics envisaged them in the first place. Very clearly the caprices of the gods – whether Greek, Indian, Nordic or else – correlate with the deeply felt and shared experience of being "defenceless, completely exposed to the dangers of nature" (Heath 2005: 61, FN 71). The Homeric epics, with their typical "representation of the sea as dangerous, [...] terrifying and unpredictable" (Schultz 2009: 301) tossing hapless heroes to and fro, are in that respect very similar to, say, *Beowulf* with its geography of "the great earth, ringed with *garsecg*, the shoreless sea, beneath the sky's inaccessible roof; whereon, as in a little circle of light about their halls, men with courage as their stay went forward to that battle with the hostile world" (Tolkien 2002: 115). Perhaps it is only due to the absence of other light in that vast and deep encircling darkness that Lukács's stars can shine so brightly. In this light (should I say, gloom?), the alleged death of the epic corresponds with a substantial and qualitative enlargement of that 'little circle of light' that, pace Tolkien, defines the tiny terrain of human agency in the 'happy ages' of 'integrated civilizations' that are not quite so happily but rather precariously set vis-à-vis an overwhelming "wilderness world" (Miller 2000: 78) ready to invade, Grendel-style, at any moment.

As far as Europe is concerned, the resurgence of epic in the early modern period – Tasso, Camoes, Spenser, Milton – is arguably tied in with the "constitution of America" and the concomitant "new geocultural *id*-entity of Europe" (Quijano 2000: 533, 537) that now configures itself as the subject in control. Here, the knight errand stands in for the explorer, conqueror and colonizer taking possession of 'wasteland' to be exploited and cultivated; or rather, and more accurately put, wasteland that had to be produced as such in the first place – produced by destruction. In a compelling reading of Book 2 of Spenser's *The Faerie Queene*, Stephen Greenblatt argues that the spoliation of the enchantress Acrasia's realm, the Bower of Bliss, by Lord Guyon, the Knight of Temperance, is an only thinly masked representation of the conquest and devastation of the Americas – that historical event that, for Quijano and many others, enables the fashioning of European '*id*-entity' as the subject of modernity. Spenser nominates this masterful subject 'a perfect gentleman', and it is against this specific subjectivity that Francis Nyamnjoh rallies his reading of Tutuola's *Palm-Wine Drinkard* as a celebration of incompleteness. For in Tutuola, it is the "complete gentleman" (Tutuola 1988: 18) who serves as the grotesque embodiment of a well-nigh demonic destructive self-alienation. Tutuola's 'complete gentleman' is in fact a biopolitical parasite: essentially only a skull, this bounded self, incarcerated in his own monadism, vampirically feeds on the vitalities of his 'incomplete' victims. Similarly, Spenser's 'perfect gentleman' lays Acrasia's realm to waste "with rigour pitiless", destroys a whole world of sumptuous beauty and "of the fairest late, now made the fowlest place" (Spenser 1978: 381). The epic world that the knight travels in is now no longer an overwhelming wilderness but an object to be acquired or destroyed, and its threat consists now more in its sensuous allure than its mortal dangers.

To be sure, the threat of allurement is very well known to the classical epic, too, with its seductive sirens or Circes. With luck and cunning seduction in the *Odyssey* may be evaded, however the seductresses herself will not be destroyed but continue to lure other wayfarers into her dangerous domain. This changes drastically with the onset of modernity where the new European '*id*-entity' fashions itself premised on mastery over the outer world as much as the self. This subjectivity can secure itself "only through a restraint that involves the destruction of something immensely beautiful; to succumb to that beauty means to lose the shape of manhood and be transformed into a beast" (Greenblatt 1980: 175) like the victims of Circe. To gain and retain the 'shape of manhood' – Greenblatt's masculinized term for 'humanity' is probably deliberately chosen – therefore entails not only the annihilation of the Other (in Spenser, the female temptress, in the Renaissance scene that he writes to, the Amerindian) but also the self-deprivation that comes with this erasure, so that "each self-constituting act is haunted by inadequacy and loss" (Greenblatt 1980: 179). The modern lament of the world's disenchantment is only one among many dirges sung over the smoking embers of Acrasia's bower. With this "the subjugation of everything natural to the sovereign subject" (Horkheimer and Adorno 2002: xviii) is complete and nature has been rendered fully into a storehouse of extractable resources. Yet while the early modern epic configures a world that has lost its threat for the emergent masterful European self and become an object of domination, the contemporary epic as a gutter text focuses on "the dominated subjects of the domination of nature" (ibid.: 172), subjugated like, or *as*, nature to the regime of modern power. That world is dangerous as ever, the state of exception the norm and defenceless vulnerability to global risks inescapable. Yet there is nothing 'archaic' about this. In *Omeros* the threat is not located in nature but in the *control* of nature. Both overpowering and enveloping, nature is the non-transcendable setting within which human life is nested; to the extent that this envelope has been subdued to an object of extraction and destruction, human life is itself endangered. All of this renders the planet at large one vast danger zone full of portents of things to come: "Man was an endangered ‖ species now, a spectre, just like the Aruac | or the egret [...] once men were satisfied ‖with destroying men they would move on to Nature. | And those were the omens" (O 300). The genocide encoded as Guyon's raid on the Bower of Bliss now returns as planetary ecocide – an 'epic horizon' that calls for a cooperative rescue mission of minor cosmopolitans all over the world.

If the gutter texts grouped in this book envision the planet as process rather than object, then they contribute to an imaginary that may overcome the exploitative matrix of the 'domination of nature' so deeply engrained in Western modernity. This, to repeat, is not a return to a pristine premodernity that is neither accessible nor desirable and that, most importantly, never actually was. To the contrary, if there are any eulogies to the stars in these texts, then these are based not on some version of the sublime but, as in *Vela*, on the rotating reciprocity of the spectacle and the spectator, the constellation and the gazer: "We read the stars as they in turn | observed and read us into existence" (V 243). Situational transcendence here can hardly be held apart from situational congruence. The same goes for the perplexity that Carson's Geryon experiences as he and Herakles speculate that many of the visible stars must have "burned out then thousand years ago" so that seeing them in fact means to "see memories" (R 65). There is no nostalgia here, no invocation of some irretrievable 'happy ages', but also no modernist euphoria of mastery and self-centredness. The world *is* dangerous in these gutter texts: not as overpowering nature but because other people make it uninhabitable – colonial, racist, capitalist, homophobic, antisemitic, enslavist 'perfect gentlemen' to whom the subjects of these texts are vulnerably exposed and against whom they rally their creative solidarities.

Next to the notion of the epic as a narrative that gives form to the experience of the world as danger zone there is a second speculative layer loosely wrapped around the epic that I would briefly like to superimpose on that first one; namely the assumption that the epic is an exceptionally hospitable form, or, as Wai Chee Dimock asserts with reference to the ancient Greek epic, "a kind of linguistic sponge": "Springing up at contact zones, it is also superresponsive to its environment, picking up all those non-Greek words that come its way, but not necessarily dissolving them, perhaps keeping them simply as alien deposits, grains or lumps that stick" (Dimock 2006: 82). Indeed polyglossia is extremely conspicuous in all the texts under discussion here – from the French and Patois that Walcott weaves into the fabric of *Omeros* and the Greek and Quechua 'deposits' in Carson's verse novel; from the saturation of *Vela* with Samoan lexemes and *The Folding Cliffs* with Hawai'ian terms; from Evaristo's Latinizing manipulation of modern English to Agbabi's jukebox jive, not to speak of the disjunct configuration of Fon and Dutch, Yoruba and Portuguese, Hebrew and Shona "words and phrases overheard on board the *Zong*" (Z 183). In both its incompletely articulated segmentivity and its internal polyglossia, then, the gutter text constellates heterogeneities rather than a coherently grouted composite. By virtue of this gappiness, each of these texts evokes an essentially incomplete, weakly articulated and hence open-ended 'world': one that never closes in as a fully rounded whole and therefore allows for multiple worlds to coexist. Thus, Walcott's alter ego in *Omeros* muses on how the loosely sutured eastern and western hemispheres of the globe are reciprocal mirror images of each other while Wendt's Nafanua informs the supreme deity of the Samoan pantheon that 'there are other worlds and realities', 'other atua with greater | mana in worlds outside our comprehension' (V 125). The world is thus not only a process but a plural: there is not one but many minor cosmopolitanisms. The countermeasuring of the sequential and the segmentive, concretized by each text in its own way, is the basic poetic device with which gutter texts displace prose as the supreme literary connectivity principle and procedure to generate syntagms. To displace is not to replace: gutter textuality contains in itself a certain measure of 'prosaic' sequentiality and can for that reason alone never serve as the complete other of prose. As an alternate mode of meaning-making the gutter text will therefore not supplant but supplement prose similar to which they are driven by connexionist energies. But unlike prose, the gutter text figures connections through gap negotiation, through composed relationalities across distances in a space that fosters potential connections rather than separations. Brian McHale (2004: 15–16) has proposed to read such texts – especially the hybrid forms of narrative poetry that are at the centre of this study – as figurations of "a world made up of fragments of many worlds, a heterotopia". Much in the readings presented in this book is in principal agreement with this assertion only that I would prefer not to speak of fragments but segments (a term that McHale himself otherwise seems to prefer too). Where fragments are shards of a lost whole, the affordance of segments is that they may or may not at some point become component parts of a larger assemblage. Fragments point to the past, segments to possible futures. More than that, they do not assume wholeness but a non-teleological aggregation without closure. Reading gutter texts is therefore similar to stargazing where "what we see is a partial image of a universe which, in reality, is formed by traces of light from stars in movement" (Camargo 2020: 35). In this sense, the gutter text speaks of and to a world that is neither whole nor broken but always becoming.

BIBLIOGRAPHY

Primary sources

Agbabi, Patience. (2014). *Telling Tales*. Edinburgh: Cannongate.
Alighieri, Dante. ([*c*.1321] 1928). *The Inferno: The Divine Comedy, Book One*. Transl. S. Fowler Wright. New York: Cosmopolitan.
Carson, Anne. (1998). *Autobiography of Red: A Novel in Verse*. New York: Vintage.
Carson, Anne. (2013). *Red Doc>*. New York: Vintage.
Chaucer, Geoffrey. ([*c*.1381] 1970a). *The Canterbury Tales*. Trans. into modern English by Nevill Coghill. Harmondsworth: Penguin.
Coghill, Nevill. (1970b). 'Introduction'. In Geoffrey Chaucer, *The Canterbury Tales*. Transl. into Modern English by Nevill Coghill, 11–18. Harmondsworth: Penguin.
Conrad, Joseph. ([1899] 2006). *Heart of Darkness*. Edited by Paul B. Armstrong. New York: Norton.
Doyle, Arthur Conan. ([1912] 2008). *The Lost World*. Edited by Ian Duncan. Oxford: Oxford University Press.
Ellis, Brett Easton. (1991). *American Psycho*. New York: Vintage.
Evaristo, Bernardine. (2001). *The Emperor's Babe*. London: Penguin.
Gibson, William. (2003). *Pattern Recognition*. New York: Berkley.
Green, Michael Cawood. (1997). *Sinking: A Verse Novella*. London: Penguin.
Isherwood, Christopher. ([1939] 2001). *Goodbye to Berlin*. London: Vintage.
Kipling, Rudyard. (1922). *Rudyard Kipling's Verse*. Garden City: Doubleday, Page.
Lang, Andrew. (1888). *Grass of Parnassus: Rhymes Old and New*. London: Longman.
Merwin, W. S. (1998). *The Folding Cliffs: A Narrative of 19th-Century Hawaii*. New York: Knopf.
Merwin, W. S. (2013). *Collected Poems 1996-2011*. New York: The Library of America.
Mitchell, David. (2004). *Cloud Atlas*. London: Sceptre.
Ngugi Wa Thiongo. (2020). *The Perfect Nine: The Epic of Gikuyu and Mumbi*. New York: The New Press.
Philip, M. NourbeSe. (2008). *Zong! As Told to the Author by Setaey Adamu Boateng*. Middletown, CT: Wesleyan University Press.
Pynchon, Thomas. ([1973] 2000). *Gravity's Rainbow*. London: Vintage.
Rice, William Hyde. (1923). *Hawaiian Legends*. Honolulu: The Museum.
Rushdie, Salman. (1981). *Midnight's Children*. London: Viking.

Spenser, Edmund. ([1590–1609] 1978). *The Faerie Queene*, edited by Thomas R. Roche Jr. Harmondsworth: Penguin.
Tempest, Kae. (2016). *Let Them Eat Chaos: A Poem*. New York: Bloomsbury.
Tutuola, Amos. ([1952] 1988). *The Palm-Wine Drinkard*. London: Faber and Faber.
Walcott, Derek. (1990). *Omeros*. New York: Farrar, Straus and Giroux.
Wendt, Albert. (1986). 'The Contest'. *Landfall* 40, no. 2, 144–53.
Wendt, Albert. (2009). *The Adventures of Vela*. Auckland: Huia.
Wilde, Oscar. ([1893] 2008). 'Lady Windermere's Fan'. In *The Importance of Being Earnest and Other Plays*, edited by Peter Raby, 1–61. Oxford: Oxford University Press.

Secondary sources

Abate, Michelle Ann. (2018). 'Verse-ality: The Novel in Verse and the Revival of Poetry'. *The Lion and the Unicorn* 42, no. 2: v–viii.
Aboulafia, Mitchell. (2013). *Transcendence: On Self-Determination and Cosmopolitanism*. Stanford: Stanford University Press.
Addison, Catherine. (2009). 'The Verse Novel as Genre: Contradiction or Hybrid?' *Style* 43, no. 4: 539–62.
Addison, Catherine. (2012). 'The Contemporary Verse Novel: A Challenge to Established Genres?' *English Studies in Africa* 55, no. 2: 85–101.
Addison, Catherine. (2017). *A Genealogy of the Verse Novel*. Newcastle: Cambridge Scholars.
Addison, Catherine. (2018). 'Verse Novel: Generic Hybridity and the Chamber-Pot'. *Style* 53, no. 3: 326–43.
Adorno, Theodor W. ([1970] 1997). *Aesthetic Theory*. Transl. Robert Hullot-Kenter. London: Continuum.
Agard-Jones, Vanessa. (2012). 'What the Sands Remember'. *GLQ: A Journal of Gay and Lesbian Studies* 18, nos. 2–3: 325–46.
Agbabi, Patience. (2011). 'Dark and Light'. https://patienceagbabi.wordpress.com/2011/10/27/dark-and-light/ (accessed 28 January 2023).
Agbabi, Patience. (2014). 'NOT "The Rap Canterbury Tales"'. https://patienceagbabi.wordpress.com/2014/09/01/not-the-rap-canterbury-tales/ (accessed 28 January 2023).
Agbabi, Patience. (2018). 'Stories in Stanza'd English: A Cross-Cultural *Canterbury Tales*'. *Literature Compass* 16, no. 5. https://doi.org/10.1111/lic3.12455 (accessed 28 January 2023).
Ahmed, Sara. (2000). *Strange Encounters: Embodied Others in Post-Coloniality*. London: Routledge.
Aikau, Hokulani K. (2019). 'From Malihini to Hoaʻina: Reconnecting People, Places, and Practices'. In *The Past Before Us: Moʻokūʻauhau as Methodology*, edited by Nālani Wilson-Hokowhitu and Marie Alohalani Brown, 81–93. Honolulu: University of Hawaii Press.
Albin, Andrew. (2013). 'The Prioress's Tale, Sonorous and Silent'. *The Chaucer Review* 48, no. 1: 91–112.

Alexander, Joy. (2005). 'The Verse-Novel: A New Genre'. *Children's Literature in Education* 36, no. 3: 269–83.
Al-Nakib, Mai. (2020). 'Finding Common Cause: A Planetary Ethics of "What Could Happen If"'. *Interventions* 22: 228–45.
Althusser, Louis. (2006). *Philosophy of the Encounter: Later Writings, 1978–1987*. Trans. G. M. Goshgarian. Edited by Francois Matheron and Oliver Corpet. London: Verso.
Anae, Melani. (2017). 'Nafanua and Reflections on Samoan Female Sexual Personhood'. In *The Relational Self: Decolonizing Personhood in the Pacific*, edited by Upolu Luma Va'ai and Unaisi Nabobo-Baba, 203–23. Suva: University of the South Pacific Press.
Anderson, Benedict. (1991). *Imagined Communities: Reflections on the Origins and Spread of Nationalism*. London: Verso.
Appadurai, Arjun. (1996). *Modernity at Large: Cultural Dimensions of Globalization*. Minneapolis: University of Minnesota Press.
Apter, Emily. (2013). *Against World Literature: On the Politics of Untranslatability*. London: Verso.
Arditi, Benjamin. (2005). 'Populism as an Internal Periphery of Democratic Politics'. In *Populism and the Mirror of Democracy*, edited by Francisco Panizza, 72–98. London: Verso.
Armstrong, Tim (2007). 'Catastrophe and Trauma: A Response to Anita Rupprecht'. *The Journal of Legal History* 28, no. 3: 347–56.
Arvin, Maile. (2019). *Possessing Polynesians: The Science of Settler Colonial Whiteness in Hawai'i and Oceania*. Durham: Duke University Press.
Ashcroft, Bill (2018). 'Singing the Spiral of Time: Albert Wendt's *The Adventures of Vela*'. In *Postcolonial Past and Present: Negotiating Literary and Cultural Geographies*, edited by Anne Collett and Leigh Dale, 183–95. Amsterdam: Brill.
Austenfeld, Thomas. (2006). 'How to Begin a New World: Dante in Walcott's *Omeros*'. *South Atlantic Review* 71, no. 3: 15–28.
Badiou, Alain. (1999). *Manifesto for Philosophy*. Albany, NY: SUNY Press.
Badiou, Alain. (2001). *Ethics: An Essay on the Understanding of Evil*. London: Verso.
Badiou, Alain. (2003). *Infinite Thought: Truth and the Return to Philosophy*. London: Continuum.
Badiou, Alain. (2006). *Polemics*. Trans. Steven Corcoran. London: Verso.
Badiou, Alain. (2007). *The Century*. Cambridge: Polity.
Bakhtin, Mikhail M. ([c.1920–3] 2006). 'Author and Hero in Aesthetic Activity'. In *Art and Answerability: Early Philosophical Essays by M. M. Bakhtin*, edited by Michael Holquist. Trans. Vadim Liapunov, 4–256. Austin: Texas University Press.
Bakhtin, Mikhail M. ([1975] 2011). *The Dialogic Imagination: Four Essays*. Transl. Caryl Emerson and Michael Holquist. Austin: University of Texas Press.
Barolini, Teodolinda. (1992). *The Undivine Comedy: Detheologizing Dante*. Princeton: Princeton University Press.
Baron, Scarlett. (2020). 'Joyce's Art of Mosaic'. *James Joyce Quarterly* 57, nos. 1–2: 21–34.
Barthold, Lauren Swayne. (2016). *A Hermeneutic Approach to Gender and Other Social Identities*. New York: Palgrave.

Baucom, Ian. (2005). *Spectres of the Atlantic: Finance Capital, Slavery, and the Philosophy of History*. Durham: Duke University Press.

Beattie, Pamela, and Simona Bertacco. (2017). 'Philoctete's Healing: Echoes of Dante's *Purgatorio* in Walcott's *Omeros*'. *Altre Modernità/Other Modernities* 18, no. 11: 84–105.

Beckwith, Martha Warren. (1972). *The Kumulipo: A Hawaiian Creation Chant*. Honolulu: University of Hawaii Press.

Beebee, Thomas O. (1994). *The Ideology of Genre: A Comparative Study of Generic Instability*. University Park: University of Pennsylvania Press.

Beecroft, Alexander. (2015). *An Ecology of World Literature: From Antiquity to the Present Day*. London: Verso.

Beller, Jonathan. 2016). 'Informatic Labor in the Age of Computational Capital'. *Lateral* 5, no. 1: 1–26. https://doi.org/10.25158/L5.1.4, accessed 5 February 2023.

Belting, Hans. (2010). 'The Double Perspective: Arab Mathematics and Renaissance Art'. *Third Text* 24, no. 5: 521–7.

Belting, Hans. (2011). *Florence and Baghdad: Renaissance Art and Arab Science*. Transl. Deborah Lucas Schneider. Cambridge, MA: Harvard University Press.

Benjamin, Bret. (2007). *Invested Interests: Capital, Culture, and the World Bank*. Minneapolis: University of Minnesota Press.

Benjamin, Walter. ([1940] 1968). 'Theses on the Philosophy of History'. In *Illuminations: Essays and Reflections*, edited by Hannah Arendt. Trans. Harry Zohn, 253–64. New York: Schocken.

Bennett, Jane. (2009). *Vibrant Matter: A Political Ecology of Things*. Durham: Duke University Press.

Benyousky, Daniel. (2019). '"Circle Yourself and Your Island": The "O" as a Generative Tension in Derek Walcott's *Omeros*'. *Anthurium* 15, no. 1: 1–11.

Bernard, Catherine. (2015). 'John Lanchester's *Capital* (2012): Fiction and Crisis'. *Études britanniques contemporaines* 49. https://doi.org/10.4000/ebc.2753 (accessed 28 January 2023).

Bersani, Leo. (1989). 'Pynchon, Paranoia and Literature'. *Representations* 25: 99–118.

Besserman, Lawrence. (2004). 'Chaucer, Spain and the Prioress's Antisemitism'. *Viator* 35: 329–53.

Bhabha, Homi K. (1990). 'DissemiNation: Time, Narrative and the Margins of the Modern Nation'. In *Nation and Narration*, edited by Homi K. Bhabha, 291–322. London: Routledge.

Bhabha, Homi K. (1994). *The Location of Culture*. London: Routledge.

Biebricher, Thomas. (2020). 'Neoliberalism and Authoritarianism: Politics, Governance and the Law'. *Global Perspectives*, no. 1: 1–18.

Binney, Mathew. (2010). 'Milton, Locke, and the Early Modern Framework of Cosmopolitan Right'. *Modern Language Review* 105, no. 1: 31–52.

Blaser, Mario, and Marisol de la Cadena. (2018). 'Pluriverse: Proposal for a World of Many Worlds'. In *A World of Many Worlds*, edited by Marisol de la Cadena and Mario Blaser, 1–22. Durham: Duke University Press.

Bleikasten, André. (1995). 'Faulkner from a European Perspective'. In *The Cambridge Companion to William Faulkner*, edited by Philip M. Weinstein, 75–95. Cambridge: Cambridge University Press.

Bloomfield, Morton W. (1972). '"The Man of Law's Tale": A Tragedy of Victimization and a Christian Comedy'. *PMLA* 87, no. 3: 384–90.

Blurton, Heather, and Hannah Johnson. (2017). *The Critics and the Prioress: Antisemitism, Criticism, and Chaucer's 'Prioress's Tale'*. Ann Arbor: University of Michigan Press.

Boltanski, Luc, and Ève Chiapello. (2005). *The New Spirit of Capitalism*. London: Verso.

Boose, Lynda E., and Richard Burt. (1997). 'Totally Clueless? Shakespeare Goes Hollywood in the 1990s'. In *Shakespeare, the Movie: Popularizing the Plays on Film, TV and Video*, edited by Lynda E. Boose and Richard Burt, 8–22. London: Routledge.

Borges, Jorge Luis. ([1951] 2007). 'The Argentine Writer and Tradition'. *Labyrinths: Selected Stories and Other Writings*. Edited and transl. by Donald A. Yates and James E. Irby, 171–8. New York: New Directions.

Bradley, Adam. (2009). *Book of Rhymes: The Poetics of Hip Hop*. New York: Basic Civitas.

Bratton, Benjamin H. (2013). 'Some Trace-Effects of the Post-Anthropocene: On Accelerationist Geopolitical Aesthetics'. *e-flux journal* 46: 1–12.

Brivic, Sheldon. (1991). *The Veil of Signs: Joyce, Lacan, and Perception*. Urbana: University of Illinois Press.

Broeck, Sabine. (2018). *Gender and the Abjection of Blackness*. New York: SUNY Press.

Brouillette, Sarah. (2007). *Postcolonial Writers and the Global Literary Marketplace*. New York: Palgrave Macmillan.

Brown, Christopher Leslie. (2006). *Moral Capital: Foundations of British Abolitionism*. Chapel Hill: University of North Carolina Press.

Brown, Wendy. (2015). *Undoing the Demos: Neoliberalism's Stealth Revolution*. New York: Zone Books.

Brown, Wendy. (2019). *In the Ruins of Neoliberalism: The Rise of Antidemocratic Politics in the West*. New York: Columbia University Press.

Bruff, Ian, and Cemal Burak Tansel. (2019). 'Authoritarian Neoliberalism: Trajectories of Knowledge Producton and Praxis'. *Globalizations* 16, no. 3: 233–44.

Bundgaard, Peer F. (2013). 'Roman Ingarden's Theory of Reader Experience: A Critical Assessment'. *Semiotica* 194: 171–88.

Bundschuh, Jessica. (2015). '"Volcano Time": Temporal Plurality in Anne Carson's *Autobiography of Red*'. In *Anglistentag 2015: Proceedings*, edited by Christoph Ehland, Ilka Mindt and Merle Tönnies, 219–31. Trier: Wissenschaftlicher Verlag.

Burkitt, Katharine. (2012). *Literary Form as Postcolonial Critique: Epic Proportions*. Farnham: Ashgate.

Burt, John. (2015). 'History and Narrative in Merwin's *The Folding Cliffs*'. https://www.academia.edu/14853272/History_and_Narrative_in_Merwins_The_Folding_Cliffs (accessed 18 May 2022).

Butler, Judith. (2000). 'Restaging the Universal: Hegemony and the Limits of Formalism'. In Judith Butler, Ernesto Laclau and Slavoj Žižek. *Contingency, Hegemony, Universality: Contemporary Dialogues on the Left*, edited by Judith Butler, Ernesto Laclau and Slavoj Žižek, 11–43. London: Verso.

Cachey Jr., Theodore. (2010). 'Cartographic Dante'. *Italica* 87, no. 3: 325–54.

Camargo, Marina. (2020). 'Notes on the Representation of Time and Space'. In *Minor Cosmopolitan: Thinking Art, Politics, and the Universe Together Otherwise*, edited by Zairong Xiang, 33–40. Berlin: Diaphanes.

Casanova, Pascale. (2006). *The World Republic of Letters*. Cambridge, MA: Harvard University Press.

Cassirer, Ernst. ([1923] 1980). *The Philosophy of Symbolic Forms. Vol. 1: Language*. Trans. Ralph Manheim. New Haven: Yale University Press.

Chakrabarty, Dipesh. (2000). *Provincializing Europe: Postcolonial Thought and Historical Difference*. New Delhi: Oxford University Press.

Chang, David A. (2019). 'Transcending Settler Colonial Boundaries with Moʻokuʻauhau: Genealogy as Transgressive Methodology'. In *The Past Before Us: Moʻokūʻauhau as Methodology*, edited by Nālani Wilson-Hokowhitu and Marie Alohalani Brown, 94–105. Honolulu: University of Hawaii Press.

Charlot, John. (1990). 'Aspects of Samoan Literature I: The Structure of the Samoan Single Story Form and Its Uses'. *Anthropos* 85: 415–30.

Chatman, Seymour. (1980). 'What Novels Can Do That Films Can't (And Vice Versa)'. *Critical Inquiry* 7, no. 1: 121–40.

Cheah, Pheng. (2016). *What Is a World? On Postcolonial Literature as World Literature*. Durham: Duke University Press.

Clark, Nigel. (2010). *Inhuman Nature: Sociable Life on a Dynamic Planet*. London: Sage.

Clark, Nigel, Alexandra Gormally and Hugh Tuffen. (2018). 'Speculative Volcanology: Time, Becoming, and Violence in Encounters with Magma'. *Environmental Humanities* 10, no. 1: 273–94.

Clark, R. J. (1995). 'Giles of Viterbo on the Phlegraean Fields: A Vergilian View?' *Phoenix* 49, no. 2: 150–62.

Click, Melissa. (2015). 'Fifty Shades of Postfeminism: Contextualizing Readers' Reflections on the Erotic Romance Series'. *Cupckaes, Pinterest and Ladyporn: Feminized Popular Culture in the Early Twenty-First Century*, edited by Elana Levine, 15–31. Urbana: University of Illinois Press.

Clifford, James. (1986). 'On Ethnographic Allegory'. In *Writing Culture: The Poetics and Politics of Ethnography*, edited by James Clifford and George E. Marcus, 98–121. Berkeley: University of California Press.

Clifford, James. (2001). 'Indigenous Articulations'. *The Contemporary Pacific* 13, no. 2: 468–90.

Colley, Linda. (2002). *Britons: Forging the Nation 1707–1837*. London: Pimlico.

Collins, Timothy. (2017). 'Wu-Tang Clan versus Jean Baudrillard: Rap, Poetics and Simulation'. *Journal of Popular Culture* 50, no. 2: 1–21.

Compton, Todd. (1994). 'The Herodotean Mantic Session at Delphi'. *RhM* 137, no. 3–4: 217–23.

Cooney, Brian C. (2014). '"Nothing is Left Out": Kenneth Goldsmith's *Sport* and Erasure Poetry'. *Journal of Modern Literature* 37, no. 4: 16–33.

Creaser, John. (2008). '"Fear of Change": Closed Minds and Open Form in Milton'. *Milton Quarterly* 42, no. 3: 161–82.

Crosby, A.W. (1992). 'Hawaiian Depopulation as a Model for the Amerindian Experience'. In *Epidemics and Ideas: Essays on the Historical Perception of Pestilence*, edited by Terence Ranger and Paul Slack, 175–201. Cambridge: Cambridge University Press.

Cuder-Domínguez, Pilar. (2004). 'Ethnic Cartographies of London in Bernardine Evaristo and Zadie Smith'. *European Journal of English Studies* 8, no. 2: 173–88.

Culler, Jonathan. (2015). *Theory of the Lyric*. Cambridge, MA: Harvard University Press.

D'abdon, Raphael, and Natalia Molebatsi. (2011). 'Behind the Scenes: An Exploration of the Process of Creation, Self-Production and Performance in the All-Female Spoken Word Poetry Show *Body of Words*'. *Scrutiny2* 16, no. 2: 56–61.

Damrosch, David. (2006). 'World Literature in a Postcanonical, Hypercanonical Age'. In *Comparative Literature in an Age of Globalization*, edited by Haun Saussy, 43–53. Baltimore: Johns Hopkins University Press.

Davies, M., and P. J. Finglass. (2014). *Stesichoros: The Poems*. Cambridge: Cambridge University Press.

Davis, Gregson. (1999). '"Pastoral Sites": Aspects of Bucolic Transformation in Derek Walcott's *Omeros*'. *The Classical World* 93, no. 1: 43–9.

Dean, James. (1991). 'Gower, Chaucer, and Rhyme Royal'. *Studies in Philology* 88, no. 3: 251–75.

De Boever, Arne. (2013). *Narrative Care: Biopolitics and the Novel*. London: Bloomsbury.

DeGroot, Jerome. (2016). *Consuming History: Historians and Heritage in Contemporary Popular Culture*. Abingdon: Routledge.

de la Cadena, Marisol. (2015). *Earth Beings: Ecologies of Practice Across Andean Worlds*. Durham: Duke University Press.

Deleuze, Gilles. (1997). *Essays Critical and Clinical*. Trans. Daniel W. Smith and Michael A. Greco. Minneapolis: University of Minnesota Press.

Dellarossa, Franca. (2014). *Talking Revolution: Edward Rushton's Rebellious Poetics, 1782–1814*. Liverpool: Liverpool University Press.

DeLoughrey, Elizabeth. (1999). 'The Spiral Temporality of Patricia Grace's *Potiki*'. *ARIEL* 30, no. 1: 59–83.

De Man, Paul. (1979). *Allegories of Reading: Figural Language in Rousseau, Nietzsche, Rilke, and Proust*. New Haven: Yale University Press.

Derrida, Jacques. (1976). 'The Supplement of Copula: Philosophy Before Linguistics'. *The Georgia Review* 30, no. 3: 527–64.

Derrida, Jacques. ([1972] 1992). 'Signature Event Context'. Trans. Samuel Weber and Jeffrey Mehlman. In *Limited Inc*, edited by Gerald Graff, 1–24. Evanston, IL: Northwestern University Press.

Derrida, Jacques. (2010). *Athens, Still Remains*. Trans. Pascale-Anne Brault and Michael Naas. New York: Fordham University Press.

Despres, Denise L. (1994). 'Anti-Judaism and Chaucer's Little Clergeon'. *Modern Philology* 9, no. 4: 413–27.

Dimock, Wai Chee. (2006). *Through Other Continents: American Literature Across Deep Time*. Princeton: Princeton University Press.

Dimock, Wai Chee. (2007). 'African, Caribbean, American: Black English as Creole Tongue'. In *Shades of the Planet: American Literature as World Literature*, edited by Wai Chee Dimock and Lawrence Buell, 274–300. Princeton: Princeton University Press.

Dimock, Wai Chee. (2015). '*Gilgamesh*'s Planetary Turns'. In *The Planetary Turn: Relationality and Geoaesthetics in the Twenty-First Century*, edited by Amy J. Elias and Christian Moraru, 125–41. Evanston, IL: Northwestern University Press.

Docherty, Thomas. (2006). *Aesthetic Democracy*. Stanford: Stanford University Press.

DuPlessis, Rachel. (1996). 'Manifests'. *Diacritics* 26, nos. 3–4: 31–53.

DuPlessis, Rachel. (2006). *Blue Studios: Poetry and Its Cultural Work*. Tuscaloosa: University of Alabama Press.

During, Simon. (1990). 'Waiting for the Post: Some Relations Between Modernity, Colonization and Writing'. In *Past the Last Post: Theorizing Post-Colonialism and Post-Modernism*, edited by Ian Adam and Helen Tiffin, 23–45. Calgary: University of Calgary Press.

Durix, Jean-Pierre. (2016). 'Fantasy, Myth, and the Pacific World: Albert Wendt's The Adventures of Vela'. In *New Soundings in Postcolonial Literature: Critical and Creative Contours*, edited by Janet Wilson and Chris Ringrose, 171–92. Amsterdam: Brill.

Dworkin, Craig. (2020). *Radium of the Word: A Poetics of Materiality*. Chicago: University of Chicago Press.

Easthope, Antony. (1983). *Poetry as Discourse*. London: Methuen.

Eckstein, Lars, and Anja Schwarz. (2019). 'The Making of Tupaia's Map: A Story of the Extent and Mastery of Polynesian Navigation, Competing Systems of Wayfinding on James Cook's *Endeavour*, and the Invention of an Ingenious Cartographic System'. *Journal of Pacific Hisotry* 51, no. 1: 1–95.

Eisner, Will. ([1996] 2008). *Graphic Storytelling and Visual Narrative*. New York: Norton.

Eldridge, David. (2008). 'The Generic American Psycho'. *Journal of American Studies* 42, no. 1: 19–33.

Ercolino, Stefano. (2014). *The Maximalist Novel: From Thomas Pynchon's Gravity's Rainbow to Roberto Bolano's 2666*. Trans. Albert Sbagria. London: Bloomsbury.

Eve, Martin Paul. (2019). 'Reading Redaction: Symptomatic Metadata, Erasure Poetry, and Mark Blacklock's *I'm Jack*'. *Critique: Studies in Contemporary Fiction* 60, no. 3: 330–41.

Eyers, Tom. (2017). *Speculative Formalism: Literature, Theory and the Critical Present*. Evanston, IL: Northwestern University Press.

Fanon, Frantz. ([1952] 1986). *Black Skin, White Masks*. Trans. by Charles Lam Markmann. London: Pluto Press.

Fasselt, Rebecca. (2016). '(Post)Colonial We-Narratives and the "Writing Back" Paradigm: Joseph Conrad's *The Nigger of the "Narcissus"* and Ngugi Wa Thiong'o's *A Grain of Wheat*'. *Poetics Today* 37, no. 1: 155–79.

Faubert, Michelle. (2017). 'Granville Sharp's Manuscript Letter to the Admiralty on the *Zong* Massacre: A New Discovery in the British Library'. *Slavery and Abolition* 38, no. 1: 178–95.

Faubert, Michelle. (2019). *Granville Sharp's Uncovered Letter and the Zong Massacre*. Houndmills: Palgrave Macmillan.

Federici, Silvia. (2004). *Caliban and the Witch: Women, the Body and Primitive Accumulation*. Automedia.
Fehskens, Erin M. (2012). 'Accounts Unpaid, Accounts Untold: M. NourbeSe Philip's *Zong!* and the Catalogue'. *Callaloo* 35, no. 2: 407–24.
Felski, Rita. (2009). 'After Suspicion'. *Profession* 1: 28–35.
Ferguson, Moira. (1992). *Subject to Others: British Women Writers and Colonial Slavery, 1670–1834*. London: Routledge.
Fisher, Mark. (2017). *The Weird and the Eerie*. London: Repeater.
Flusser, Villém. (2002). *Writings*, edited by Andreas Ströhl. Minneapolis: University of Minnesota Press.
Fox, Karen M., and Lisa McDermott. (2019). 'The Kumulipo, Native Hawaiians, and Well-Being: How the Past Speaks to the Present and Lays the Foundation for the Future'. *Leisure Studies*: 1–15.
Frazier, Frances. (2001). *The True Story of Kaluaikoolau as Told by His Wife, Piilani*. Lihue: The Kauai Historical Society Press.
Freud, Sigmund. ([1923] 1984). 'The Ego and the Id'. In *Standard Works. Vol. 11: On Metapsychology*, edited by James Strachey, 339–407. London: Penguin.
Freud, Sigmund. ([1933] 1989). 'The Dissection of the Psychical Personality'. In *New Introductory Lectures on Psycho-Analysis*, edited by James Strachey. Transl. W. J. H. Sprott, 71–101. New York: Norton.
Gabbard, Caroline Sinavaiana. (2018). 'Samoan Literature and the Wheel of Time: Cartographies of the Va'. *symploke* 26, nos. 1–2: 33–49.
Gandhi, Leela. (2014). *The Common Cause: Postcolonial Ethics and the Practice of Democracy, 1900–1955*. Chicago: University of Chicago Press.
Ganguly, Debjani. (2016). *This Thing Called the World: The Contemporary Novel as Global Form*. Durham: Duke University Press.
Gardner, Jared. (2006). 'Archives, Collectors, and the New Media Work of Comics'. *Modern Fiction Studies* 52, no. 4: 787–806.
Gilbert, Stuart. ([1930] 1958). *James Joyce's Ulysses: A Study*. New York: Vintage.
Gilroy, Paul. (2016). 'Antiracism and (re)Humanization'. In *The Common Growl: Towards a Poetics of Precarious Community*, edited by Thomas Claviez, 111–35. New York: Fordham University Press.
Girard, René. *The Scapegoat*. (1986). Trans. Yvonne Freccero. Baltimore: Johns Hopkins University Press.
Girouard, Mark. (1981). *The Return to Camelot: Chivalry and the English Gentleman*. New Haven: Yale University Press.
Glissant, Édouard. (1990). *Poetics of Relation*. Trans. Betsy Wing. Ann Arbor: University of Michigan Press.
Gourgouris, Stathis. (2013). *Lessons in Secular Criticism*. New York: Fordham University Press.
Gowers, Emily. (2005). 'Virgil's Sybil and the "Many Mouths" Cliché'. *Classical Quarterly* 55, no. 1: 170–82.
Greenblatt, Stephen. (1980). *Renaissance Self-Fashioning: From More to Shakespeare*. Chicago: University of Chicago Press.
Greenblatt, Stephen. (1990). *Learning to Curse: Essays in Early Modern Culture*. New York: Routledge.

Grossberg, Lawrence. (1986). 'On Postmodernism and Articulation'. *Journal of Communication Inquiry* 10, no. 2: 45–60.

Guillory, John. (2017). 'Mercury's Words: The Ends of Rhetoric and the Beginning of Prose'. *Representations* 138, no. 1: 59–86.

Habermas, Jürgen. (1988). *Nachmetaphysisches Denken: Philosophische Aufsätze*. Frankfurt/Main: Suhrkamp.

Halberstam, Judith. (2011). *The Queer Art of Failure*. Durham: Duke University Press.

Hale, Dorothy J. (1998). *Social Formalism: The Novel in Theory from Henry James to the Present*. Stanford: Stanford University Press.

Hale, Dorothy J. (2009). 'Aesthetics and the New Ethics: Theorizing the Novel in the Twenty-First Century'. *PMLA* 124, no. 3: 896–905.

Hall, Catherine. (2012). 'Afterword: Britain 2007, Problematizing Histories'. In *Imagining Transatlantic Slavery*, edited by Cora Kaplan and John Oldfield, 191–202. Houndmills: Palgrave.

Hall, Edith. (2009). 'The Autobiography of the Western Subject: Carson's Geryon'. In *Living Classics: Greece and Rome in Contemporary English Poetry*, edited by S. J. Harrison, 218–37. Oxford: Oxford University Press.

Hallward, Peter. (2001). *Absolutely Postcolonial: Writing between the Singular and the Specific*. Manchester: Manchester University Press.

Haraway, Donna. (1988). 'Situated Knowledges: The Science Question in Feminism and the Privilege of Partial Perspective'. *Feminist Studies* 14, no. 3: 575–99.

Haraway, Donna. (2016). *Staying with the Trouble: Making Kin in the Chthulucene*. Durham: Duke University Press.

Hardt, Michael, and Antonio Negri. (2000). *Empire*. Cambridge, MA: Harvard University Press.

Hardt, Michael, and Antonio Negri. (2004). *Multitude: War and Democracy in the Age of Empire*. New York: Penguin Press.

Härtl, Kathrin. (2019). '"They Keep Shifting Shapes": Derek Walcott's *Omeros* and Its Fluid Genre'. In *Poem Unlimited: New Perspectives on Poetry and Genre*, edited by David Kerler and Timo Müller, 139–54. Berlin: De Gruyter.

Hartman, Saidiya. (1997). *Scenes of Subjection: Terror, Slavery and Self-Making in Nineteenth-Century America*. Oxford: Oxford University Press.

Hartman, Saidiya. (2007). *Lose Your Mother: A Journey along the Atlantic Slave Route*. New York: Farrar, Straus and Giroux.

Harvey, David. (2010). *A Companion to Marx's Capital*. London: Verso.

Harvey, Paul Dean Adshead. (1987). 'Local and Regional Cartography in Medieval Europe'. In *The History of Cartography. Vol. 1: Cartography in Prehistoric, Ancient and Medieval Europe and the Mediterranean*, edited by J. B. Harley and David Woodward, 464–501. Chicago: University of Chicago Press.

Hawas, May. (2019). *Politicizing World Literature: Egypt, between Pedagogy and the Public*. New York: Routledge.

Hayot, Eric. (2012). *On Literary Worlds*. Oxford: Oxford University Press.

Harzewski, Stephanie. (2006). 'Tradition and Displacement in the New Novel of Manners'. In *Chick Lit: The New Woman's Fiction*, edited by Suzanne Ferris and Mallory Young, 29–46. New York: Routledge.

Hearon, Todd. (2004). 'One Hell of a Ride: Glynn Maxwell's *Time's Fool: A Tale in Verse*'. *Paranassus* 27, no. 2: 254–69.

Heath, John. (2005). *The Talking Greeks: Speech, Animals, and the Other in Homer, Aeschylus, and Plato*. Cambridge: Cambridge University Press.
Henderson, April K. (2010). 'Gifted Flows: Making Space for a Brand New Beat'. *The Contemporary Pacific* 22, no. 2: 293–315.
Henderson, April K. (2016). 'The I and the We: Individuality, Collectivity, and Samoan Artistic Responses to Cultural Change'. *The Contemporary Pacific* 28, no. 2: 316–45.
Henke, Suzette. (1978). *Joyce's Moraculous Sindbook: A Study of Ulysses*. Columbus: Ohio State University Press.
Hereniko, Vilsoni. (2006). 'Interview with Albert Wendt: Art, Writing, and the Creative Process'. *The Contemporary Pacific* 18, no. 1: 59–69.
Hipsky, Martin. (2011). *Modernism and the Women's Popular Romance in Britain, 1885–1925*. Athens: Ohio University Press.
Hitchcock, Peter. (2010). *The Long Space: Transnationalism and Postcolonial Form*. Stanford: Stanford University Press.
Hogue, Bev. (2013). 'Pain Worth More Than a Penny: Performance of Suffering in *Omeros* and *The America Play*'. In *Making Sense of Suffering: A Collective Attempt*, edited by Anja Drautzenberg and Jackson Oldfield, 127–33. Amsterdam: Brill.
Holden, Philip. (2010). 'Reading for Genre: The Short Story and (Post)colonial Governmentality'. *Interventions* 12, no. 3: 442–58.
hoʻomanawanui, kuʻualoha. (2014). *Voices of Fire: Reweaving the Literary Lei of Pele and Hiʻiaka*. Minneapolis: University of Minnesota Press.
hoʻomanawanui, kuʻualoha. (2019). 'E Hoʻi ka Piko (Returning to the Center): Theorizing Moʻokuʻauhau as Methodology in an Indigenous Context'. In *The Past Before Us: Moʻokūʻauhau as Methodology*, edited by Nālani Wilson-Hokowhitu and Marie Alohalani Brown, 50–68. Honolulu: University of Hawaii Press.
Horkheimer, Max, and Theodor W. Adorno. ([1944] 2002). *Dialectic of Enlightenment: Philosophical Fragments*. Transl. Edmund Jephcott. Durham: Duke University Press.
Hsy, Jonathan. (2021). *Antiracist Medievalisms: From 'Yellow Peril' to Black Lives Matter*. Leeds: Arc Humanities Press.
Hühn, Peter. (2010). 'Plotting the Lyric: Forms of Narration in Poetry'. *Literator* 31, no. 3: 17–47.
Ingarden, Roman. (1973). *The Cognition of the Literary Work of Art*. Evanston: Northwestern University Press.
Irr, Caren. (2011). 'Toward the World Novel: Genre Shifts in Twenty-First-Century Expatriate Fiction'. *American Literary History* 23, no. 3: 660–79.
Irr, Caren. (2014). *Toward the Geopolitical Novel: U.S. Fiction in the Twenty-First Century*. New York: Columbia University Press.
Jameson, Fredric. (1979). *Fables of Aggression: Wyndham Lewis, the Modernist as Fascist*. Berkeley: University of California Press.
Jameson, Fredric. (1988). 'Cognitive Mapping'. In *Marxism and the Interpretation of Culture*, edited by Cary Nelson and Lawrence Grossberg, 347–60. Basingstoke: Macmillan.

Jameson, Fredric. (1990). 'Modernism and Imperialism'. In *Nationalism, Colonialism, and Literature*, edited by Seamus Deane, 43–66. Minneapolis: University of Minnesota Press.

Jameson, Fredric. (1995). *The Geopolitical Aesthetic: Cinema and Space in the World System*. London: BFI.

Jameson, Fredric. (1998). *The Cultural Turn: Selected Writings on the Postmodern, 1983–1998*. London: Verso.

Jameson, Fredric. (1999). 'Marx's Purloined Letter'. In *Ghostly Demarcations: A Symposium on Jacques Derrida's 'Specters of Marx'*, edited by Michael Sprinker, 26–67. London: Verso.

Jameson, Fredric. (2003). 'The End of Temporality'. *Critical Inquiry* 29, no. 4: 696–718.

Jameson, Fredric. (2013). *The Antinomies of Realism*. London: Verso.

Jay, Paul. (2010). *Global Matters: The Transnational Turn in Literary Studies*. Ithaca: Cornell University Press.

Jenemann, David. (2013). 'Stupider and Worse: The Cultural Politics of Stupidity'. *Parallax* 19, no. 3: 34–49.

Johnson, Rubellite Kawena. (2000). *The Kumulipo Mind: A Global Heritage*. Honolulu: Anoai Press.

Johnston, Andrew James. (2015). 'Chaucer's Postcolonial Renaissance'. *Bulletin of the John Rylands Library* 91, no. 2: 5–20.

Jolles, André. ([1958] 2017). *Simple Forms*. Transl. Peter J. Schwartz. London: Verso.

Julien, Eileen. (2006). 'Arguments and Further Conjectures on World Literature'. In *Studying Transcultural Literary History*, edited by Gunilla Lindberg-Wada, 122–32. Berlin: DeGruyter.

Kanahele, Pualani Kanaka'ole. ([1897] 1997). 'Forward' [sic]. In *The Kumulipo: An Hawaiian Creation Myth*, edited by Kimo Campbell, i–ii. Trans. Lili'oukalani. Kentfield, CA: Pueo Press.

Kant, Immanuel. ([1788] 2002). *Critique of Practical Reason*. Trans. Werner S. Pluhar. Indianapolis: Hackett.

Kaplan, Gregory. (2019). *Jewish Poetry and Cultural Coexistence in Late Medieval Spain*. Berlin: De Gruyter.

Kellner, Douglas. (2019). *American Nightmare: Donald Trump, Media Spectacle, and Authoritarian Populism*. Rotterdam: Sense.

Kempton, Adrian. (2018). *The Verse Novel in English: Origins, Growth and Expansion*. Oxford: Peter Lang.

Kennedy, Curry. (2019). 'Milton's Ethos, English Nationhood, and the Fast-Day Tradition in *Areopagitica*'. *Studies in Philology* 116, no. 2: 375–400.

Kenyatta, Jomo. (1961). *Facing Mount Kenya: The Tribal Life of the Gikuyu*. London: Mercury Books.

Khan, Almas. (2015). 'Poetic Justice: Slavery, Law, and the (Anti-)Elegiac Form in M. NourbeSe Philip's *Zong!*'. *Cambridge Journal of Postcolonial Literary Inquiry* 2, no. 1: 5–32.

Knapp, Peggy A. (2004). 'Chaucer Imagines England (in English)'. In *Imagining a Medieval English Nation*, edited by Kathy Levezzo, 131–60. Minneapolis: University of Minnesota Press.

Kneale, James. (2011). 'Plots: Space, Conspiracy, and Contingency in William Gibson's *Pattern Recognition* and *Spook Country*'. *Environment and Planning* 29: 169–86.
Knowles, Joanne. (2004). 'Editorial: Chick Lit'. *Diegesis* 8: 1–3.
Kofman, Sarah. ([1973] 1998). *Camera obscura: Of Ideology*. Trans. Will Straw. Ithaca: Cornell University Press.
Kornbluh, Anna. (2019). *The Order of Forms: Realism, Formalism, and Social Space*. Chicago: University of Chicago Press.
Kristeva, Julia. (1980). *Desire in Language: A Semiotic Approach to Literature and Art*. Trans. Thomas Gora, Alice Jardine and Leon S. Roudiez. New York: Columbia University Press.
Kristeva, Julia. ([1974] 1984). *Revolution in Poetic Language*. Trans. Margaret Waller. New York: Columbia University Press.
Kroll, Jeri. (2010). 'Living on the Edge: Creative Writers in Higher Education'. *Text* 14, no. 1: 1–16.
Kroll, Jeri, and Leslie Jacobson. (2014). 'A Fine Balancing Act: Adapting the Verse Novel to the Stage'. *New Writing* 11, no. 2: 182–201.
Kroonenberg, Salomon. (2011). *Why Hell Stinks of Sulfur: Mythology and Geology of the Underworld*. London: Reaktion.
Kruger, Steve. (2006). *The Spectral Jew: Conversion and Embodiment in Medieval Europe*. Minneapolis: University of Minnesota Press.
Laclau, Ernesto. (2000). 'Structure, History and the Political'. In *Contingency, Hegemony, Universality: Contemporary Dialogues on the Left*. Judith Butler, Ernesto Laclau and Slavoj Žižek, 182–212. London: Verso.
Laclau, Ernesto. (2005). 'Populism: What's in a Name?' In *Populism and the Mirror of Democracy*, edited by Francisco Panizza, 32–49. London: Verso.
Laclau, Ernesto, and Chantal Mouffe. (2001). *Hegemony and Socialist Strategy: Towards a Radical Democratic Politics*. 2nd edn. London: Verso.
Lacoue-Labarthe, Phillipe, and Jean-Luc-Nancy. (1988). *The Literary Absolute: The Theory of Literature in German Romanticism*. New York: SUNY Press.
Lanham, Richard A. (1993). *The Electronic Word: Democracy, Technology, and the Arts*. Chicago: University of Chicago Press.
Larkin, Graham, and Lisa Pon. (2001). 'The Materiality of Printed Words and Images'. *Word and Image* 17, nos. 1–2: 1–6.
Larner, Wendy. (2014). 'The Limits of Post-Politics: Rethinking Radical Social Enterprise'. In *The Post-Political and Its Discontents: Spaces of Depoliticization, Spectres of Radical Politics*, edited by Japhy Wilson and Erik Swyngedouw, 189–207. Edinburgh: Edinburgh University Press.
Lawrence, Karen. (1990). 'Joyce and Feminism'. In *The Cambridge Companion to James Joyce*, edited by Derek Attridge, 237–58. Cambridge: Cambridge University Press.
Lesuma, Caryn. (2019). 'Sā Nafanuā: Reconstituting Nafanua as Female Empowerment in Samoan Diasporic Literature'. *Journal of American Folklore* 132, no. 525: 260–74.
Levin, Stephenie Seto. (1968). 'The Overthrow of the Kapu System in Hawaii'. *Journal of the Polynesian Society* 77, no. 4: 402–30.

Levine, Caroline. (2013). *Forms: Whole, Rhythm, Hierarchy, Network*. Princeton: Princeton University Press.
Lieberman, Laurence. (2012). 'W. S. Merwin: Apotheosis of the Lepers'. *The American Poetry Review* 41, no. 2: 41–8.
Lili'oukalani. ([1897] 1997). 'Introduction'. In *The Kumulipo: An Hawaiian Creation Myth*, edited by Kimo Campbell, 10–12. Trans. Lili'oukalani. Kentfield, CA: Pueo Press.
Lilomaiava-Dokter, Sailiemanu. (2009). 'Beyond "Migration": Samoan Population Movement (Malaga) and the Geography of Social Space (Va)'. *The Contemporary Pacific* 21, no. 1: 1–34.
Linebaugh, Peter, and Martin Rediker. (2000). *The Many-Headed Hydra: Sailors, Slaves, Commoners, and the Hidden History of the Revolutionary Atlantic*. Boston: Beacon Press.
Locher, Hubert. (2011). 'Ut pictura poesis – Malerei und Dichtung'. In *Metzler Lexikon Kunstwissenschaft*, edited by Ulrich Pfisterer, 454–9. Stuttgart: Metzler.
Lock, Charles. (2000). 'Derek Walcott's *Omeros*: Echoes from a White-Throated Vase'. *The Massachusetts Review* 41, no. 1: 9–31.
Lodge, David. (1977). *The Modes of Modern Writing: Metonymy, Metaphor, and the Typology of Modern Literature*. London: Edward Arnold.
Lukács, Georg. ([1920] 1988). *The Theory of the Novel: A Historico-Philosophical Essay on the Great Forms of Epic Literature*. Trans. Anna Bostock. London: Merlin Press.
Lukács, Georg. ([1937] 1989). *The Historical Novel*. Transl. Hannah and Stanley Mitchell. London: Merlin Press.
Lynch, Kathryn L. (1999). 'Storytelling, Exchange, and Constancy: East and West in Chaucer's "Man of Law"s Tale'. *The Chaucer Review* 33, no. 4: 409–22.
Macpherson, Sandra. (2015). 'A Little Formalism'. *ELH* 82, no. 2: 385–405.
Madörin, Anouk. (2022). *Shadow Archives of the European Border Regime: Border Surveillance Technology between Colony and Crisis*. Lanham: Rowman and Littlefield.
Mannheim, Karl. ([1929] 1979). *Ideology and Utopia: An Introduction to the Sociology of Knowledge*. Transl. Louis Wirth and Edward Shills. London: Routledge and Kegan Paul.
Marsh, Selina Tusitala. (1999). 'Theory 'Versus' Pacific Islands Writing'. In *Inside Out: Literature, Cultural Politics, and Identity in the New Pacific*, edited by Vilsoni Hereniko and Rob Wilson, 337–56. Lanham: Rowman and Littlefield.
Martin, Jonathan. (1992). 'Nightmare History: Derek Walcott's *Omeros*'. *The Kenyon Review* 14, no. 4: 197–204.
Marx, Karl. ([1852] 1973). 'The Eighteenth Brumaire of Louis Bonaparte'. Transl. Ben Fowkes. In *Surveys from Exile: Political Writings. Vol.2*, edited by David Fernbach, 143–249. Harmondsworth: Penguin.
Marx, Karl. ([1867] 1976). *Das Kapital: Kritik der politischen Ökonomie. Vol. 1*. Frankfurt/Main: Verlag Marxistische Blätter.
Mazza, Cris. (2006). 'Who's Laughing Now? A Short History of Chick Lit and the Perversion of a Genre'. In *Chick Lit: The New Woman's Fiction*, edited by Suzanne Ferriss and Mallory Young, 17–28. New York: Routledge.
Mazzoni, Guido. (2017). *Theory of the Novel*. Transl. Zakiya Hanafi. Cambridge, MA: Harvard University Press.

Mbembe, Achille. (2001). *On the Postcolony*. Berkeley: University of California Press.
Mbembe, Achille. (2017). *Critique of Black Reason*. Durham: Duke University Press.
McCloud, Scott. (1993). *Understanding Comics: The Invisible Art*. New York: HarperCollins.
McClure, John. (1994). *Late Imperial Romance*. London: Verso.
McConnell, Justine. (2016). 'Crossing Borders: Bernardine Evaristo's *The Emperor's Babe*'. *Callaloo* 39, no. 1: 103–14.
McHale, Brian. (2004). *The Obligation toward the Difficult Whole: Postmodernist Long Poems*. Tuscaloosa: University of Alabama Press.
McHale, Brian. (2009). 'Beginning to Think about Narrative in Poetry'. *Narrative* 17, no. 1: 11–27.
McHale, Brian. (2010). 'Affordances of Form in Stanzaic Narrative Poetry'. *Litterator* 31, no. 3: 49–60.
McKinsey, Martin. (2008). 'Missing Sound and Mutable Meanings: Names in Derek Walcott's *Omeros*'. *Callaloo* 31, no. 3: 891–902.
McNulty, Tess. (2019). 'Chick Lit Meets the Avantgarde'. In *Think in Public: A Public Books Reader*, edited by Sharon Marcus and Caitlin Zaloom, 439–51. New York: Columbia University Press.
Melas, Natalie. (2005). 'Forgettable Vacations and Metaphor in Ruins: Derek Walcott's *Omeros*'. *Callaloo* 28, no. 1: 147–68.
Miller, Dean A. (2000). *The Epic Hero*. Baltimore: Johns Hopkins University Press.
Milton, John. ([1643] 1959). 'The Doctrine and Discipline of Divorce'. In *The Complete Works of John Milton. Vol. 2*, edited by Ernest Sirluck, 229–343. New Haven: Yale University Press.
Milton, John. ([1670] 1991). *The History of Britain*. Stamford: Paul Watkins.
Milton, John. ([1644] 1999). 'Areopagitica'. *Areopagitica and Other Political Writings of John Milton*, edited by John Alvis, 3–51. Indianapolis: Liberty Fund.
Mirzoeff, Nicholas. (2016). *How to See the World: An Introduction to Images, from Self-Portraits to Selfies, Maps to Movies, and More*. New York: Basic Books.
Missler, Heike. (2017). *The Cultural Politics of Chick Lit: Popular Fiction, Postfeminism and Representation*. London: Routledge.
Montoro, Rocío. (2012). *Chick Lit: The Stylistics of Cappuccino Fiction*. London: Continuum.
Montroso, Alan S. (2020). 'Skin Black and Wrinkled: The Toxic Ecology of the Sybil's Cave'. *Postmedieval* 11, no. 1: 91–101.
Moore, Jason W. (2015). *Capitalism in the Web of Life: Ecology and the Accumulation of Capital*. London: Verso.
Moran, Michelle T. (2008). 'Telling Tales of Koʻolau: Containing and Mobilizing Disease in Colonial Hawaii.' In *Moving Subjects: Gender, Mobility, and Intimacy in an Age of Global Empire*, edited by Tony Ballantyne and Antoinette Burton, 315–35. Urbana: University of Illinois Press.
Moretti, Franco. (1996). *Modern Epic: The World System from Goethe to García Márquez*. London: Verso.
Moretti, Franco. (2000). 'Conjectures on World Literarure'. *New Left Review* 1: 54–68.

Moretti, Franco. (2013). *The Bourgeois: Between History and Literature*. London: Verso.
Moten, Fred. (2003). *In the Break: The Aesthetics of the Black Radical Tradition*. Minneapolis: University of Minnesota Press.
Mouffe, Chantal. (2005). *The Return of the Political*. 1993. London: Verso.
Mudde, Cas, and Cristóbal Rovira Kaltwasser. (2017). *Populism: A Very Short Introduction*. Oxford: Oxford University Press.
Mufti, Aamir R. (2016). *Forget English! Orientalisms and World Literatures*. Cambridge, MA: Harvard University Press.
Mukherjee, Ankhi. (2014). *What Is a Classic? Postcolonial Rewriting and Invention of the Canon*. Stanford: Stanford University Press.
Müller, W. G. (1991). 'Interfigurality. A Study of Interdependence of Literary Figures'. In *Intertextuality*, edited by Heinrich F. Plett, 101–21. Berlin: De Gruyter.
Munos, Delphine, and Bénédicte Ledent. (2018). '"Minor" Genres in Postcolonial Literatures: New Webs of Meaning'. *Journal of Postcolonial Writing* 54, no. 1: 1–5.
Muñoz-Valdivieso, Sofía. (2010). 'Africa in Europe: Narrating Black British History in Contemporary Fiction'. *Journal of European Studies* 40, no. 2: 159–74.
Nakley, Susan. (2010). 'Sovereignty Matters: Anachronism, Chaucer's Britain, and England's Future's Past'. *The Chaucer Review* 44, no. 4: 368–96.
Neumann, Birgit, and Gabriele Rippl. (2020). *Verbal-Visual Configurations in Postcolonial Literature: Aesthetic Configurations*. London: Routledge.
Ngai, Sianne. (2012a). 'Network Aesthetics: Juliana Spahr's *The Transformation* and Bruno Latour's *Reassembling the Social*'. In *American Literature's Aesthetic Dimensions*, edited by Cindy Weinstein and Chrsitopher Looby, 367–91. New York: Columbia University Press.
Ngai, Sianne. (2012b). *Our Aesthetic Categories: Zany, Cute, Interesting*. Cambridge, MA: Harvard University Press.
Nikulin, Dmitri. (2006). *On Dialogue*. Lanham: Lexington.
Novak, Julia. (2020). 'Performing Black British Memory: Kat François's Spoken-Word Show Raising Lazarus as Embodied Auto/biography'. *Journal of Postcolonial Writing* 56, no. 3: 324–41.
Nuʻuhiwa, Kalei. (2019). 'Papaku-Makawalu: A Methodology and Pedagogy of Understanding the Hawaiian Universe'. In *The Past before Us: Moʻokūʻauhau as Methodology*, edited by Wilson-HokowhituNālani and Marie Alohalani Brown, 39–49. Honolulu: University of Hawaii Press.
Nyamnjoh, Francis. (2017). *Drinking from the Cosmic Gourd: How Amos Tutuola Can Change Our Minds*. Mankon: Langaa Research.
O'Connor, Ralph. (2012). 'Victorian Saurians: The Linguistic Prehistory of the Modern Dinosaur'. *Journal of Victorian Culture* 17, no. 4: 492–504.
Osborne, Peter. (2013). *Anywhere or Not at All: Philosophy of Contemporary Art*. London: Verso.
Palleau-Papin, Françoise. (2016). 'W. S. Merwin's *The Folding Cliffs*: Epic Poetry as Postcolonial Revision'. *Revue française d'études américaines* 147, no. 2: 27–43.
Panofsky, Erwin. ([1927] 1991). *Perspective as Symbolic Form*. Trans. Christopher S. Wood. New York: Zone.

Parrinder, Patrick. (2008). *Nation and Novel: The English Novel from Its Origins to the Present Day*. Oxford: Oxford University Press.

Paul, Anthony. (2014). 'From Stasis to Ekstasis: Four Types of Chiasmus'. In *Chiasmus and Culture*, edited by Boris Wiseman and Anthony Paul, 19–39. New York: Berghahn.

Pittel, Harald. (2019). 'Romance and Irony: Oscar Wilde and the Political'. PhD diss., University of Potsdam.

Postero, Nancy, and Eli Elinoff. (2019). 'Introduction: A Return to Politics'. *Anthropological Theory* 19, no. 1: 3–28.

Pratt, George. ([1894] 2009). *Pratt's Grammar and Dictionary Samoan: English / English – Samoan*. Papkura, NZ: McMillan.

Propp, Vladimir. ([1928] 2009). *Morphology of the Folk Tale*. 2nd edn, edited by Louis A. Wagner. Trans. Lawrence Scott. Austin: University of Texas Press.

Quijano, Anibal. (2000). 'Coloniality of Power, Eurocentrism, and Latin America'. *Nepantla: Views from South* 1, no. 3: 533–80.

Rae, Ian. (2000). 'Dazzling Hybrids: The Poetry of Anne Carson'. *Canadian Literature* 166: 17–42.

Raghavan, Anjana. (2017). *Towards Corporeal Cosmopolitanism: Performing Decolonial Solidarities*. Lanham: Rowman and Littlefield.

Ramazani, Jahan. (1997). 'The Wound of History: Walcott's *Omeros* and the Postcolonial Poetics of Affliction'. *PMLA* 113, no. 3: 405–17.

Rancière, Jacques. (2004a). *The Flesh of Words: The Politics of Writing*. Trans. Charlotte Mandell. Stanford: Stanford University Press.

Rancière, Jacques. (2004b). *The Politics of Aesthetics*. Trans. Gabriel Rockhill. London: Continuum.

Rancière, Jacques. (2010). *Dissensus: On Politics and Aesthetics*. Transl. Steven Corcoran. London: Continuum.

Rancière, Jacques. (2011). *The Politics of Literature*. Trans. Julie Rose. Cambridge: Polity.

Renfrew, Alastair. (2015). *Mikhail Bakhtin*. London: Routledge.

Richter, Jean Paul. ([1802–12,] 1990). *Vorschule der Ästhetik*, edited by Wolfgang Heckmann. Hamburg: Meiner.

Ricks, Christopher. (1963). *Milton's Grand Style*. Oxford: Clarendon Press.

Rohrer, Judy. (2016). *Staking Claim: Settler Colonialism and Racialization in Hawai'i*. Tucson: University of Arizona Press.

Rosenberg, Ingrid von. (2010). 'If …: Bernardine Evaristo's (Gendered) Reconstructions of Black European History'. *ZAA* 58, no. 4: 381–95.

Rothberg, Michael. (2019). *The Implicated Subject: Beyond Victims and Perpetrators*. Stanford: Stanford University Press.

Rouse, Marylynn. (2018). '"A Double Portion of My Thoughts and Prayers": John Newton's Letters to William Wilberforce'. *Midwestern Journal of Theology* 17, no. 2: 15–41.

Roy, Sneharika. (2018). *The Postcolonial Epic: From Melville to Walcott and Ghosh*. London: Routledge.

Rupprecht, Anita. (2007). '"A Very Uncommon Case": Representation of the *Zong* and the British Campaign to Abolish the Slave Trade'. *The Journal of Legal History* 28, no. 3: 329–46.

Said, Edward. (1994). *Culture and Imperialism*. London: Vintage.

Sauerberg, Lars Ole. (2004). 'Repositioning Narrative: The Late-Twentieth-Century Verse Novels of Vikram Seth, Derek Walcott, Craig Raine, Anthony Burgess, and Bernardine Evaristo'. *Orbis Litterarum* 59: 439–64.

Sauerberg, Lars Ole. (2013). 'Monumentalism and Contemporary Verse Novels'. *Anglia* 131, nos. 2–3: 248–61.

Scafe, Suzanne. (2015). 'Unsettling the Centre: Black British Writing'. In *The History of British Women's Writing, 1970 – Present*, edited by Mary Eagleton and Emma Parker, 214–28. Houndmills: Palgrave.

Scarth, Alwyn. (2002). *La Catastrophe: The Eruption of Mount Pelée, the Worst Volcanic Disaster of the 20th Century*. Oxford: Oxford University Press.

Schoo, Jan. (1969). *Hercules' Labors: Fact or Fiction?* Chicago: Argonaut.

Schudson, Michael. (2003). 'Click Here for Democracy: A History and Critique of an Information-Based Model of Citizenship'. In *Democracy and New Media*, edited by Henry Jenkins and David Thorburn, 49–60. Cambridge, MA: MIT Press.

Schultz, Elizabeth. (2009). 'Odysseus Come to Know His Place: Reading *The Odyssey* Ecocritically'. *Neohelicon* 36: 299–310.

Sedgwick, Eve Kosovsky. (1985). *Between Men: English Literature and Male Homosocial Desire*. New York: Columbia University Press.

Sexton, Jared, and Huey Copeland. (2003). 'Raw Life: An Introduction'. *Qui Parle* 13, no. 2: 53–62.

Shapiro, James. (1996). *Shakespeare and the Jews*. New York: Columbia University Press.

Sharpe, Christina. (2016). *In the Wake: On Blackness and Being*. Durham: Duke University Press.

Sharpe, Jenny. (2014). 'The Archive and Affective Memory in M. NourbSe Philip's *Zong!*'. *Interventions* 16, no. 4: 465–82.

Sharrad, Paul. (2002). 'Albert Wendt and the Problem of History'. *The Journal of Pacific History* 37, no. 1, 109–116.

Sharrad, Paul. (2003). *Albert Wendt and Pacific Literature: Circling the Void*. Manchester: Manchester University Press.

Sharrad Paul, and Karen M. Peacock. (2003). 'Albert Wendt: Bibliography'. *The Contemporary Pacific* 15, no. 2: 378–420.

Shineberg, Dorothy. (1967). *They Came for Sandalwood: A Study of the Sandalwood Trade in the South-west Pacific, 1830–1865*. Melbourne: University of Melbourne Press.

Shklovsky, Victor. ([1925] 2015). *Theory of Prose*. Transl. Benjamin Sher. Champaign, IL: Dalkey Archive Press.

Shockley, Evie. (2011). 'Going Overboard: African Poetic Innovation and the Middle Passage'. *Contemporary Literature* 52, no. 4: 791–817.

Siskin, Clifford. (1996). 'Epilogue: The Rise of Novelism'. In *Cultural Institutions of the Novel*, edited by Deidre Lynch and William B. Warner, 423–40. Durham: Duke University Press.

Siskind, Mariano. (2010). 'The Globalization of the Novel and the Novelization of the Global: A Critique of World Literature'. *Comparative Literature* 62, no. 4: 336–60.

Smith, Barbara Herrnstein. (1968). *Poetic Closure: A Study of How Poems End*. Chicago: University of Chicago Press.
Smith, Caroline J. (2008). *Cosmopolitan Culture and Consumerism in Chick Lit*. New York: Routledge.
Somers-Willett, Susan B. A. (2005). 'Slam Poetry and the Cultural Politics of Performing Identity'. *The Journal of the Midwest Modern Language Association* 38, no. 1: 51–73.
Sorensen, Eli Park. (2021). *Postcolonial Realism and the Concept of the Political*. New York: Routledge.
Southward, John. ([1875] 2010). *A Dictionary of Typography and Its Accessory Arts*. Cambridge: Cambridge University Press.
Spivak, Gayatri Chakravorty. (1990). *The Postcolonial Critic*. New York and London: Routledge.
Spivak, Gayatri Chakravorty. (1999). *A Critique f Postcolonial Reason: Toward a History of the Vanishing Present*. Cambridge, MA: Harvard University Press.
Spivak, Gayatri Chakravorty. (2003). *Death of a Discipline*. New York: Columbia University Press.
Spivak, Gayatri Chakravorty. ([1987] 2006). *In Other Worlds*. New York: Routledge.
Spivak, Gayatri Chakravorty. (2012). *An Aesthetic Education in the Age of Globalization*. Cambridge, MA: Harvard University Press.
Spivak, Gayatri Chakravorty. (2015). 'Planetarity'. *Paragraph* 38, no. 2: 290–2.
Stafford, Emma. (2012). *Herakles*. London: Routledge.
Staudigel, Hubert, Stanley R. Hart, Adele Pile, Bradley E. Bailey, Edward T. Baker, Sandra Brooke, Douglas P. Connelly, Lisa Haucke, Christopher R. German, Ian Hudson, Daniel Jones, Anthony A. P. Koppers, Jasper Konter, Ray Lee, Theodore W. Pietsch, Bradley M. Tebo, Alexis S. Templeton, Robert Zierenberg, and Craig M. Young. (2006). 'Vailululu'u Seamount, Samoa: Life and Death on an Active Submarine Volcano'. *PNAS* 103, no. 17: 6448–53.
Stein, Mark. (2004). *Black British Literature: Novels of Transformation*. Columbus: Ohio State University.
Steyerl, Hito. (2017). *Duty Free Art: Art in the Age of Planetary Civil War*. London: Verso.
Steyerl, Hito. (2018). 'A Sea of Data: Pattern Recognition and Corporate Animism (Forked Version)'. In *Pattern Discrimination*, edited by Clemens Apprich, Wendy Hui Kyong Chun, Florian Cramer and Hito Steyerl, 1–23. Minneapolis: University of Minnesota Press.
Stinson, Timothy. (2017). '(In)Completeness in Middle English Literature: The Case of the Cook's Tale and the Tale of Gamelyn'. *Manuscript Studies* 1, no. 1: 115–34.
Swyngedouw, Erik. (2009). 'The Antinomies of the Postpolitical City: In Search of a Democratic Politics of Environmental Production'. *International Journal of Urban and Regional Research* 33, no. 3: 601–20.
Tansel, Cemal Burak. (2018). 'Authoritarian Neoliberalism and Democratic Backsliding in Turkey: Beyond the Narratives of Progress'. *South European Society and Politics* 18, no. 2: 197–217.
Tavita, Tupuola Terry. (2010). 'Nafanua Dead in Vela's Verse'. *Pacific Scoop*. https://pacific.scoop.co.z/category/samoa/page21/ (accessed 29 January 2023.

Theis, Jeffery S. (2005). 'Milton's Principles of Architecture'. *English Literary Renaissance* 35, no. 1: 102–22.
Theweleit, Klaus. ([1977] 1992). *Male Fantasies. Vol.1: Women – Floods – Bodies – History*. Transl. Stephen Conway. Minneapolis: University of Minnesota Press.
Thomas, Helen. (2000). *Romanticism and Slave Narratives: Transatlantic Testimonies*. Cambridge: Cambridge University Press.
Thurston, Martin. (2009). *The Underworld in Twentieth-Century Poetry: From Pound and Eliot to Heaney and Walcott*. New York: Palgrave.
Todorov, Tzvetan. (1984). *The Conquest of America: The Question of the Other*. Transl. Richard Howard. New York: Harper Colophon.
Tolkien, John Ronald Reuel. ([1936] 2002). 'Beowulf: The Monster and the Critics'. In *Beowulf: A New Verse Translation*, edited by Daniel Donoghue, 103–30. New York: Norton.
Tomasch, Sylvia. (2000). 'Postcolonial Chaucer and the Virtual Jew'. In *The Postcolonial Middle Ages*, edited by Jeffrey Jerome Cohen, 243–60. Houndmills: Palgrave.
Tschofen, Monique. (2004). '"First I Must Tell about Seeing": (De)monstrations of Visuality and the Dynamics of Metaphor in Anne Carson's *Autobiography of Red*'. *Canadian Literature* 180: 31–50.
Tuagalu, l'uogafa. (2008). 'Heuristics of the Va'. *AlterNative: An International Journal of Indigenous Peoples* 4, no. 1: 107–26.
Tui Atua, Tupua Tamasese Ta'isi Efi. (2009). *Su'esu'e Manogi: In Search of Fragrance*. Wellington: Huia.
Tymocko, Maria. (1994). *The Irish Ulysses*. Berkeley: University of California Press.
Ulbrich, Hans-Joachim. (1992). 'Archäologie der Cañadas del Teide'. *Almogaren* 23, no. 2: 41–76.
Va'ai, Sina Mary Theresa. (1999). *Literary Representations in Western Polynesia: Colonialism and Indigeneity*. Le Papa-I-Galagala: National University of Samoa.
Van Sickle, John. (1999). 'The Design of Derek Walcott's *Omeros*'. *Classical World* 93: 7–27.
Varughese, Emma Dawson. (2012). *Beyond the Postcolonial: World Englishes Literature*. Houndmills: Palgrave.
Vogl, Joseph. (2015). *The Specters of Capital*. Transl. Joachim Redner and Robert Savage. Stanford: Stanford University Press.
Wacker, Julian. (2019). 'Grime Poetry: Black British Rap Lyric(s) in the Twenty-First Century'. *Poem Unlimited: New Perspectives on Poetry and Genre*, edited by David Kerler and Timo Müller, 255–69. Berlin: De Gruyter.
Wacks, David A. (2015). *Double Diaspora in Sephardic Literature: Jewish Cultural Production before and after 1492*. Bloomington: Indiana University Press.
Wagner, Eva Sabine. (2020). *Narrativity, Coherence and Literariness: A Theoretical Approach with Analyses of Laclos, Kafka and Toussaint*. Berlin: De Gruyter.
Walkowitz, Rebecca L. (2015). *Born Translated: The Contemporary Novel in the Age of World Literature*. New York: Columbia University Press.
Walvin, James. (1994). *Black Ivory: A History of British Slavery*. Washington: Howard University Press.

Walvin, James. (2011). *The Zong: A Massacre, the Law, and the End of Slavery*. New Haven: Yale University Press.
Watt, Ian. ([1957] 1972). *The Rise of the Novel: Studies in Defoe, Richardson and Fielding*. Harmondsworth: Penguin.
Weheliye, Alexander. (2014). *Habeas Viscus: Racializing Assemblages, Biopolitics, and Black Feminist Theories of the Human*. Durham: Duke University Press.
Weinig, Siegfried. (1998). 'Aristotelian Foundations of German Novella Theory'. *seminar* 34, no. 1: 46–62.
Wells, Juliette. (2006). 'Mothers of Chick Lit? Women Writers, Readers, and Literary History'. In *Chick Lit: The New Woman's Fiction*, edited by Suzanne Ferriss and Mallory Young, 47–70. New York: Routledge.
Wendt, Albert. ([1976] 2019). 'Towards a New Oceania'. In *Global Modernists on Modernism: An Anthology*, edited by Alys Moody and Stephen J. Ross, 385–397. London: Bloomsbury.
Werbner, Pnina. (2018). 'De-orientalising Vernacular Cosmopolitanism: Towards a Local Cosmopolitan Ethics'. In *Beyond Cosmopolitanism: Towards Planetary Transformations*, edited by Nanata Kumar Giri, 275–95. New York: Palgrave.
Westover, Jeff. (2019). 'Story, Discourse, and the Voice of the Other in W. S. Merwin's *The Folding Cliffs*'. In *Genre* 52, no. 1: 51–75.
West-Pavlov, Russell. (2013). *Temporalities*. London: Routledge.
White, Hayden. (1973). *Metahistory: The Historical Imagination in Nineteenth-Century Europe*. Baltimore: Johns Hopkins University Press.
White, Hayden. (1987). *The Content of the Form: Narrative Discourse and Historical Representation*. Baltimore: Johns Hopkins University Press.
Wiemann, Dirk. (2005). 'News from Nowhere: Vikram Seth's *An Equal Music*'. In *Transgressions: Interventions in the Global Manifold*, edited by Renate Brosch and Rüdiger Kunow, 127–41. Trier: WVT.
Wiemann, Dirk. (2007). 'From Forked Tongue to Forked Tongue: Milton and Rushdie in the Postcolonial Conversation'. *Journal of Commonwealth Literature* 42, no. 2: 47–63.
Wiemann, Dirk. (2022). 'Network Realism/Capitalist Realism'. In *Realism: Aesthetics, Experiments, Politics*, edited by Jens Elze, 209–27. New York: Bloomsbury.
Wilderson III, Frank B. (2009). 'Grammar & Ghosts: The Performative Limits of African Freedom'. *Theatre Survey* 50, no. 1: 119–25.
Wilderson III, Frank B. (2014). '"We're Trying to Destroy the World": Anti-Blackness and Police Violence after Ferguson'. *Ill Will Editions*. https://illwilleditions.noblogs.org/files/2015/09/Wilderson-We-Are-Trying-to-Destroy-the-World-PRINT.pdf, accessed 28 January 2023.
Wilsbacher, Gregory J. (2005). 'Lumiansky's Paradox: Ethics, Aesthetics, and Chaucer's "Prioress's Tale"'. *College English* 32, no. 4: 1–28.
Wilson, Japhy, and Erik Swyngedouw. (2014). 'Seeds of Dystopia: Post-Politics and the Return of the Political'. In *The Post-Political and Its Discontents: Spaces of Depoliticization, Spectres of Radical Politics*, edited by Japhy Wilson and Erik Swngedouw, 1–22. Edinburgh: Edinburgh University Press.
Wilson, Nick. (2020). *The Space that Separates: A Realist Theory of Art*. London: Routledge.

Wilson-Hokowhitu, Nalani. (2012). 'He Pukoa Kaniʻaina: Kanaka Maoli Approaches to moʻokuuʻauhau as Methodology'. *AlterNative: An International Journal of Indigenous Peoples* 8, no. 2: 137–47.

Wood, Marcus. (2010). 'Significant Silence: Where Was Slave Agency in the Popular Imagery of 2007?' In *Imagining Transatlantic Slavery*, edited by Cora Kaplan and John Oldfield, 162–90. Houndmills: Palgrave.

Woodcock, Bruce. (2001). 'Derek Walcott, *Omeros*'. In *A Companion to Twentieth-Century Poetry*, edited by Neil Roberts, 547–58. Oxford: Blackwell.

Worden, Blair. (2007). *Literature and Politics in Cromwellian England: John Milton, Andrew Marvell, Marchamont Nedham*. Oxford: Oxford University Press.

Wright, Patrick. (2009). *On Living in an Old Country: The National Past in Contemporary Britain*. Oxford: Oxford University Press.

Yesilbas, Emre. (2020). 'The Polyphonic Novel in Contemporary British Fiction: Neoliberal Individualism and Collective Narratives'. PhD diss., University of Rostock.

Zatti, Sergio. (2006). *The Quest for Epic: From Ariosto to Tasso*. Toronto: University of Toronto Press.

Žižek, Slavoj. (1999). *The Ticklish Subject: The Absent Centre of Political Ontology*. London: Verso.

Žižek, Slavoj. (2004). *Organs without Bodies: On Deleuze and Consequences*. London: Routledge.

Zupancic, Alenka. (2008). *The Odd One In: On Comedy*. Cambridge, MA.: MIT Press.

INDEX

abolitionism (anti-slavery) 174, 175, 177–9, 192
Addison, Catherine 18–20, 31, 63
Adorno, Theodor W. 4, 151, 197
Afropessimism 182–4
Agbabi, Patience 58, 133, 172, 179, 198
　Telling Tales 158–71
anachronism 32–3, 64, 80, 98, 100, 146, 152
Anderson, Benedict 33, 65, 134, 136, 138, 140, 160, 161, 165, 166
antisemitism 58, 162, 164, 169
apartheid 51–6
apophenia 142–3
Appadurai, Arjun 160
articulation 6–7, 10, 11–12, 29, 39, 46, 71, 79, 87, 96, 101, 106, 129, 135
　incomplete 14, 16, 23, 39, 41, 44, 45, 47, 70, 72
assemblage 3, 7, 11, 23, 34, 47, 79, 105, 135, 183, 185, 199

Badiou, Alain 39, 140–4
Bakhtin, Mikhail M. 7, 29, 32, 41, 54, 72, 134
Beecroft, Alexander 12, 58, 64, 100
Benjamin, Walter 23, 39, 49, 50, 171, 195
Bhabha, Homi K. 76, 180, 190
Blackness/Black condition 49, 179, 182, 185, 187, 195
　anagrammatical (Sharpe) 176, 179
　fact of 69, 178
　universalization of (Mbembe) 49, 195
Blue Marble (NASA photographs) 8–10, 29, 74, 136

Boltanski, Luc 45–6
Borges, Jorge Luis 111
Broeck, Sabine, *see also* enslavism 63
Brown, Wendy 14, 37
Burkitt, Katharine 21, 30, 31, 75, 85
Bush, George W. 151

capitalism 35, 36, 102, 194–5
　network 45–6
Carson, Anne 30, 57, 65, 69, 90, 101, 112, 116, 127, 132, 198
　Autobiography of Red 74–89
　The Beauty of the Husband 30
Casanova, Pascale 27, 29, 31
　Greenwich meridian of world literature 31, 33
Cassirer, Ernst 13, 14, 23
Castillo, Ana 30
central-point perspective 13–16
Chakrabarty, Dipesh 33, 98
Chaucer, Geoffrey
　anti-Judaism 162–6
　'The Prioress's Tale' 162–6, 167, 168, 169
　'remix' by Patience Agbabi 58, 158–61
Cheah, Pheng 34, 35, 38
Chiapello, Eve 45–6
chick lit 149–56
claustrophobia 12, 13, 38, 47, 103, 143
Clifford, James 71, 92, 102
colonial pedagogy / 'civilizing mission' 152, 96, 97, 147, 148, 152
colonialism 73, 95–6, 115, 152, 158, 171, 172
　anti- 35, 42, 50
　computational 174, 175, 177
　settler 114, 127, 131, 132

connexionism 41, 42, 45–50, 65, 73, 78, 104, 105, 106, 112, 141–5, 189, 190
Conrad, Joseph 147–8, 158
continuity, see also seamlessness 3, 4, 10, 12, 15, 79, 87, 89, 96, 102, 106, 136, 160
  editing (film) 6, 7
  Milton 43–4
  text 7, 10, 16, 22
copula 107, 108, 109, 181
cosmopolitanism, minor 13, 48–50, 93, 100, 109, 120, 164, 197, 199
cuaderna vía (stanza form) 169–71

D'Aguiar, Fred 30
danger 49, 62, 153, 194–5, 197, 198
Dante (Alighieri) 101, 116, 189, 194
  Geryon in *Divine Comedy* 75–7, 80
  and *Omeros* 61, 63, 67, 69, 71
  and *The Adventures of Vela* 102–3
decompletion 8, 12, 23, 40
deep time 28, 33, 57, 122, 133
Deleuze, Gilles 47, 105
  molar/molecular 41, 44, 45, 58, 135, 143, 144
DeLillo, Don 59, 143, 194
de Man, Paul 107
Derrida, Jacques 86–8, 107, 128
Dickinson, Emily 88
Dimock, Wai Chee 24–6, 32, 48, 66, 139, 198

Ellis, Bret Easton 102
enslavement/Atlantic slave trade 50, 63, 172, 173–6, 179, 182, 191–2
  historical trauma of 63, 65, 66, 73, 181, 189
enslavism 58, 63, 76, 173, 175, 179, 186, 188, 190, 192
entrelacement / interlacement 4, 12–13, 58, 63, 65, 76, 77, 125, 133, 188
epic 14, 19, 23, 32–3, 193–7
  and *Autobiography of Red* 75, 77, 79, 89
  and *The Emperor's Babe* 155–8
  as linguistic sponge (Dimock) 32, 196
  and migratory poetics (Roy) 32–3
  and *Omeros* 61–7, 71–3
Equiano, Olaudah 177–8
erasure poetry 23
Eurochrony 33, 93
Evaristo, Bernardine 31, 58, 172, 179, 198
  Girl, Woman, Other 59
  The Emperor's Babe 30, 133, 145–58
Eyers, Tom 8, 17, 40, 42, 43

Fisher, Mark 194, 195
form 1–4, 7, 12, 15–17, 20, 29, 42–5, 63, 79, 81, 85, 106, 113, 128, 138, 139, 143, 164, 169–71, 180, 193–5
  affordances of (Levine) 18, 31, 89, 160
  and content 15, 20–1
  formativeness of (Eyers) 8, 12
  nation- 51, 54, 133, 160
  plurality of 30, 31, 39, 59, 167–8
  politics of 17, 23, 35, 38, 167
  symbolic 13, 15, 16
formalism 15–18, 21, 43
  planetary, see also Dimock 27, 28
  political 15, 18, 31, 43
  social 7, 8, 12, 13, 21, 33, 123, 134, 160, 170
Freud, Sigmund 81, 84, 87

Gandhi, Leela 42
  imperfectionism 42–5
gap
  as connector/bridge 4, 6, 11, 28, 41, 45, 74, 190
  negotiation 7, 11, 13, 22, 26, 43, 58, 89, 113, 119, 123, 136, 199
  non-negotiable 186, 190
gappiness, gappy textuality 4, 6, 8, 14, 17, 22, 25, 34, 35–59, 74, 78, 89, 93, 106, 160, 180, 193, 198
Gates, J., Henry Louis 7
Gendersternchen 12, 39
Geryon
  Dante 75–6
  Greek mythology 77
  Stesichoros 77, 79

Gibson, William 143
Glissant, Edouard 65, 71, 104
globalization 24, 27, 34, 48, 51, 133, 160
  plot of (Beecroft) 12, 58, 64, 133
Green, Michael Cawood
  Sinking 24–6, 51–6
Greenblatt, Stephen 94–6, 104, 196, 197
gutter
  in graphic narrative 4–7, 106, 136
  Oscar Wilde 1–3, 5, 193, 195
  in printing 5–7, 55
  as separator and connector 5, 17, 27, 28, 34, 44, 45, 46, 66, 70, 79, 106, 107, 135, 139, 140, 145, 157, 190, 199

Halberstam, Jack 150–1
Hansen's disease 114–16, 120, 131
Haraway, Donna 40, 44, 47, 105
Hardt, Michael 15, 36, 46, 47
Hartman, Saidiya 173–5, 195
Hayot, Eric 8
Herrera, Juan Felipe 30
hip hop
  in *The Adventures of Vela* 99–100, 105
hoa'ina (Hawaiian epistemology) 131–2
Homer 32, 61, 101, 156, 157, 196
  in *Autobiography of Red* 77, 78, 87
  in *The Emperor's Babe* 155, 176
  in *Omeros* 63–8, 71, 72, 195
homogeneous empty time (Benjamin) 15, 98, 124, 127, 134, 135, 138, 140, 160
homogeneous space 13, 14, 52
Horkheimer, Max 151, 197

imperial romance 146, 147–52, 155, 156
incompleteness 3, 8, 11, 16, 17, 33, 65, 79, 90, 93, 104, 125, 158–60, 187, 193
  pace Francis Nyamnjoh 40, 41, 50, 196
Ingarden, Roman 4, 5, 8
isomorphism 34, 42, 43, 57, 87

Jameson, Fredric 12, 35, 44, 95, 113
Jolles, André 2, 10
Joyce, James 4, 54, 139
  in *Omeros* 72, 73, 77
  in *The Emperor's Babe* 157

Kant, Immanuel 107, 195
kapu (Hawaiian social stratification) 118, 131, 132
Kempton, Adrian 19
Kenyatta, Jomo 62
Kipling, Rudyard 53, 152
Kornbluh, Anna 3, 17, 43–5, 138
  composed relationalities 3, 17, 39, 79, 81, 90, 138, 139, 142, 144, 160, 199
Kroll, Jeri 30
Kumulipo (Hawaiian creation chant) 61, 116–21, 127, 128, 129, 132, 135

Laclau, Ernesto 7, 16, 17, 37, 41, 46
Lennon, John 98, 111
Levine, Caroline 16, 17
Lili'oukalani 117
Lukàcs, Georg 61, 113, 120, 138, 193, 196

Mannheim, Karl 1–2, 138, 140
  situational congruence 1, 2, 12, 17, 35, 37, 38, 198
  situational transcendence 1–3, 8, 12, 17, 37, 38, 39, 42, 47, 49, 138, 140, 198
Marx, Karl 15, 53, 117
masculinism 11, 55, 83, 151–5
Mbembe, Achille 49–50, 95, 190, 195
McCloud, Scott 4–6
McHale, Brian 6, 22, 23, 26, 28, 44, 123, 199
  countermeasure 25, 26, 28, 106, 193, 199
  segmentivity 7, 8, 10, 17, 22–6, 28, 34, 38, 42, 59, 61, 74, 79, 87, 106, 136, 158, 198
  sequentiality 6, 7, 17, 22–6, 28, 44, 58, 199
Merwin, W. S. 57, 65, 135

INDEX

The Folding Cliffs 61, 113–32
metaphor 72, 75, 87
   architecture as 43–5
   lei (Hawaiian wreath) as 124–5
metonymy 72, 87
Middle Passage 50, 66, 173–7, 179, 181, 189
Milton, John 47, 48, 63, 123, 128, 147, 196
   Areopagitica 43–5
Mirzoeff, Nicholas 8–10, 13
missionaries 97, 108, 110, 114
Mitchell, David 58, 64, 107
modernity 14, 15, 32, 50, 93, 98, 102, 108, 132, 193–8
moʻokuʻauhau (Hawaiian genealogy) 118–19, 122, 123, 127
Moretti, Franco 3, 27, 28, 31, 133
Moten, Fred 176
Mouffe, Chantal 7, 16, 17, 36, 41, 46
Murray, Les 30

Nafanua (Samoan queen/deity) 61, 91
   in *The Adventures of Vela* 92, 94–101, 110, 111
   volcano 112
nation 32, 44, 47, 51, 140, 191
   narrative address of 173, 179, 180, 190–2
   and (prose) novel 34, 54–5, 57, 133, 160
   and verse novel 57, 58, 62, 133, 135–9, 143–5, 158, 163, 165–6, 171
Negri, Antonio 15, 36, 46, 47
neoliberalism 35, 36, 45, 46, 48, 49, 50, 195
   authoritarian 37, 39
Ngai, Sianne 45–7, 134, 141
Ngugi Wa Thiongo 61, 62, 67, 135
night sky 3–5, 74, 107, 193, 195, 196
novel 6, 7, 13, 64
   historical 113–14, 115
   and nation 34, 54–5, 57, 133, 160
   prose 18–21, 28, 29, 34, 58, 133
novelism – novel-centrism 29, 30
novelization of the global 29, 34, 58, 59

Nyamnjoh, Francis, *see also* incompleteness 40, 41, 45, 196

Oesterle, Kathy 30
opacity 102, 103, 104, 179, 190
orature 32, 145, 194
   South Pacific 91, 92, 94, 118, 120

Panowsky, Erwin 13–15
paranoia 12, 13, 143
Paris Commune (1871) 39
Pele (Hawaiian volcano deity) 112, 129, 130
performance poetry 20, 134, 145, 158, 170
Philip, M NourbeSe 58, 133
   anagrammaticality 183, 184, 186, 190, 192
   Zong! 171–92
photography 8–10, 85–90
planetarity 3, 24, 27, 33, 34, 47, 51, 55, 57, 62, 65–7, 73, 93, 112, 119, 128–9, 134, 137, 139, 197
plantation 70, 131, 172, 173, 174, 175
populism 36, 37, 39, 151, 153
Porter, Dorothy 30, 58
postcolonial 18, 21, 57, 169
   critique 21, 30, 33, 35, 68, 93, 195
   temporalities 30–5, 123–5
   writing 18, 31, 32, 63, 67, 71, 98, 145, 146, 156, 160
post-politics 35–7, 39
precolonial Samoa 90–2, 93, 97, 110, 111 (FN)
prose 6, 18, 20–3, 24, 59, 61, 133, 156, 193, 199
Pynchon, Thomas 143

racism 36, 55, 82, 114, 147, 149, 167, 199
   anti- 35, 80
Raine, Craig 30
Ramayana 61
Rancière, Jacques 16, 35, 45, 143, 171, 176
   dissensus 17, 23, 34, 36, 39, 171
   distribution of the sensible 16, 118, 151, 187

INDEX

gap in the sensible 17, 35, 38, 39
rap 20, 99
   in *Let Them Eat Chaos* 134, 145
   in *Telling Tales* 166, 168–9
realism 5, 19, 43, 135, 138, 141
   formal (Watt) 19, 64
   magic 90, 91, 98
   melancholy 175, 178
rime royal (stanza form) 164, 168
Rushdie, Salman 34, 146

Said, Edward 69, 190
Sauerberg, Lars Ole 19–21, 31
seamlessness, *see also* continuity 11, 15, 36, 96, 103, 106
segments 2, 3, 6, 7, 14, 16, 25, 44, 47, 58, 79, 106, 135, 190
   distinct from fragments 2, 42, 89, 183, 184, 199
   foregrounded in gutter texts 22–3, 26, 34, 42, 157
Seth, Vikram 30, 31, 59
Shakespeare, William 68, 69, 76, 95
Sharp, Granville 177–8
Sharpe, Christina 174, 176
Siskin, Clifford 29
Spenser, Edmund 32, 196–7
Spivak, Gayatri Chakravorty 48, 51, 54, 56, 57, 107, 171, 192
Stesichoros 75–80, 87, 89, 120
Steyerl Hito 143
stupidity
   as male privilege 149–52
   as misogynist trope 153, 155
Sylbaris, Louis-Auguste 82–4

Tempest, Kae 58, 133, 158, 179
   Let Them Eat Chaos 134–45
temporality
   homogeneous 15, 57, 92, 98, 124, 127, 134, 135, 138, 140, 160
   planetray, *see* deep time
   postcolonial 31, 33–5
   spiral 98, 99, 124–6, 127
Theweleit, Klaus 83
Truax, Tammi J. 30
Trump, Donald 38, 151
Turner, Tina 103

Tutuola, Amos 196
typography 3, 5, 7, 22, 59, 113, 156, 168, 181

Va (Samoan epistemology) 104–12, 118, 139, 142
Vergil 61, 63, 101, 155, 194
verse novel 51, 54, 56–8, 61, 81, 88, 103, 108, 113, 133, 151, 192, 194, 198
   formal feautures 17–34
   as hybrid 18, 33, 149, 199
   as literary misfit (Burkitt) 30
   Omeros as 65, 74
   Let Them Eat Chaos as 134–5
   Telling Tales as 158
   Zong! as 172, 180
Vidal, Gore 30
Vogl, Josef 194–5
volcano, volcanism 33, 57, 61–3, 65, 67, 85, 87, 111, 128–32
   Icchantikas 88
   Mt Pelée 82
   Nafanua 112
   Soufrière 67, 68, 70, 75
   Teide 80, 83
voyage in (Said) 68, 114, 146

Walcott, Derek 31, 75–8, 82, 83, 89, 116, 127, 195, 198
   Omeros 63–74
Watt, Ian 18, 19, 61, 64
web of life 65, 119, 121
Weheliye, Alexander 11, 175, 176, 195
Wendt, Albert 57, 61, 65, 116, 117, 118–20, 125, 127, 135, 145, 199
   The Adventures of Vela 89–112
Wilberforce, William 174, 175, 178, 179, 189
Wilde, Oscar 1–4, 193
world literature 12, 18, 21, 23–9, 34, 68–9, 74, 92, 133, 158
   as ecology 24, 26, 27–9, 34, 100
worlding 33, 34, 48, 73, 90, 103, 107, 109, 114

Zizek, Slavoj 36, 171
Zong massacre (1781) 172, 176–9, 180, 182, 183

www.ingramcontent.com/pod-product-compliance
Lightning Source LLC
Chambersburg PA
CBHW052036300426
44117CB00012B/1846